Playing Politics with Science

Practical and Professional Ethics Series

Published in conjunction with the Association for Practical and Professional Ethics

General Editors
Robert Audi, University of Notre Dame
Patrick E. Murphy, University of Notre Dame

Published in the Series

Playing Politics with Science

Balancing Scientific Independence and Government Oversight

David B. Resnik

OXFORD
UNIVERSITY PRESS

2009

OXFORD
UNIVERSITY PRESS

Oxford University Press, Inc., publishes works that further
Oxford University's objective of excellence
in research, scholarship, and education.

Oxford New York
Auckland Cape Town Dar es Salaam Hong Kong Karachi
Kuala Lumpur Madrid Melbourne Mexico City Nairobi
New Delhi Shanghai Taipei Toronto

With offices in
Argentina Austria Brazil Chile Czech Republic France Greece
Guatemala Hungary Italy Japan Poland Portugal Singapore
South Korea Switzerland Thailand Turkey Ukraine Vietnam

Copyright © 2009 by Oxford University Press, Inc.

Published by Oxford University Press, Inc.
198 Madison Avenue, New York, New York 10016

www.oup.com

Oxford is a registered trademark of Oxford University Press

Library of Congress Cataloging-in-Publication Data
Resnik, David B.
Playing politics with science: balancing scientific independence and government oversight /
David B. Resnik.
p. cm. — (Practical and professional ethics series)
Includes bibliographical references and index.
ISBN 978-0-19-537589-3
1. Science—Political aspects.   2. Research—Moral and ethical aspects.   3. Science and state.
I. Title.
Q175.5.P58 2009
509.73—dc22   2008026680

9 8 7 6 5 4 3 2 1

Printed in the United States of America
on acid-free paper

In memory of Jay F. Rosenberg, teacher, scholar, friend

Acknowledgments

This research was supported by the Intramural Program of the National Institute of Environmental Health Sciences, National Institutes of Health. It does not represent the views of the National Institute of Environmental Health Sciences or the National Institutes of Health. For useful comments and criticism, I would like to thank Christina Gutierrez-Ford and two anonymous reviewers at Oxford University Press.

Contents

Abbreviations

AAALAC	Association for the Accreditation and Assessment of Laboratory Animal Care International
AAAS	American Association for the Advancement of Science
AAHRPP	Association of Accreditation of Human Research Protection Programs
ACHRE	Advisory Committee on Human Radiation Experiments
AE	adverse event
AEC	Atomic Energy Commission
AHRQ	Agency on Healthcare Research and Quality
AIDS	acquired immunodeficiency syndrome
BTWC	Biological and Toxin Weapons Convention
CDC	Centers for Disease Control and Prevention
C.F.R.	*Code of Federal Regulations*
CHEERS	Children's Environmental Exposure Research Study
CI	categorical imperative
CRO	contract research organization
DHHS	Department of Health and Human Services
DHS	Department of Homeland Security
DNA	deoxyribonucleic acid
DOD	Department of Defense
DOE	Department of Energy
EPA	Environmental Protection Agency
FBI	Federal Bureau of Investigation
FCC	Federal Communications Commission
FDA	Food and Drug Administration
FTC	Federal Trade Commission
GAO	Government Accounting Office
GSA	General Services Administration
HES	human embryonic stem
HIPAA	Healthcare Insurance Portability and Accountability Act
HIV	human immunodeficiency virus

ID	intelligent design
IRB	institutional review board
JCAHO	Joint Commission on the Accreditation of Healthcare Organization
K–12	kindergarten through 12th grade
NAC	national advisory committee
NAS	National Academy of Sciences
NASA	National Aeronautics and Space Administration
NIH	National Institutes of Health
NIOSH	National Institute for Occupational Safety and Health
NOAA	National Oceanic and Atmospheric Administration
NRC	National Research Council
NSA	National Security Administration
NSABB	National Science Advisory Board for Biosecurity
NSF	National Science Foundation
OGE	Office of Government Ethics
OHRP	Office of Human Research Protections
OTA	Office of Technology Assessment
OTC	over the counter
PCB	President's Council on Bioethics
PHrMA	Pharmaceutical Research and Manufacturers of America
PNAS	*Proceedings of the National Academy of Sciences*
PP	precautionary principle
RAC	Recombinant DNA Advisory Committee
R & D	research and development
SBU	sensitive but unclassified
SEA	Scientists and Engineers for America
UN	United Nations
UNSCOM	United Nations Special Commission
USA PATRIOT	Uniting and Strengthening America by Providing Appropriate Tools Required to Intercept and Obstruct Terrorism
USDA	U.S. Department of Agriculture
USNRC	U.S. Nuclear Regulatory Commission
USPTO	U.S. Patent and Trademark Office
VA	Department of Veterans Affairs
WMD	weapon of mass destruction

Playing Politics with Science

I

Introduction

Scientific progress on a broad front results from the free play of free intellects, working on subjects of their own choice, in the manner dictated by their curiosity for exploration of the unknown. Freedom of inquiry must be preserved under any plan for government support of science.

—Vannevar Bush

Science and the Government

It has been over sixty years since Vannevar Bush, director of the Office of Scientific Research and Development for presidents Franklin Delano Roosevelt and Harry Truman, prepared his report *Science: The Endless Frontier*, a document that shaped U.S. science policy in the second half of the 20th century and continues to hold influence today (Guston 2000). In this report, Bush outlined a vision for a partnership between scientists and the state: The government would fund research in the physical, biomedical, and social sciences and provide scientists with access to resources and a labor force. In return, scientists would produce knowledge and train the next generation of researchers. The fruits of this partnership would be national security, economic prosperity, and health and wellbeing. Scientists receiving funding from the government would have control over decisions concerning their methods, theories, analyses, and publications, but they would still be held financially, legally, and ethically accountable to the public. Although the government would share in the decisions concerning funding priorities, freedom of inquiry would be preserved (Bush 1945). The government would have broad oversight over scientific research, but scientists would still have considerable freedom to make decisions within their own sphere of influence. Scientists would have significant independence and autonomy.

The ideal of scientific independence envisioned by Bush has withstood many different threats from all sides of the political spectrum over the years, as politicians have attempted to limit scientific decision-making in various ways. These limitations on decision-making have included restricting funding, regulating some aspects of scientific practice, dictating science curricula, controlling the composition of science advisory committees for political purposes, rewriting scientific reports, and censoring scientific publications. While a convincing case can be made that the administration of President George W. Bush has posed an unprecedented threat to the independence of science (Shulman 2007, Union of Concerned Scientists 2004), for many years Democrats, Republicans, liberals, conservatives, presidents, members of Congress, lobbyists, and interest groups have tried to influence, manipulate, spin, or subvert decisions made by scientists working for the U.S. government (Mooney 2005, Pielke 2007). Playing politics with science is a sport as old as modern government.

The tension between science and politics is not new. At various times, scientists and scholars have fought for intellectual freedom. The Greek philosopher Socrates (470–399 B.C.) was ordered to drink hemlock for corrupting youth through his teachings and methods; English philosopher and scientist Roger Bacon (1214–94) was imprisoned for heresies, such as finding logical inconsistencies in the Bible; Italian anatomist Andreas Vesalius (1514–64) defied a ban against dissecting the human body; Italian philosopher and cosmologist Giordano Bruno (1548–1600) was burned at the stake for heresy; and Italian astronomer and physicist Galileo Galilei (1564–1642) was placed under house arrest for refusing to recant his defense of a heliocentric solar system (Burke 1995). The public has also had to manage some of the social and political consequences of research, including the Copernican revolution, which shattered the idea that man is the center of the universe; steam power, which paved the way for the Industrial Revolution; Einstein's theory of relativity, which provided the conceptual foundation for nuclear weapons; the development of the computer, which transformed the electronics industry and the workplace; and the discovery of the structure of deoxyribonucleic acid (DNA), which led to the biotechnology revolution (Burke 1995).

Since science and politics have always interacted in complex and often dangerous ways, the themes investigated in this book are perennial. It may seem like the politicalization of science became much worse under the administration of George W. Bush and the Republican-controlled Congress (Mooney 2005), but science has always been politicized to some degree (Ziman 2000). More significant, the relationship between science and politics takes place in new social, economic, cultural, and technological settings. Scientific research now plays a greater role in government decision-making and has more of an immediate impact on society than in previous eras. Countries around the globe continue to increase the amount of money they spend on science, and the scientific labor force continues to grow. Science has evolved from an avocation practiced by a few hundred people, financed by their own means or by wealthy patrons, to a profession composed of hundreds of different disciplines, practiced by millions of people, and financed by governments and corporations (Ziman 2000).

Without a doubt, the public has both a right and an obligation to oversee scientific research so that scientists can be held financially, legally, and ethically accountable for their activities. Government regulations, laws, and policies are necessary to maximize the benefits of science and minimize its adverse effects on individuals, society, and the environment. However, excessive or inappropriate interference with scientific practice can undermine scientific creativity, innovation, education, and progress. In the most extreme cases, such as the Soviet Union's suppression of scientists who supported Mendelian genetics and opposed Lysenkoism, government control of science can interfere with basic human rights, such as freedom of thought, speech, and association. Restrictions on scientific practice must be developed and implemented in a manner that does not threaten scientific freedom and independence. Government oversight of science should not shackle or strangle the geese that lay the golden eggs.

Several recent examples, discussed below, illustrate some troubling episodes of the politicalization of science by U.S. politicians.[1] These examples demonstrate how politicians have used a variety of tactics to influence or control scientific research.

1. One of the most important cases involving the politicalization of science, the manipulation of national security intelligence prior to the invasion of Iraq in 2003, is discussed in chapter 6.

The Global Climate Change Debate

Scientists have been studying the impacts of human activity on the global climate for decades. Since the early 1800s, scientists have known about the greenhouse effect, which occurs when gases in the earth's atmosphere, such as carbon dioxide, water vapor, ozone, and methane, capture and recycle radiant heat (infrared radiation). During the 1980s, many environmental scientists and climatologists began to accept the hypothesis that the earth is getting warmer and that human activities, such as emissions of greenhouse gases and the destruction of forests, are making a significant contribution to this increase in temperatures. By the mid-1990s, an overwhelming majority of scientists accepted this view, although they continued to debate over specific details concerning global climate change, such as how much the earth is warming, when this warming began, how much warmer the earth will become, the contributions of human activities, the consequences of global warming for the environment and humankind, and ways to mitigate or adapt to global warming. In 1997, over 150 nations ratified the Kyoto Protocol, an agreement to limit the emission of greenhouse gases. The United States signed the protocol but did not ratify it. At that time, the United States produced more greenhouse gases than any other country in the world. China is now the world's largest producer of carbon dioxide (Dessler and Parson 2006).

George W. Bush had been an oil industry executive for many years before becoming governor of Texas. Oil companies have been opposed to restrictions on greenhouse gas emissions, since these restrictions could hurt their business. The oil industry supported Bush's presidential candidacy in 2000, and he demonstrated his loyalty to the industry when he took office in 2001. Bush proposed that the United States open up areas of the Alaska wilderness to oil drilling, supported additional offshore drilling, and opposed the Kyoto Protocol. He also expressed skepticism on global warming, arguing that there was not enough evidence to decide whether to take action to avert or mitigate global climate change. He favored additional research instead of taking any preventative measures, such as restricting greenhouse gas emissions, on the basis that such measures might harm the economy. As the scientific consensus concerning global climate change continued to solidify, the Bush administration gave up its skeptical stance in 2006 and officially admitted that the earth is growing warmer. The administration insisted, however, that human activity probably does not play a large role in this change, and it remained opposed to the Kyoto Protocol or taking steps to reduce greenhouse gas emissions (Dessler and Parson 2006).

In 2001, the Bush administration hired Philip Cooney to serve as chief of staff of the White House Council on Environmental Quality. Cooney, who had worked for about ten years as an attorney for the American Petroleum Institute, has a law doctorate and a bachelor's degree in economics, but no scientific training. One of his primary responsibilities in the Bush administration was to censor, distort, or edit government reports relating to the global climate in order to raise doubts about global climate change and humanity's role in this process. He altered many government documents, including a report issued by the Climate Change Science Program. Specifically, he deleted a paragraph from the report that discussed how global warming could adversely affect the availability of drinking water by reducing glaciers and mountain snowpacks. Cooney made over 650 changes in all to this report (Shulman 2007).

In June 2003, the Bush administration attempted to make the Environmental Protection Agency (EPA) change its *Report on the Environment*. The Bush administration wanted the EPA to delete data on global temperatures for the last thousand years, remove any reference to humankind's role in climate change, and eliminate the claim, accepted by most climate researchers, that global warming has significant consequences for the environment and human health. The administration also attempted to insert qualifying words, such as "may," "could," "might," and so on, to soften the impact of the report. Cooney and other government lawyers with little knowledge of the science of global climate change were involved in rewriting the report (Union of Concerned Scientists 2004).

In January 2006, National Aeronautics and Space Administration (NASA) scientist James Hansen told the press that officials at NASA had tried to prevent him and his colleagues from conveying information to the public about global climate change and the importance of restricting greenhouse gas emissions. He said that NASA officials were reviewing his publications, Web site postings, and media interviews and trying to intimidate him. Officials at NASA denied that they were trying to intimidate Hansen or stop him from speaking to the public about global climate change. They said he was free to express his own opinions but that he was not permitted to represent the administration's policies. Hansen also charged that officials at the National Oceanic and Atmospheric Administration (NOAA) had prevented scientists from communicating their findings about global climate change to the public. He claimed that in 2004 the Bush administration had rewritten NASA and NOAA press releases and reports to minimize the risks of climate change. Hansen also stated that the Clinton administration had tweaked assumptions used in economic models to downplay the costs and impacts of restricting greenhouse gas emissions. In February 2006, NASA spokesman George Deutsch resigned following allegations that he changed written comments made by NASA scientists to conform to the Bush administration's stance on global climate change (Revkin 2006).

The Bush administration's pattern of censoring scientific communications with the public was apparent in October 2007, when the White House Office of Management and Budget deleted passages from Centers for Disease Control and Prevention (CDC) director Julie Gerberding's testimony to a Senate committee on the health risks of global warming. Testimony was removed that described global warming as a serious public health concern, hypothesizing that global warming could exacerbate allergic disease, broaden the range of infectious diseases, and increase mortality due to heat waves (Kintisch 2007). The testimony that remained was much more ambiguous concerning the health effects of global warming. Administration officials said the cuts were part of the normal review process. Gerberding said that press coverage of the story had made a mountain out of a molehill (Revkin 2007).

Stem Cells and Bioethics

Stem cells are cells that can differentiate into different tissue types. Stem cells found in adult tissues, such as bone marrow stem cells, can change into different tissue types but cannot become a viable embryo. Multipotent stem cells taken from five-day-old human embryos can differentiate into any cell type and can become a new embryo. Totipotent stem cells taken from older embryos or found in the umbilical cord and placenta can differentiate into any cell type but cannot become an embryo. These cells are also pluripotent. In 1998, James Thompson and his colleagues at the University of Wisconsin discovered a method for growing human embryonic stem (HES) cells taken from the inner cell mass of an embryo in a culture medium. The HES cells were derived from embryos donated by couples seeking in vitro fertilization. Most couples who seek in vitro fertilization as an infertility treatment create many more embryos than they will use, and most embryos that are not used are discarded. The significance of Thompson's research is that HES cells, or cells derived from HES cells, could be used to treat diseases that involve damage to cells or tissues, such as diabetes, spinal cord injuries, Parkinson's disease, Alzheimer's disease, liver cirrhosis, kidney disease, and heart disease. Some researchers are developing methods for making replacement tissues and organs from stem cells. Researchers have used embryonic stem cells to repair spinal injuries in laboratory rodents, but no clinical trials on human subjects have been initiated as of the writing of this book (Pucéat and Ballis 2007). Human embryonic stem cells may have some advantages over other types of stem cells for tissue regeneration because they are less likely to be rejected by the body.

Human embryonic stem cells are morally controversial because the procedure developed by Thompson and his colleagues to derive these cells involves the destruction of the human embryo, which many people regard as having as much moral value as a newborn child. Many abortion opponents oppose HES cell research because it involves the destruction of embryos. Though scientists have been developing different methods for producing HES cells, as of July 2008 these methods have not been perfected. Scientists have also been conducting research on using stem cells taken from adult tissues in therapy (Green 2007, Klimanskaya et al. 2006, Weissman 2006).

In 1980, President Ronald Reagan signed an order that prohibited federal agencies from funding research on human embryos. President William Clinton lifted this ban when he took power in 1993, but then in 1995 Congress enacted a ban that prohibited the use of federal funds to create or destroy embryos for research purposes. President Clinton interpreted this ban to mean that the government could fund research on cell lines derived from human embryos, although it could not actually fund the derivation of cell lines from embryos, as this would involve the creation or destruction of embryos for research. Thus, private companies derived HES cell lines used by government-funded scientists from the National Institutes of Health (NIH) in research. In August 2001, President George W. Bush announced a new policy on government funding of human embryonic stem cell research. Bush told the American public in a nationally televised speech that only government-funded research on the cell lines that the NIH had already procured from private vendors would be permitted. No new cell lines would be used. The Bush administration originally estimated that sixty cell lines would be available, but it turned out that only twenty-one cell lines were actually available, and most of those cell lines cannot be used on human beings because they were grown in mouse cell cultures. According to Mooney (2005), Bush made his announcement without taking steps to ensure that he had an accurate estimate of the number of viable cell lines. The estimate was based on a phone survey of NIH institutes, not on a careful accounting of the actual cell lines. In July 2006, Congress passed a bill that would override Bush's policy and allow the NIH to expand its funding of embryonic stem cell research beyond the ones approved by the administration, but Bush vetoed the measure (Stout 2006). Bush vetoed a similar bill passed in 2007.

When Bush made his stem cell announcement he also said that he would appoint the President's Council on Bioethics (PCB) to study stem cell research and other bioethics issues. Bush appointed a well-known conservative Christian bioethicist, Leon Kass, to chair the PCB. Kass has opposed abortion, physician-assisted suicide, in vitro fertilization, and surrogate motherhood in his writings (Kass 2004). The PCB was originally composed of nineteen members, including Kass. Members came from the disciplines of political science, religious studies, philosophy, ethics, law, molecular biology, neuroscience, cell biology, medicine, and psychiatry. Kass had communicated to members of the PCB the importance of considering different sides of the issues and said that he would welcome a dissenting view (Blackburn 2004). However, some commentators charged that Bush had stacked the PCB with conservative members in order to ensure that it would render opinions consistent with the conservative, prolife political agenda, and that his administration had also tried to manipulate other scientific advisory committees to achieve political goals (Mooney 2005, Union of Concerned Scientists 2004).

Elizabeth Blackburn, a cell biologist from the University of California at Berkeley, was the most distinguished scientist on the PCB. Blackburn had received international recognition for her discovery of telomeres, segments on the ends of chromosomes that become shorter after each cell division. When telomeres become too short, the chromosome unravels and the cell dies. Her discovery has important implications for understanding cancer and aging. In February 2004, Blackburn received a phone call on a Friday afternoon from the White House informing her that her services on the PCB were no longer needed; no other explanation was offered. William May, an ethicist and PCB member, was told the same thing. Blackburn and May had spoken in favor of some types of HES cell research as important for the advancement of science and medicine and had dissented from the PCB's recommendation to ban all forms of cloning. Blackburn and May favored cloning for research purposes, but not cloning for reproduction. President George W. Bush replaced Blackburn and May with three other members who opposed HES cell research and cloning. In an editorial in the *New England Journal of Medicine*, Blackburn accused the Bush administration of manipulating scientific advisory panels for political purposes:

> In late September 2001, I was asked to serve on the President's Council on Bioethics. My initial instinct was not to accept, because I was concerned that the Bush Administration would not be interested in considering fully the potential of certain controversial advances in basic biomedical research. Indeed, the administration was already on record as opposing federal funding for somatic-cell nuclear transplantation and therapeutic cloning... Two factors, however, tipped the balance in favor of accepting the appointment. First, as the country mourned after the tragedy of September 11, 2001, I felt that I wanted to contribute something. Second, I received strong assurance from the council's newly appointed chairman Leon Kass (and later from President George W. Bush himself) that the wisdom of a full range of experts was needed. I believed that, especially at this juncture in history, it was important to serve in this potentially critical way.... Unfortunately, my initial misgiving proved to be prescient. In a telephone call from the White

House one Friday afternoon in February [2004], I was told that my services were no longer needed. The only explanation I was offered was that "the White House has decided to make some changes in the bioethics council." Persons who are versed in such matters have since suggested that the prearranged timing of the call was not a coincidence: this administration commonly takes controversial action on Friday afternoons, when the news is expected to fall into a weekend void. How might perceived bias in a federal commission such as the bioethics council affect the ability of the nation to receive the best available scientific information on which to base policy decisions? Will researchers be unwilling to provide their expert opinions regarding their field of research for fear that they will be used to promote a particular view held by the council? I am afraid that this effect is already occurring. (Blackburn 2004, 1379–80)

The Bush administration denied the charge that the termination was politically motivated, but Blackburn's assertion rang true with many people who have kept an eye on the administration's handling of scientific advisory bodies (Mooney 2005, Shulman 2007). Ironically, Kass also was asked to step down from the leadership of the PCB due to his own political activities. Kass had been lobbying Congress to adopt a conservative bioethics agenda while serving as chair of the PCB. Bush replaced Kass with another Christian thinker, Edmund Pellegrino, who is a well-respected bioethicist and physician (Holden 2005).

Peerless Review

There have been several incidents where politicians have interfered with the peer review process to stop projects from being funded or have tried to bypass it to ensure funding for their pet projects. For example, in a hearing of the House Energy and Commerce Committee in July 2003, lawmakers considered cutting four grants that had been approved by a peer review panel at the NIH. The Traditional Values Coalition had sent a list of 198 NIH grants that it regarded as a waste of taxpayers' money. The grants were for research on a variety of topics related to human sexuality, such as human immunodeficiency virus (HIV)/acquired immunodeficiency syndrome (AIDS) risks of drug users, teen-pregnancy prevention methods, the use of prostitutes by truck drivers, and sexual dysfunction. The committee decided not to cut off funding for the grants after hearing testimony from NIH director Elias Zerhouni in January 2004 (Kaiser 2004). In 2005, the House of Representatives voted to cancel two NIH grants related to research on human and animal psychology. One study would have examined the factors that contribute to a successful marriage; the other would have investigated visual perception and cognition in pigeons (Cohen 2005).

In May 2006, Senator Kay Bailey Hutchison (R-TX) inserted a provision into the Department of Veterans Affairs (VA) budget to earmark $15 million for research on Gulf War illness at the University of Texas Southwestern Medical Center. Many scientists objected to this special allocation of funds because (a) it bypassed the normal scientific peer review channels; and (b) the Gulf War illness theory has little support among mainstream scientists. In 2004, the Institute of Medicine concluded that there was insufficient evidence to prove the main hypothesis of the Gulf War illness theory—that is, that symptoms experienced by Gulf War veterans were caused by exposure to low levels of neurotoxins released during the war (Couzin 2006). In 2006, Congress spent nearly $2.5 billion on special, earmarked science projects that bypassed peer review (Mervis 2006a). Though many legislators regard these projects as wasteful, pork-barrel spending, other earmarked scientific projects are seen as a way of bringing federal dollars to their constituencies (Malakoff 2001).

In that same month, Senator Hutchison questioned whether the social sciences should be included in a ten-year plan to double the budget of the National Science Foundation (NSF). Hutchison also suggested that the NSF should not fund social science research at all so the agency could focus on engineering, mathematics, and the natural sciences (biology, physics, and chemistry) (Mervis 2006c).

In April 2005, Stephen Johnson, who had recently been appointed as administrator of the EPA, decided to cancel the Children's Environmental Exposure Research Study (CHEERS), a field monitoring study on young children's in-home exposures to pesticides and other chemicals in Duvall County, Florida. During Johnson's nomination hearings, senators Barbara Boxer (D-CA) and William Nelson (D-FL) threatened to stop his nomination for the EPA position if he did not cancel the study. The CHEERS study had been approved by a special panel of EPA scientists and outside reviewers as well as institutional review boards (IRBs) at three different institutions. The study came under fire in the fall of 2004, when environmental groups charged that parents would be required to intentionally expose their children to pesticides. Although these allegations were false, environmental interest groups and politicians used them to attack Bush's record on the environment and score political points against the Bush administration. Scientists who helped to develop and review the study regretted that it had become a political football and that society would lose out on an important opportunity to learn more about children's pesticide exposures and promote children's health (Janofsky 2005). In the summer of 2005, Boxer introduced an amendment to an appropriations bill that placed some restrictions on the EPA's funding and review of research. The amendment placed a one-year moratorium on the EPA's acceptance of data from pesticide experiments conducted on human subjects by private companies and prohibited the EPA from funding intentional exposure studies on children or pregnant women. The EPA adopted new regulations consistent with Boxer's amendment (Resnik 2007b).

The Politics of Health

In 1999, the U.S. Congress mandated that the Department of Health and Human Services (DHHS) prepare a report on health disparities as part of a nationwide effort to address differences in health among various racial, ethnic, and socioeconomic groups. Some of the disparities in health were well known prior to the release of the report, such as racial, ethnic, and socioeconomic differences in cancer rates, infant mortality, HIV/AIDS, heart disease, and access to health care. When the Agency on Healthcare Research and Quality (AHRQ) completed its report in 2003, political appointees at the DHHS whitewashed it, deleting important information about health disparities. An AHRQ scientist with an uncensored copy of the report leaked it to the media, which led to a congressional investigation by Representative Henry Waxman (D-CA), chair of the House Committee on Government Reform. The report found that political appointees in DHHS had manipulated the document to mollify the bad news about health disparities. The uncensored document reinforced findings by the Institute of Medicine that there was overwhelming evidence of racial, ethnic, and socioeconomic differences in health and access to health care, but the "official" version of the document only acknowledged that some differences exist (Shulman 2007).

In August 2006, after more than three years of deliberation and debate, the Food and Drug Administration (FDA) decided to approve Barr Laboratories' application to make a form of emergency contraception known as Plan B available over the counter (OTC), provided that it would not be not sold to women younger than eighteen years old. Acting FDA commissioner Andrew Eschenbach did not announce any plans to enforce the age requirement, but asked pharmacies to voluntarily comply with the new rules (Harris 2006). Conservative Christian groups had opposed Plan B because it can interfere with the implantation of the embryo in the uterus. In August 2005, the FDA had refused to approve Plan B. Then FDA commissioner Lester Crawford cited the need to protect the health of teenage women as a reason to withhold approval of Plan B as an OTC drug. Opponents of Plan B also argued that making it available OTC could encourage promiscuity in teenage women. Susan Wood, director of women's health at the FDA, resigned her position to protest the FDA's decisions concerning Plan B and other actions related to women's health. An FDA advisory committee composed of scientific and medical experts had recommended OTC status for Plan B by a 23–4 vote. Several physician groups, including the American Medical Association, had developed similar recommendations. According to several former FDA employees, the agency's decision on Plan B was based on abortion politics, not science (Couzin 2005).

This was not the first time that political interests had affected FDA decisions. In September 2000, the FDA finally approved the birth control drug RU-486 (mifepristone) after delaying its decision for many years. The drug had been available in Europe since 1990. When used in conjunction with a drug that induces uterine contractions, RU-486 is about 95% effective in causing an abortion when used within the first seven weeks of pregnancy. Abortion opponents had also opposed the adoption of RU-486. In another instance, in 1992, gay rights groups opposed the adoption of a home HIV test, which the FDA eventually approved (Hawthorne 2005).

From 2002 to 2006, Richard Carmona served as the surgeon general for the Bush administration. He was not reappointed when his termed ended in 2006. In July 2007, he told a congressional panel that the Bush administration had repeatedly censored, weakened, or suppressed health policy reports for political purposes and had prevented him from speaking to the public about stem cell research, sex education, emergency contraception, and global health issues (Harris 2007). Carmona said that the Bush administration had blocked publication of a report titled "A Call to Action on Global Health," which urged Americans to help tackle global health problems. He said that officials suppressed publication of the report because it did not tout the Bush administration's accomplishments. According to Carmona, officials told him that the report could be published if he made some changes to it, but he refused to do so (Lee and Kaufman 2007). Carmona also said that administration officials had tried and failed to water down a report on the dangers of secondhand smoke (Harris 2007).

A Plea for Scientific Autonomy and Independence

These cases illustrate some of the different ways that politicians have attempted to control, manipulate, or influence scientific decisions to achieve political ends, and there are numerous other cases of political meddling in scientific matters that we do not need to discuss here (see Mooney 2005, Shulman 2007). Some of the strategies politicians have used to control scientific decisions include:

- Censoring or rewriting scientific communications, such as reports or other publications
- Stacking science advisory committees with experts sympathetic to a particular political agenda
- Refusing to heed the advice of scientific advisory committees when their advice is not consistent with a political agenda
- Interfering with or bypassing scientific peer review
- Restricting government-funded science for political aims

Inappropriate government control over scientific decision-making can have many negative consequences for science and society, including eroding the integrity and trustworthiness of research, hampering scientific creativity and innovation, undermining the fairness and effectiveness of government actions and policies, discouraging talented researchers from working for the government, and violating the freedom of scientists. To prevent these negative outcomes, it is important to clearly delineate scientific and political realms. Scientists should control aspects of their practice where the public has little or no expertise or authority, such as research design, hypothesis testing, and analysis and interpretation of data. Scientists need be free to make careful and well-reasoned decisions, unfettered by political intimidation, manipulation, and harassment. Although scientists should have some independence and autonomy, the public should have some input into different aspects of science where public opinion and oversight is warranted, including government funding of research, the use of science to make public policy decisions, experiments that pose risks to human or animal subjects or the environment, science education, and publication of information with implications for national security. Political control over scientific decisions should occur in such a way that it benefits society without undermining scientific practice. Scientific autonomy and government oversight must be properly balanced. Some types of oversight are appropriate and necessary; others are not. The difficult task for science policy is trying to specify how the government should be involved in scientific decisions. I hope to do so in the remaining chapters of this book.

Plan for the Book

The plan for the book is as follows. In chapter 2, I will develop a conceptual framework for thinking about the relationship between politics and science. I will argue that science is valuable because it is generally reliable and aspires to be objective, and that it is generally reliable and aspires to be objective because it adheres to methods that are designed to minimize personal, political, economic, and other forms of bias. In chapter 3, I will argue that science should be protected from economic, political, and other biases that can undermine the objectivity of research. Science should be independent and autonomous. I will also argue that society should still have oversight authority over science to ensure that science does not undermine important social values. I will set forth some principles and strategies for promoting the autonomy of science while allowing for adequate public oversight. In chapters 4 through 8, I will examine five areas where science needs to be protected from political gaming: peer review, scientific advice panels, science education, publication, and military science (intelligence). In chapter 9, I will conclude the book with some recommendations for policy makers and scientists.

Philosophical Foundations

For a successful technology, reality must take precedence over public relations, for Nature cannot be fooled.

—Richard Feynman

The previous chapter gave an overview of the book and described some cases that raise important questions concerning the relationship between politics and science. In this chapter, I will develop a conceptual framework for thinking about these cases and others like them by examining some central issues in the philosophy of science. These issues include the definition of science, the value of science for society, the reliability of science, the methods of science, and the objectivity of science. The abstract ideas and arguments discussed in this chapter will also provide the philosophical basis for concrete policies discussed in subsequent chapters.

Science and Politics

Since this book is about the relationship between science and politics, it is important to have a firm understanding of what we mean by these two key terms. I shall follow the *American Heritage Dictionary* (2008) in defining politics as the art of "government or governing, especially the governing of a political entity, such as a nation, and the administration and control of its internal and external affairs." Politics has to do with the affairs of state and the operations of the different branches of government—legislative, executive, and judicial. Political questions concern issues of social justice, criminal justice, allocation of resources, taxation, national defense, human rights, and modes of governance (democratic, bureaucratic, autocratic, and so forth). Some of the disciplines that study politics include political science, which describes and explains politics, and political philosophy, which explores the normative and conceptual foundations of politics.

Defining science is much more difficult than defining politics. Many 20th-century philosophers, from Karl Popper (1959) to Paul Thagard (1978), spilled much ink trying to answer the question, "What is science?" The U.S. Supreme Court has even entered the debate in its decisions on the admissibility of expert testimony in court (*Daubert v. Dow Merrell Pharmaceuticals, Inc.* 1993; *Kumho Tire Co. v. Carmichael*, 1999). For many years, the problem of distinguishing science from unscientific activities, such as pseudoscience, religion, philosophy, and superstition, was regarded as one of the fundamental problems in the philosophy of science. Today, however, many philosophers of science regard this problem as unsolvable, because none of the definitions of science proposed by philzosophers, sociologists, or historians have withstood rigorous scrutiny (Kitcher 1993).

I will not review each proposed definition of science in this book, but I will examine two influential ones: Popper's idea that science must be testable (or falsifiable) and Thagard's notion of science as a progressive enterprise. According to Popper (1959), the difference between science and nonscience is that the statements of scientific disciplines are testable, whereas statements from nonscientific disciplines are not. A statement is testable if one could perform a test of a statement, such as an experiment, in which the statement could be proven false (or falsified) by the outcome of the test. For example, the statement "water boils at 100 degrees centigrade" is testable because we could test it by raising the temperature of water to 100 degrees centigrade at sea level and observing whether water boils. If water did not boil under these conditions, then the statement would be proven false. A statement like "God is omniscient" is not testable because there is no test we can do that would tend to prove it false. We cannot perform an experiment to prove whether God is omniscient, because we cannot establish experimental conditions in which the outcome of the experiment would show that God is not omniscient. We cannot establish experimental conditions for this experiment, because there are difficulties in defining the term "God" and observing God's knowledge (or lack of it).

While testability is an important principle of scientific reasoning and methodology, it does not distinguish science from nonscience.

The main problem with Popper's view is that there are some statements that we would regard as scientific that may not be directly
testable. For example, consider the principle of the conservation of
mass-energy, which holds that the sum of all the mass and energy in
the universe must remain unchanged. Energy can be converted to mass
and vice versa, but the total mass-energy must remain constant. What
type of evidence would it take to falsify this statement? If someone
observed an apparent loss of matter or energy in the universe, most
scientists would assume that the matter or energy has not really been
lost: it has been transported or transformed in some way, but it has not
disappeared from the universe. Conservation of mass-energy is a fundamental principle that most scientists would defend against contrary
evidence. For another example, consider a scientific definition, such as
"Electrons have a negative charge." How could we prove this false? If
we observed a particle that behaved like an electron but had a positive
charge, we would call it something else, such as a positron. The general
point here is that scientific disciplines contain many important statements, such as fundamental principles and definitions, which are not
testable in any direct way. The statements are confirmed or discon-
firmed by virtue of their connection to other statements and the role
they play in scientific research. They can be justified but they are not
directly testable. Testability is not the sine qua non of science (Haack
2003, Kitcher 1993).

Thagard argues for his definition by reflecting on the problems with
Popper's definition. According to Thagard (1978), many pseudosciences
and other nonscientific disciplines have testable statements. One can test
astrology's main principle that the positions of the planets and stars affect
human behavior. The problem is that practitioners of astrology are not
trying to test this principle, or, even worse, that they have held onto this
principle despite considerable evidence against it. The problem with
pseudoscience is that it is not progressive, whereas science is. A discipline
is pseudoscientific if it has been less progressive than competing disciplines over time and faces many unsolved problems, and if the community of practitioners makes little attempt to deal with these problems or
compare their discipline to others (Thagard 1978). By implication, a
discipline is scientific if it is more progressive than other disciplines and
if its practitioners attempt to address outstanding problems and evaluate
the discipline in relation to other disciplines.

Thagard's proposal, like Popper's, does not provide necessary and sufficient conditions for defining "science." Some disciplines that we would call sciences have made very little progress in recent years. For example, most would consider human anatomy to be a science, but anatomy has not changed very much since the 1700s. We would also regard many activities that make progress to be unscientific. For example, cosmetology has made considerable progress since the 1900s, yet we would not consider it to be a science. Though I am skeptical of Thagard's attempt to define science, I agree that the notion of progress is essential to our understanding of science. My point is simply that science cannot be defined in terms of progress alone; other characteristics are important for thinking about science.

There are other definitions that equate science with a set of necessary and sufficient conditions, but these have fared no better than Popper's or Thagard's definitions. Suffice it to say that most people who have studied the problem of distinguishing science from nonscience have concluded that there is no universally agreed-upon set of necessary and sufficient conditions for defining science (Resnik 2000). The best we can expect to do is draw up a list of criteria that most of those human activities that we call "science" have in common. This is the approach I will take in this book. Most of the human activities that we call science are composed of people who aspire to and often succeed at the following:

- Rationality (scientists make decisions by means of argument and reasoning, not by rhetoric, force, or appeals to emotion)
- Empiricism (scientists adopt hypotheses, theories, beliefs, and principles on the basis of empirical evidence)
- Naturalism (scientists appeal to natural forces, properties, and causes, not supernatural ones)
- Methodology (scientists develop and use methods to test hypotheses, theories, beliefs, and principles)
- Progress (scientists seek to make progress: they avoid intellectual stagnation and dogmatism and value new and original ideas)
- Objectivity (scientists take steps to minimize social, political, religious, economic, and other biases)

I will make two comments about this proposed account of science. First, this account has a sociological dimension because it focuses on the activities of people we will call scientists, not on scientific theories, concepts, or hypotheses. Second, this account is not simply a description of scientific behavior, since it is a list of aspirations of scientists. The account focuses not on what scientists do but on what they aspire to do. A baseball player who strikes out is still a baseball player, and a musician who hits a wrong note is still a musician. Likewise, scientists who fail to achieve objectivity, rational consensus, or even progress would still be scientists, provided that they were trying to achieve these goals and making reasonable progress. The significance of these points will become more apparent later in this chapter.

Having given an account of science, I will now consider the value of science to society.

The Value of Science to Society

The U.S. government allocated $137 billion for research and development (R & D) in 2007, a 2.6% increase over the previous year. Defense-related research accounted for 32% ($61.4 billion) of the budget, followed by the NIH at 20.9% ($28.6 billion), NASA at 12.3% ($16.8 billion), the NSF at 4.4% ($6 billion), and the Department of Energy (DOE) at 3% ($4.1 billion) (Kintisch and Mervis 2006). Although the United States is by far the leader in government R & D spending, other industrialized nations also spend a considerable amount on scientific research each year. Trailing the United States are Japan ($33 billion), Germany ($21.3 billion), France ($20.9 billion), Great Britain ($18 billion), China ($13.4 billion), Canada ($6.3 billion), Australia ($4.2 billion), and India ($3.5 billion) (Brumfiel 2006). From this sizable fiscal commitment to R & D, one can draw the obvious inference that many people throughout the world value scientific research. But why do people value science so highly, and what do people value about science?

One might value science intrinsically, for its own sake; one might value it extrinsically, for the sake of what it can do; or one might value it both intrinsically and extrinsically. Most scientists (and many laypeople) value science for its own sake: they want to know how the world works and why things happen. They seek truth, explanation, and understanding. While I would be the last person to deny that knowledge is valuable for its own sake, belief in the intrinsic worth of scientific research does not explain why governments spend so much money on it. People value many things intrinsically that governments hardly support at all, such as poetry, ballet, music, literature, and philosophy. The main reason why governments spend so much money on scientific research is that science is useful.

Science has two important uses in society: (a) generating practical applications and (b) developing and implementing public policy. As we saw in chapter 1, Vannevar Bush appealed to the practical applications of science to justify government investments in R & D following World War II. The idea that science is valuable for its practical applications has its origins in the writings of Sir Francis Bacon (1561–1626), an English philosopher, scientist, and statesman, who inspired the first scientific association, the Royal Society of London, and coined the phrase "knowledge is power" (Simpson 2006). In the 20th century, politicians have used different aspects of this argument to justify investments in science. During the cold war, presidents Truman, Eisenhower, Kennedy, Johnson, Nixon, and Reagan regarded investments in scientific research as important for defending the country against the threat of Soviet imperialism. After the cold war, presidents George H. W. Bush, Bill Clinton, and George W. Bush argued that investments in R & D are vital to defend the nation against other threats, such as economic decline or global terrorism (Guston 2000). During the 1980s and 1990s, American presidents stressed the importance of science's contribution to technical innovation, business productivity, and economic growth and prosperity, as the country faced economic competition from Japan, Germany, and China (Greenberg 2001). Finally, the idea that science can lead to improvements in human health has also played a key role in justifying government R & D investments, and was especially important in winning support for the doubling of the NIH budget from 2000 through 2005 (Resnik 2007c).

Investing in science is also important for developing and implementing public policy (Guston 2000, Kitcher 2001). Many different agencies of the U.S. government, such as the EPA, the FDA, the U.S. Department of Agriculture (USDA), the CDC, the Department of Defense (DOD), and the Department of Homeland Security (DHS), rely heavily on scientific expertise and advice in implementing regulations and making policy decisions. Members of Congress, state legislators, governors, and even local legislators also depend on the expertise and advice from scientists (Jasanoff 1990). Scientists also play an increasingly important role in providing expert testimony in legal proceedings (Jasanoff 1997). Perhaps science's value as a policy tool is not mentioned very often because it has less political appeal than the other rationales for R & D investment: while everyone wants a cure for cancer, few people want new regulations or lawsuits. Even though science's role in shaping public policy may not receive top billing in science funding debates, it is still one of the most important ways that science can contribute to society (Pielke 2007).

The strategy for justifying public investments in scientific research by appealing to its practical value assumes an idea that has been dubbed the "linear model of science." According to the linear model, the relationship between science and practical and policy applications is straightforward and inexorable (Pielke 2007). Progress in basic research leads to progress in applied science, which leads to practical applications and public policy uses. For example, research in biochemistry has led to practical applications in medicine and pharmaceuticals. Research in toxicology has played an important role in informing regulatory decisions concerning pesticides.

One might object to this model by pointing out that it is an oversimplification. First, basic research (that is, research that is highly abstract or appears to be impractical) often does not lead to any practical applications. The practical payoffs of astrophysics, logic, mathematics, paleontology, and many other fields of basic research are highly speculative and remote. Second, some practical fields, such as parts of technology and engineering, sometimes develop on their own, with little or no input from basic or applied science. For example, people could make clay pots long before they understood the molecular structure of clay. Third, sometimes the linear order is reversed and practical applications lead to scientific advancements. For example, advances in lens making led to better light microscopes, which contributed to advances in cell biology. Fourth, sometimes public policy debates take place with very little input from science. For example, scientific research has played a minimal role in the formation of laws concerning murder and rape.

While I agree that the linear model is an oversimplification, it still holds some important insights for the relationships among science, practical applications of science, and science policy. First, although basic research often does not lead to practical applications, it often does. The applications may occur decades after the basic research has been completed, but they often occur. For example, Einstein's special theory of relativity ($E = MC^2$) did not immediately lead to any practical applications, but it laid the theoretical foundation for the development of atomic power thirty years later. Second, basic research creates a knowledge base that can be used for solving practical problems. For example, rocket scientists have used Isaac Newton's laws of motion to land spaceships on the moon, and geneticists have used Mendel's laws of inheritance to identify genetic diseases. Third, studying basic science promotes intellectual development. The study of physics may improve an engineer's analytical skills or creative insight. The study of mathematics, logic, and statistics helps scientists to develop reasoning abilities that they can use throughout their careers and apply to their work. Indeed, all education, even education in the arts and humanities, can contribute to intellectual development. Robert Boyle, Isaac Newton, Louis Pasteur, Charles Darwin, Sigmund Freud, Albert Einstein, Stephen Hawking, and many other great scientists and inventors had a keen interest in philosophy, literature, art, music, and other humanities disciplines.

Fourth, although many of the practical arts, such as technology and engineering, have made advancements with little or no input from science, the walls between science, engineering, and technology have been breaking down for many years. Pharmacogenomics is a salient example of the links between basic research, applied research, technology, and practical applications. Pharmacogenomics seeks to understand the genomic basis for human responses to drugs, such as drug metabolism, toxicity, distribution, and drug elimination. People respond differently to the same drug: a dose that is appropriate for one person may be toxic for another. Information from genetics and genomics (basic sciences) can be used to suggest strategies for adjusting doses to a person's genetic profile, or for developing new drugs tailored to specific genetic profiles (Licinio and Wong 2002). There are many other areas where basic research flows naturally into practical applications, including biomedicine and biotechnology, computer science and information technology, and materials science and materials engineering. Modern technology and engineering are very different from the technology and engineering of ancient Egypt, Greece, or China; the modern versions are often closely aligned with new advancements in basic and applied research.

Fifth, although some public policy debates have taken place with little scientific input, this is a very rare situation. Governments have relied increasingly on scientific information and advice in making all sorts of policy decisions, ranging from revising public school curricula to approving new drugs. Indeed, it would be irresponsible in most cases to have a public policy debate without making use of scientific information pertaining to the issues, including information from the social sciences and humanities.

One might admit that basic science—and even research in the arts and humanities—has important practical uses without necessarily endorsing a heavy investment in basic science. One might argue that the government's research portfolio should be heavily weighted toward research with direct, immediate, practical applications, such as biomedical or military research. The further away one goes from practical applications, the weaker the justification for government funding. A quick inspection of the U.S. R & D budget shows that it is already tilted toward applied research. In the United States, 79% of R & D funds go to defense-related research, the NIH, and NASA. Although not all of this research is applied research—the DOD and the NIH both sponsor a significant amount of basic research—most of this research deals with problems, goals, and questions.

Vannevar Bush also addressed the question of how much money the government should spend on basic research. One argument that Bush gave for investing in basic research, which still makes sense today, is that the government should invest in basic science because private industry will invest in applied science, since applied research is often economically lucrative (Bush 1945). This argument certainly rings true in the United States, where 60% of all R & D is funded by private companies (Resnik 2007c). In 2005, members of the Pharmaceutical Research and Manufactures of America (PHrMA) spent $39.4 billion on R & D (Pharmaceutical Research and Manufactures of America 2006), and members of the Biotechnology Industry Organization spent about $21 billion on R & D (Biotechnology Industry Organization

2006). The NIH, the agency that sponsors most of the biomedical research funded by the U.S. government, had a budget of $28.4 billion in 2005.

Not all scientists or politicians agreed with Bush's proposal that the government should invest heavily in basic research. Some of Bush's contemporaries argued for more spending on applied research in fields such as medicine or engineering. However, history has shown, time and again, the importance of making investments in basic research, for all of the reasons discussed earlier (Guston 2000). Although there needs to be a balance between basic versus applied research, the government should spend money on both. It is important to continually make the case to the public for investing in basic research because political support will always be strong for spending money on applied research. Indeed, one reason why Congress has decided to double the budget of the NSF is that many members of Congress believe in the importance of making investments in basic research in mathematics, physics, biology, and chemistry (Mervis 2006c).

The Reliability of Science

In the previous section of this chapter, I argue that people value science because of its usefulness or practical utility. But why is science so useful? Why does science, even basic science, often lead to practical applications? Why does science play a key role in public policy? The next two sections will address these questions.

One reason why science is useful is because it is reliable. Something is reliable (or dependable) if it does what it is supposed to do most of the time. For example, an automobile is reliable if it drives most of the time without requiring repairs, a train is reliable if it arrives on time regularly, and a newspaper is reliable if it is usually truthful and accurate. Many human activities that we would not consider to be scientific can be reliable, including train service, the news media, and manufacturing. However, science's reliability is different from the reliability we find in other human activities. The reliability of science depends on the functions of science in society: What is science supposed to do? Science's main function is to provide knowledge that is descriptive, explanatory, and predictive (Haack 2003, Kitcher 1993).

Scientific knowledge is expressed in theories, hypotheses, models, and laws.[1] Thus, one could say that science is reliable insofar as it develops theories, hypotheses, laws, and models that describe, explain, and predict natural phenomena (Goldman 1986, Haack 2003, Kitcher 1993). For example, a model of the solar system is reliable to the extent that it predicts the positions of the planets; a hypothesis concerning the relationship between hurricanes and ocean temperatures is reliable if it explains and predicts the number of hurricanes in a given year; and Newton's laws of motion are reliable insofar as they predict and explain the movements of the planets.

It is important to recognize that science's reliability should be qualified with the words "generally" or "for the most part." When new scientific fields emerge, they may lack reliability until they develop and mature. For example, chemistry has become increasingly reliable ever since it emerged from alchemy in the 1700s, and medicine has become much more reliable since it broke away from quackery in the early 1900s (Burke 1995, Butterfield 1997). Also, some sciences are more reliable than others because they are better at prediction and explanation.

---

1. A hypothesis is a descriptive statement one can use to make predictions or explanations. For example, "The patient has HIV" is a hypothesis about the health of the patient (also known as a diagnosis) that one can use to explain the patient's symptoms (such as a low white blood cell count) or predict future changes in the patient's health (such as increased infections). A theory is a unified set of descriptive statements one can use in explanation or prediction. For example, the germ theory of disease is a set of statements about how diseases are acquired, transmitted, prevented, and treated. The theory can explain how epidemics occur and how vaccines work, and it can predict outbreaks of disease. A model is a set of statements, or an image, a diagram, or a structure that represents a complex system in the world. One can use a model to explain or predict the behavior of the system. For example, the Copernican model of the solar system represents the orbits and positions of the planets around the sun. A law is a well-accepted theory or hypothesis that states a generalization. For example, F = ma (force equals mass times acceleration) is Newton's second law of motion. Newton's second law was a hypothesis before becoming a law. Sometimes, writers refer to well-accepted hypotheses or laws as "facts." For further discussion of hypotheses, theories, laws, and models, see Giere (1988).

For example, physics is more reliable than molecular biology, and the latter is more reliable than sociology. Despite these qualifications, it is still the case that science is *generally* reliable.

Why is science generally reliable? To answer this question we need to say a bit more about scientific knowledge. According to a standard view, knowledge is justified, true belief (Goldman 1986). For a belief to count as knowledge it must be properly justified. A person could have a true belief but this would not be considered knowledge unless it is also properly justified. For example, a person who correctly guesses the year in which I was born does not know that I was born in that year, because guesses are not justified beliefs. My mother knows the year in which I was born based on her memory of giving birth to me. Justified beliefs do not count as knowledge unless they are also true. For example, suppose all the evidence in a criminal case supports the conclusion that Person X committed a murder, when, in fact, Person X is innocent but someone who looks exactly like Person X committed the murder. A juror could have sufficient justification to conclude that Person X committed the murder, but this belief would not be true and would not count as knowledge.

Scientists have various rules, procedures, and standards for justifying beliefs that are also known as scientific methods. We will examine these in more detail in another section of this chapter. For now, we need to consider the idea that science develops theories, hypotheses, models, or laws, which are or could be true. What is truth? Once again, answering this question would take us deep into a philosophical jungle that I will not explore in depth here. For the purposes of this book, I will adopt a popular conception of truth known as the correspondence theory (Giere 1988, Goldman 1986, Wittgenstein 2001). According to this approach, a mental or linguistic representation (such as a belief, sentence, hypothesis, or theory) is true if it corresponds to a reality independent of human beliefs, ideas, values, and assumptions. For example, the sentence "snow is white" is true just in case there is something in reality (or the world) that we refer to as snow and that thing (or type of thing) has a white color. The sentence "gasoline is flammable" is true if and only if there is something in the world that we refer to as gasoline and it is flammable. True representations correspond to something real.

The notion of correspondence with reality must be understood metaphorically, because it is impossible to know whether our representations literally correspond to a world that is independent of us. To know whether two different things correspond, one would need to be able to perceive both of those things and compare them. For example, one can examine two photos taken at different times to determine whether the same objects occur in both photos. Although we can perceive our own representations of reality, we cannot perceive reality in itself, because we always perceive the world via our own concepts and beliefs (Kant 2003). When I perceive snow, I do not perceive the snow as it really is, but how the snow appears to me. I see it as white, in motion, fluffy, cold, solid, shaped like dots, and so on.

Philosophers have used different metaphors to explain how our representations could correspond with reality, such as isomorphism, concurrence, picturing, or similarity (Giere 1988, Goldman 1986). One way to think of correspondence is that it is like a mapping relationship (Kitcher 1993). A map corresponds to a city insofar as places on the map are linked to places in the city, and the spatial relationships represented in the map preserve the spatial relationships in the city. If the map is accurate, one will be able to use the map to navigate around the city: it will have practical value. Many scientific representations have much in common with maps. When scientists are studying structures, they often build models or diagrams to represent those structures, such as Watson and Crick's model of DNA, Bohr's model of the atom, Wegner's model of the continental plates, or Copernicus's model of the solar system. When scientists are studying processes, such as the steps of cell division, nuclear fission, photosynthesis, disease etiology, or star formation, they often develop diagrams, models, flow charts, or schemas that represent steps in processes. Representations of processes are like temporal maps. For example, a representation of an HIV infection should include the steps of infection, from contact with the virus, to propagation of the virus, to the destruction of white blood cells, and so on.

No map is a perfect representation of the world: a map is always an approximation that represents some aspects of the world. For example, a map of a city will usually not include information about parked cars, cracks in sidewalks, or sewer grates. However, a map need not be perfect in order to be very useful. As long as the map accurately represents aspects of the world that one needs for one's purposes, it will be useful. For example, if one wants to use the map to navigate the city, the map will be useful if it includes all the streets that one needs to travel. If one wants to use the map to build a housing development, the map will not be very useful if it does not contain information about elevations and sewer and gas lines. The same point also applies to scientific represen- tations. Theories, hypotheses, models, and laws are approximations that represent some aspects of the world (Cartwright 1983). They can still be useful as long as they accurately represent aspects of the world one requires for description, explanation, or prediction. For example, Newton's laws of motion are very good at describing, explaining, and predicting motion at sub-light velocities, but they do not work very well at velocities approaching the speed of light. Newton's laws are approximations, but they are still very useful (Giere 1988).

Even though scientific representations of reality will always be approximations, some are better than others for specific purposes. If we are interested in a precise measurement of the value of pi, then 3.141592653 is a better approximation than 3.141593, which is better than 3.1416, which is better than 3.14. Scientists are interested in describing, explaining, and predicting phenomena. Science makes progress over time as its theories, hypotheses, laws, and models become better at describing, explaining, and predicting events in the world (Boyd 1983, Kitcher 1993). Quantum physics is a better approximation of reality than Newtonian physics, which is a better approximation of reality than Aristotelian physics. Molecular genetics is a better approx- imation of the world than Mendelian genetics, which is a better approximation than the blending theory of inheritance. Scientific methods (discussed in more depth later) are the key to developing bet- ter approximations (Boyd 1983, Haack 2003, Kitcher 1993).

Many sociologists, historians, and philosophers of science, and even some scientists, would disagree with my claim that science makes progress toward an approximation of reality. Much of the skepticism concerning scientific progress stems from the writings of Kuhn (1970), whose book *The Structure of Scientific Revolutions* challenged the idea that science is a steady march toward the truth. According to Kuhn, scientific disciplines go through different phases of change. During the normal science phase, people in the field accept a core set of beliefs, methods, theories, and concepts known as a paradigm. Progress occurs within the paradigm as scientists solve problems that can be solved within the paradigm. However, unsolvable problems and anomalies arise, and scientists must decide whether to continue clinging to the dominant paradigm. Eventually, the weight of problems and anomalies becomes so great that a scientific revolution occurs. A new paradigm emerges, and the cycle continues again. The transition from one paradigm to another is not a rational choice like adding two numbers: it is like learning to see a Gestalt image in a different way or having a religious "conversion" experience. Because scientists do not rationally compare and choose competing paradigms, progress can occur within a paradigm, but there is no overall progress from one paradigm to the next. Although Kuhn did not reject the notion of scientific progress outright, he did argue that we need a new notion of scientific progress (Kuhn 1970). Some scholars have gone one step further than Kuhn and have asserted that science does not make progress. All scientific theories, hypotheses, and models are good only within a particular paradigm or world-view. Today's science is different from, but not better than, yesterday's science. It is not a better approximation of reality (Barnes 1977, Knorr-Cetina 1981, Latour and Woolgar 1986).

There are at least two different ways to respond to skeptical views about progress. First, one could challenge Kuhn's reading of the history of science and argue that science usually changes through the slow, cumulative changes one finds in normal science, rather than through the major upheavals that occur in revolutions. In his book, Kuhn focused on revolutionary changes in scientific disciplines, such as the shift from Newtonian physics to quantum physics. However, one could argue that most of the history of science is marked by the piecemeal changes found in fields such as optics, statistics, or biochemistry. Second, one could argue that overall progress can still happen even when a scientific revolution occurs. In normal science, the methods, theories, and concepts within the paradigm can serve as standards for measuring progress. In revolutionary science, one can appeal to standards that transcend specific paradigms to measure progress. Kuhn (1970) held that paradigms were not comparable because they do not share common theories, concepts, terms, methods, or evidence. However, one might argue that one can use epistemic values (discussed later) to compare succeeding paradigms, because epistemic values transcend any particular paradigm (Kuhn 1977). Newtonian physicists and quantum physicists would both agree that simplicity, testability, empirical support, and the like are important desiderata, even if they accept radically different theories and world-views. One could appeal to epistemic values to decide whether a new paradigm is better at description, explanation, or prediction than an older one.

Returning to the questions at the beginning of this section, we have a partial explanation of the usefulness of science. One reason why science is useful is that it is generally reliable, and it is generally reliable because it approximates reality. We can use science to control and manipulate phenomena, because it gives us an approximate representation of the world (Boyd 1983, Hacking 1983). Scientific realism—the view that scientific theories, hypotheses, models, and laws approximate reality—helps us to understand the practical success of science. For example, NASA scientists and engineers used Newton's laws of motion and gravitation to plan and execute the Apollo 11 mission that went from the earth to the moon and back. They used Newton's laws to estimate the amount of thrust needed to leave the earth, the amount of fuel needed during the trip, the trajectory of the spaceship, and the velocity needed to maintain an orbit around the moon. Newton's laws were useful to the scientists and engineers because they accurately described the path of the spaceship and made reliable predictions. It is hard to imagine how scientists and engineers could have accomplished these complex feats if Newton's laws were mere fiction with no relationship at all to reality.

Before concluding this section, it is worth considering another objection. One might object to this account of science's reliability by claiming that the reliability of science resides in its technological applications, not in its theories, hypotheses, or models. Scientific theories, hypotheses, principles, and models could be totally fictitious, with no connection to reality. As long as the technology works, the science behind it is irrelevant. For example, early hunter-gatherer societies were able to use fire without knowing anything about oxidation. The Egyptians built pyramids without a great deal of knowledge about engineering or physics. Even in modern times technological innovations occur without much input from science, such as the discovery of penicillin.

While I admit that one can have reliable technology that is totally independent of science, this is usually not the case. More often than not, the reliability of technology and science go hand-in-hand. To send a rocket to the moon, one needs many different technologies that work well, such as rocket engines, heat-resistant shields, computers, and electric wires. One cannot launch, navigate, or land a rocket successfully without using the laws of mechanics, astrophysics, thermodynamics, and aeronautics. In addition, scientific theories, principles, hypotheses, and methods play an important role in designing the technologies that are used in rockets. For example, one needs to use principles and theories of chemistry and solid-state physics to design heat shields, and one needs to conduct scientific experiments to determine whether the shields are effective. As noted previously in this chapter, in many areas of research the walls between science and technology are breaking down, since the new theories, hypotheses, and models are immediately translated into new technologies, and newly developing technologies require new theories, hypotheses, and models. The bottom line is that one needs both reliable science and technology to achieve practical results. Science and technology interact and intertwine in important ways.

The Objectivity of Science

As we have just seen, one reason why science is useful is that it is generally reliable. A second reason why science is useful is that it aspires to be objective (Resnik 2007c). The word "objective," like the word "science," is difficult to define. There are at least two distinct meanings of this word. One meaning of objective is "true or real." According to the *American Heritage Dictionary* (2008), a definition of "objective" is "having actual existence or reality." In the previous section I argued that science is (generally) objective insofar as scientific theories, hypotheses, models, and laws approximate reality. This way of defining objectivity is not my concern in this section. A second meaning of the word "objective," which shall be the focus of this section, equates objective with "unbiased." The *American Heritage Dictionary* also defines "objective" as "uninfluenced by emotions or personal prejudices." I would add to this definition the phrase "uninfluenced by politics, culture, economic interests, or religion." So, something is objective if it is not influenced by personal prejudice or emotion, politics, ideology, culture, economic interests, or religion, that is, it is unbiased (Longino 1990).

Is science unbiased? It is highly unlikely that any scientific discipline ever has been or ever will be completely unbiased, for the simple reason that every scientific discipline is composed of human beings who will sometimes allow prejudice, emotions, politics, and other biases to influence their thoughts, decisions, and actions. People are not robots. But I am not attempting to prove that science is unbiased. My claim in this chapter is less ambitious: I will argue only that (a) scientists should strive to reduce or mitigate biases in their work, and (b) scientists can make progress toward that goal. Scientists should aspire to be objective.

Scientists should strive for objectivity because objectivity is necessary for the formation of fair and effective public policy. In formulating and implementing public policies, societies require information and advice that is as free as is humanly possible from personal, political, economic, religious, or other biases. Societies need neutral arbiters. Although science is not perfectly unbiased, it is less biased than other human activities, such as politics, religion, literature, and business. Scientific information and advice can promote deliberation, compromise, and agreement about public policy issues by serving as a neutral reference point (Gutmann and Thompson 1996). Without information and advice that is relatively unbiased, public policy debates would be little more than political games, often ending in stalemates. Objectivity offers the hope of settling debates in a fair and reasonable way. Unbiased information and advice in public policy debates is especially important in pluralistic societies, like the United States, where people have different social, moral, and cultural values that can fuel political controversy (Resnik 2007c).

As an example of how science functions in policy deliberations, consider the debate about restrictions on public smoking, which pits individual rights against public health. For many years this debate was at a standstill. Smokers asserted their rights to smoke, and nonsmokers asserted their rights not to be bothered by smoke. Many restaurants and bars established smoking and nonsmoking sections to satisfy their customers, but there were no major policy changes other than this. The political landscape started to change, however, when scientific evidence on the harmful effects of secondhand smoke began to accumulate (National Cancer Institute 1999). Opponents of smoking, citing evidence of the harms of secondhand smoke, lobbied for bans on smoking in public. State and local governments, as well as private employers, began to restrict smoking in public places. Without scientific evidence concerning the risks of exposure to secondhand smoke, it is likely that this debate would not have advanced as far as it did.

Science can have a significant impact on policy debates because opposing parties view science as neutral, impartial, and trustworthy. People who disagree about politics can find common ground in science. Agreement about the scientific evidence concerning secondhand smoke helped transform the smoking debate from the rights of smokers versus the rights of nonsmokers to the rights of smokers versus public health. People who tolerated smoking in public when it was regarded as a mere nuisance objected to it once smoking came to be viewed as a threat to the health of nonsmokers. Sometimes people who disagree about political issues also disagree about scientific ones, and this makes fair and effective deliberation very difficult. In some cases, political opponents try to manipulate the science to fit their preferred version of reality (Pielke 2007). This is precisely what has happened in the debate on the global warming issue (mentioned in chapter 1). Little progress will be made in this debate until the different sides, that is, environmentalists and business interests, can find some common ground concerning the science of global climate change.

Pielke (2007) argues that scientists do not always need to be neutral arbiters in policy debates. He distinguishes between four different roles scientists have played in policy debates: (a) the pure scientist (not involved in policy debates), (b) the issue advocate (conducts research and gives advice with a political agenda in mind), (c) the science arbiter (engages in policy, but in a neutral way; sticks to the facts), and (d) the honest broker of policy alternatives (engages in policy, suggests different policy options, discusses how facts apply to the different options). I have argued that scientists should perform the role of science arbiter (or neutral arbiter), but Pielke argues that scientists ought to sometimes serve as honest brokers in policy debates, because this helps the public to think clearly about the different options. I agree with Pielke that scientists can do more than just serve as neutral arbiters: they can also take on the role of the honest broker of policy alternatives. An honest broker is an acceptable role for scientists in policy debates because the role does not surrender objectivity for advocacy or bias. Pielke warns about the dangers of issue advocacy and the politicalization of science: "If scientists evaluate the research findings of their peers on the basis of the implications for issue advocacy, then 'scientific' debates among academics risk morphing into political debates. From the perspective of the public or policy makers, scientific debate and political debate on many environmental issues already have become indistinguishable, and such cases of conflation limit the role of science in the development of feasible policy options" (Pielke 2007, 117).

I also agree with Pielke's concerns about the dangers of issue advocacy science. I would add that issue advocacy science can undermine the public's trust in scientists as neutral arbiters or honest brokers. Suppose that the scientific "evidence" in the smoking debate had been generated not by academic researchers or government agencies, but by two advocacy groups: a prosmoking study funded by cigarette manufacturers, and an antismoking study funded by an antismoking group. Neither of these studies would be perceived as neutral, fair, and impartial: they would both be viewed as highly politicized and biased. It is likely that little progress would have been made if all the studies on the effects of secondhand smoke had been advocacy studies.

As Pielke notes, issue advocacy science has been a problem in environmental debates, and I concur with him. Many of the studies on both sides of the global warming debate have been distorted or manipulated by advocates eager to prove a point. In chapter 1, I described how the administration of George W. Bush has engaged in an extreme version of advocacy science, but it is worth noting that environmentalists have also twisted the truth for political ends. Former vice president Al Gore's book and documentary *An Inconvenient Truth* helped to alert many people to the importance of taking effective action to deal with global climate change. In October 2007, Gore shared the Nobel Peace Prize for his work on climate change with the United Nations (UN) Intergovernmental Panel on Climate Change (Gibbs and Lyall 2007). However, some scientists who agree with the main ideas contained in *An Inconvenient Truth* have expressed concern that the film contains inaccuracies and hyperbole and that it is overly alarmist (Broad 2007). Indeed, a British judge ruled that Gore's film contained nine inaccuracies, and that the government could not show the film to schoolchildren without informing them that it contains inaccuracies and is a political work that promotes one side of the debate (Baram 2007). (We will examine these issues again in chapter 4.)

If objectivity is a goal worth pursuing, how can scientists achieve it? What can scientists do to minimize or mitigate biases? Scientific methods hold the key. Many of the methods of science (discussed in more depth later) help to reduce bias (Haack 2003, Kitcher 1993,

2001). One of science's most important methods is peer review. Prior to publication, scientific papers are carefully scrutinized by editors and reviewers. Papers that do not pass muster may be rejected outright or returned to the authors for revisions. Following publication, papers are read by colleagues in the field and subjected to additional criticism. Other scientists may publish their own papers challenging published papers, they may try to repeat experiments described in published papers, or they may reanalyze data described in published papers. This process helps to weed out minor errors, systematic errors, and biases. Peer review is by no means perfect at eliminating all biases from research, but it is much better at controlling biases than methods used by nonscientific disciplines (Chubin and Hackett 1990, Ziman 2000). Science's experimental methods also are designed to reduce bias. For example, in a controlled trial of the safety and efficacy of a new drug, subjects will often be randomly assigned to one of two treatment groups, one receiving the new drug and another receiving a standard therapy. Randomization helps to reduce the bias that might result from voluntary assignment to a treatment group, since a researcher might assign the healthiest patients to an experimental group, or the healthiest patients might choose this group. Controlled trials also use double-blinding: both the subjects and researchers are prevented from knowing which drug is being taken. Double-blinding helps to reduce biases that may occur when subjects or researchers change their behavior upon learning which drug is being administered. Subjects may expect that the experimental drug will be more effective than the existing one (Gallin 2002). Many other methods in science help to reduce bias, including methods for developing and conducting surveys, methods for statistical analysis, and methods for interpreting data.

Though I believe that scientific methods are the key to objectivity in science, I am well aware of scholarship from the history, sociology, and philosophy of science, which has shown that political, economic, social, or other biases often affect scientific research. For example, racist assumptions have affected research on human intelligence. During the 1800s, many scientists believed that Caucasians were intellectually superior to Africans and Native Americans. They also believed that intelligence and personality were a function of the shape of the head and face. Scientists, known as phrenologists, developed diagrams of the heads of different races and racial subgroups and used these diagrams to make inferences about intelligence. Racist assumptions about human intelligence persisted into the 1900s, even though theories developed in the 1800s had been abandoned (Gould 1981). Pharmaceutical research is another striking example of biases in science. There is now considerable evidence for a funding effect in pharmaceutical research: if a study is sponsored by a drug company, the study is likely to favor the company's products (Krimsky 2003). Drug companies have used various strategies to skew research results in favor of their products, such as manipulation of the study design, dishonest data analysis, suppression of data and results, publishing the same study twice, using ghost authors, and even fabrication or falsification of data. Although universities, scientific associations, and journals have developed rules and guidelines to deal with the various ways that financial interests can affect research, numerous problems persist (Angell 2004, Greenberg 2001, Krimsky 2003, Resnik 2007c).

Thus, there is ample evidence that science often falls far short of the goal of objectivity. In response to this striking evidence of biases in scientific research, some scholars, such as Barnes (1977), Knorr-Cetina (1981), and Latour and Woolgar (1986), have argued that the objectivity of science is a useless myth that must be abandoned. Objectivity is not even worth pursuing as a goal because science never has been and never will be objective. We should regard science as little more than politics by other means, or a battle of clashing interests and agendas.

I disagree with this harsh judgment of science. Although science is not completely unbiased and probably never will be, objectivity is not a useless myth, since the goal of objectivity is worth pursuing and some measure of success is possible. There is not now, nor will there ever be, a perfectly just legal system, but this social fact does not undermine the obligation to strive for justice. Like justice, objectivity can serve as a normative ideal, even though human beings may often fall short of the mark. Scientists can make progress toward this ideal by eliminating or counteracting social, political, economic, and other biases. For example, 21st-century psychologists have rejected the racist assumptions about human intelligence held by 19th-century psychologists. In pharmaceutical research, scientists not affiliated with a particular company can reanalyze the data produced by the company, critique the study design, or conduct their own independent research (Resnik 2007c).

Before concluding this section, it is worth considering one more objection. One might object to my account of objectivity by asserting that some sciences are and always will be so fraught with bias that objectivity is not even worth pursuing as a normative ideal. One might argue that the social sciences, that is, sociology, psychology, economics, political science, and anthropology, will always reflect human values and interests. The topics studied by social scientists, such as marriage, religion, free markets, art, political parties, crime, and warfare, are inherently value-laden. The very definition of these subjects is a function of the moral, political, or other values or interests that one holds. For instance, crime is defined as a type of behavior that is illegal and often immoral. Thus, one cannot study crime without making moral judgments about the subject matter. Also, many of the methods used in social science introduce bias because they affect the research subjects. The observer effect is a common problem in social science: research subjects who know they are being observed will change their behavior in response to this knowledge. Thus, instead of pursuing objectivity in social science, researchers should accept and embrace their biases, and develop theories, hypotheses, and models that are designed to promote specific values or interests. (For further discussion, see Rosenberg [1995].)

I admit that it can be very difficult to pursue objectivity in the social sciences, but I do not think that objectivity should be abandoned in this area, because it is possible to reduce bias or compensate for it. Social scientists have developed many different methods to try to reduce bias or deal with it. While it may never be possible to develop value-neutral concepts or theories in social science, peer review and rigorous criticism can help to counteract or eliminate some biases, because colleagues and critics can bring a different perspective to a research project. Also, achieving racial, ethnic, and gender diversity can help to reduce biases, because people with different backgrounds may be more aware of some types of biases (Longino 1990). For example, female anthropologists have pointed out some of the biases that male anthropologists incorporated into theories of hunter-gatherer societies. Concerning the observer effect, there are ethically acceptable forms of deception that social scientists can use to minimize this problem. For example, when administering a survey, a social scientist can refrain from informing the subjects about any hypotheses that are being tested. A social scientist can also ask the same question in different ways to ensure consistency in responses and reduce bias. There are also some types of experimental methods that involve deception but impose only minimal risks on human participants. For example, subjects can participate in low-risk experiments in which they are not told the precise reason for the experiment or the hypothesis being tested. They can be debriefed after the experiment is over (Benham 2008). Finally, one of the best ways to deal with biases is for the social scientist to reflect on his or her own biases and consider how they might affect his or her research. Social scientists can openly discuss their biases when reporting their research, so that other scientists can understand how their biases may have affected their results, and respond accordingly. Although the social sciences will probably always be less objective than the natural sciences, they can still aspire to the ideal of objectivity (Rosenberg 1995).

The Methods of Science

Up to this point in the chapter I have argued that science is useful because it is generally reliable and aspires to be objective. I have also argued that methodology is the key to reliability and objectivity. In this section I will describe science's methods in more detail. A method is a way of doing something well. There are methods for successful golfing, for decorating cakes, for diagnosing disease, and for conducting scientific research. Scientific methods are rules for doing (or practicing) science. Scientific methods consists of rules of varying degrees of generality, ranging from highly general rules like "choose the simplest hypothesis" to highly specific ones like "store research records for at least five years." Scientific methods include epistemological rules for developing and testing new knowledge, as well as ethical rules for interacting with other scientists and society. Methods play a key role in the progress of science (Boyd 1983, Haack 2003, Kitcher 1993). As mentioned earlier, methods can help to distinguish the scientist from the charlatan and the physician from the quack (Kitcher 1983).

So what are the methods of science? Epistemological methods consist of rules, strategies, techniques, and procedures used by scientists to develop and test theories, hypotheses, and models. Philosophers and scientists often talk about "the scientific method" as if there was

---

Box 2.1. Steps of scientific research

---

1. Select a problem, question, or topic for research
2. Review the relevant literature
3. Generate a hypothesis (theory or model) to test
4. Design procedures to test the hypothesis
5. Collect data through observation or experimentation
6. Analyze and interpret data
7. Submit research for peer review
8. Publish/disseminate research
9. Other scientists evaluate, test, and criticize research
10. Acceptance of research by the scientific community

---

only a single method followed by all scientists. While there are some methods, procedures, and standards common to all scientific disciplines, scientific disciplines also have their own special standards. For example, physicists do not conduct surveys or interviews to test models of the electron, anthropologists do not conduct controlled clinical trials to learn about cultures, and so on. Science is methodologically diverse (Dupre 1993, Kitcher 1993). Even though there is no single scientific method, most different scientific disciplines adhere to the steps shown in box 2.1 (Shamoo and Resnik 2003).

These steps provide a rough description of most scientific research, but they are somewhat of an oversimplification. First, scientists may not always follow these steps in precisely this order. Some preliminary data collection often precedes hypothesis generation, and some form of preliminary peer review often occurs before problem selection. Second, scientists may go back and forth between and among steps. For example, researchers may decide to revise their hypotheses or research design after conducting some pilot studies. Third, more than one step may occur at the same time. For example, a researcher may conceive of a hypothesis while reviewing the literature or thinking about a problem.

The various epistemological methods used by scientists did not emerge all at once: scientists, philosophers, logicians, and statisticians developed them over the last 2,500 years (Ronan 1982). Such distinguished thinkers as Aristotle (384–322 B.C.), Bacon, Galileo Galilei (1564–1642), William Harvey (1578–1657), René Descartes (1596–1650), Robert Boyle (1627–91), Isaac Newton (1642–1727), Pierre de Laplace (1749–1827), William Whewell (1794–1866), John Stuart Mill (1806–73), Claude Bernard (1813–78), Louis Pasteur (1882–95), Francis Galton (1822–1911), and Ronald Fischer (1890–1962) have made important contributions to the advancement of scientific methods through their writings, scientific work, or both. While there is no need to review this rich history here, some milestones are worth noting. Aristotle and Bacon wrote about the importance of observation and induction, and Galileo, Harvey, and Boyle were instrumental in the development of experimentation as a means of making controlled observations (Aristotle 2000, Bacon 2005). While scientists have always published their ideas in books or other manuscripts, it became much easier and quicker with the emergence of the first scientific journals in the late 1600s. The practice of peer review, which is now so fundamental to science, did not become a formal part of research until the 1700s, when journals began to require it. Modern science makes extensive use of statistics in research design and data analysis, but many of the statistical methods and techniques used in research were not developed until the 1800s and 1900s (Boorstin 1983).

For many years, philosophers who wrote about scientific methods devoted most of their time and energy to thinking only about the steps of the method where scientists draw inferences and justify their beliefs, such as data analysis, data interpretation, and the evaluation of scientific research by the scientific community. These writers equated the scientific method with the logic and epistemology of science (see, for example, Hempel 1965, Nagel 1961, Popper 1959). During the 1960s, 1970s, and 1980s, historians of science, such as Kuhn (1970); sociologists of science, such as Merton (1973), Barnes (1977), and Latour and Woolgar (1986); and philosophers of science, such as Lakatos (1970) and Laudan (1977), convinced philosophers and other science scholars that the methodology of science should also address historical, social, psychological, political, ethical, and economic aspects of research. Although there is an ongoing dispute concerning the degree to which scientific choices are influenced by reasoning and evidence, as opposed to historical, social, and other factors, a consensus has emerged that these other factors play a large role in problem selection, publication and dissemination, research design, and testing (Haack 2003, Kitcher 2003, Shamoo and Resnik 2008). For example, political and economic interests play a large role in problem selection, because most research is paid for by the government or private industry. Ethical concerns influence research design and testing involving human or animal subjects, because people want to protect humans and animals from harm. Economic and political interests can influence the dissemination of data and results, since governments may seek to prevent the publication of dangerous research, and private companies may want to prevent proprietary information from being distributed to the public (Resnik 1998, 2007c).

At one time, philosophers hoped to design a rigorous, formal system of inductive logic that scientists could use to decide when to accept or reject scientific theories, hypotheses, and models (Klee 1997, Nagel 1961). The system could tell one the degree of confirmation (or proof) of a hypothesis, theory, or model, given the evidence. In theory, the whole process of research could be formalized, so that a computer could execute an algorithm (that is, a set of formal rules and procedures) for making scientific discoveries. This formal approach to scientific decision-making did not work for a variety of reasons. First, the approach made no attempt to come to terms with the processes by which scientists conceive of hypotheses, theories, or models to test. Proposing a new idea to test involves creativity and insight, and we are not likely to develop a computer that can simulate these human traits any time soon (Kantorovich 1993). Second, very often competing hypotheses, theories, or models are equally supported by the data, and one must appeal to nonevidentiary factors, such as simplicity or novelty, to decide which one to accept or reject (Haack 2003, Kitcher 1993). Third, systems of inductive logic, which are used to draw inferences from data, are plagued by several philosophical and logical problems that have resisted easy solutions. (For a review of these problems, see Haack [2003].)

Although some philosophers, logicians, and statisticians are still pursuing formal approaches to scientific decision-making (see, for example, Howson and Urbach 2005), many philosophers, historians, and sociologists of science now accept the idea that scientific decision-making is best understood as an informal process in which researchers weigh and consider different epistemological values (or criteria or

Box 2.2.   Epistemological values in scientific research

Testability	A good hypothesis (theory, model, or method) can be tested.
Empirical support	A good hypothesis is well supported by the evidence.
Consistency	A good hypothesis is internally consistent.
Precision	A good hypothesis is clearly defined and quantifiable.
Coherence	A good hypothesis coheres with other well-accepted theories, hypotheses, laws, or models.
Parsimony (Occam's Razor)	A good hypothesis is simple, economical, and elegant.
Generality	A good hypothesis is widely applicable.
Consilience (or unification)	A good hypothesis brings together disparate phenomena under a common scheme.
Novelty	A good hypothesis is new, original, or innovative.
Fruitfulness	A good hypothesis opens up new avenues of inquiry and leads to the development of new concepts, theories, hypotheses, models, and methods.

desiderata).[2] Accepting a new scientific theory is like the decision to buy a new car. When deciding to buy a new car, one carefully considers many different factors, such as price, fuel economy, safety, reliability, and so on. Though some of these decision-making factors, such

2. The values I am discussing here are epistemological, not social, political, or religious. They are values that guide research and inquiry. Although scientists should try to minimize the impact of social, political, or religious values on their work, they cannot avoid epistemological values.

as cost and fuel economy comparisons, can be formalized, others, such as style and reputation, cannot. One does not follow an algorithm when deciding to purchase a car. Likewise, scientists must consider different values, such as empirical support and simplicity, when choosing among competing theories, models, hypotheses, or methods. Box 2.2 shows a list of some of the values that guide scientific decision-making (see Haack 2003, Kitcher 1993, Kuhn 1977, Longino 1990, Quine and Ullian 1978, and Thagard 1992 for further discussion).

Some epistemological values, such as empirical support or consistency, can be formalized. For example, deductive logical systems can be viewed as rules for preserving logical consistency, and inductive logical systems and statistical methods can be viewed as rules for assessing the strength of the connection between a hypothesis and the evidence (Copi 1986). Other values, such as novelty, parsimony, and fruitfulness, resist formalization.

Very few theories, models, hypotheses. or methods satisfy all of these values, but many satisfy most of them. Very often, scientists will need to choose among theories, models, hypotheses, or methods that satisfy different values. For example, one theory might satisfy empirical adequacy, testability, simplicity, and precision, while another satisfies empirical adequacy, testability, consilience, and novelty (Kitcher 1993, Resnik 2007c, Shamoo and Resnik 2008).

In addition to the steps of research and epistemological values, scientific methods also include ethical principles (Resnik 1998, Shamoo and Resnik 2008). Ethical principles have received less attention in the philosophical literature than epistemological ones, but ethical principles are still very important in achieving the goals of science. Fabricating or falsifying data to "prove" a hypothesis is not a good way of reaching the truth. Manipulating a statistical analysis to achieve a result that supports one's economic interests is not a good way to reduce bias. Ethical principles help to promote the reliability of research, objectivity, and progress of research, along with cooperation and trust among researchers. Furthermore, ethical principles help to ensure that science is trustworthy and publicly accountable. Box 2.3 is a list of some ethical principles for scientific research.

The ethical principles described in box 2.3 apply to the various steps of scientific research as well as other aspects of science, such as grant reviewing, hiring and promotion, personal relationships,

Box 2.3.   Ethical principles for scientific research

Honesty	Honestly report data, results, methods and procedures, publication status, research contributions, and conflicts of interest. Do not fabricate, falsify, or misrepresent data.
Objectivity	Strive for objectivity in matters involving other scientists (such as personnel decisions), as well as interactions with the public (such as scientific advising and expert legal testimony).
Carefulness	Avoid careless errors and negligence; carefully and critically examine your own work and the work of your peers. Keep good records of research activities.
Openness	Share data, results, ideas, tools, and resources. Be open to criticism and new ideas.
Confidentiality	Protect confidential communications, such as papers or grants submitted for publication, personnel records, trade or military secrets, and patient records.
Respect for colleagues	Respect your colleagues and students; avoid harming them and promote their well-being. Treat your colleagues fairly.
Respect for intellectual property	Honor patents, copyrights, and other forms of intellectual property. Do not use unpublished data, methods, or results without permission. Give credit where credit is due.

Freedom	Research institutions, research sponsors, and governments should promote freedom of thought, inquiry, and communication.
Social responsibility	Strive to do good for society and avoid or prevent harm.
Stewardship	Make effective use of human, financial, and technological resources.
Education	Educate, mentor, advise, and train the next generation of scientists.
Competence	Maintain and improve your own professional competence and expertise through lifelong education and learning.
Equality of opportunity	Promote equality of opportunity for science students and colleagues; avoid discrimination in admissions decisions, personnel decisions, and peer review decisions.
Legality	Know and obey relevant laws, regulations, and policies.
Animal care	Demonstrate proper care for animals when using them in research. Do not conduct unnecessary or poorly designed animal experiments.
Human subject protection	Show appropriate care and respect for human subjects when using them in research. Protect the rights and welfare of human subjects.

Source: Based on Shamoo and Resnik (2008).

education, and interactions with research subjects. Some of the principles, such as honesty, objectivity, carefulness, and openness, are closely connected to epistemological values. For example, honesty promotes the search for truth. Objectivity serves as an epistemological goal and an ethical principle in science. These ethical principles are best understood as guidelines for conduct rather than absolute rules. Since these principles may sometimes conflict, scientists may need to choose which principle merits a higher priority, given the circumstances. For example, if a researcher working for a private company discovers that the company's decision to keep some research results secret could harm the public, the researcher may need to choose between honoring the confidentiality of proprietary information and acting in a socially responsible manner. Since ethical dilemmas, such as this one, can arise in scientific research, it is important for scientists to learn how to think clearly about moral choices (Shamoo and Resnik 2008, Steneck 2004).

Conclusion

In this chapter, I have constructed a philosophical framework to support arguments and conclusions that will be defended in successive chapters. I will apply the ideas developed in this chapter to concrete problems related to the politics of science in subsequent chapters. In this chapter, I have argued that science is useful (and valuable) because it is generally reliable and it aspires to the goal of objectivity. Science's epistemological and ethical methods hold the key to the value of science, because methods promote reliability and objectivity. One implication of this view is that social, political, economic, or other circumstances that interfere with the practice and methods of science, such as the situations described in chapter 1, could have dire implications for the reliability and objectivity of science. The next chapter will examine some of the consequences of government interference in scientific practice, as well as the consequences of unregulated science, and argue for the autonomy of science, within limits.

3

The Autonomy of Science

The only freedom that is of enduring importance is the freedom
of intelligence, that is to say, freedom of observation and of
judgment, exercised in behalf of purposes that are intrinsically
worth while.

—John Dewey

The previous chapter developed a philosophical foundation for think-ing about the nature of scientific research and science's role in society. I argued that science is valuable for its practical applications and policy implications, and that it is able to perform these functions because it is generally reliable and aspires to be objective (that is, unbiased). Reli-ability and objectivity depend, in large part, on the epistemological and ethical methods of scientific practice. An immediate implication of this view is that outside interference in the practice and methods of science could have grave implications for the usefulness of science to society. In this chapter, I will use ethical theories and historical exam-ples to argue for the autonomy of science, within limits. Scientific autonomy and government oversight must be appropriately balanced. The government should have broad oversight over scientific organiza-tions/institutions and processes for conducting scientific research, but the government should refrain from controlling the content of science or micromanaging science. Government oversight should be well mea-sured and fair; it should give direction without being intrusive.

What Is Autonomy?

Before developing my argument for the autonomy of science, it will be useful to say a bit more about what I mean by "autonomy." Autonomy comes from the idea of self-governance or self-rule. Many different entities may be considered to be autonomous, including human beings, organizations, institutions, and states. Although the type of self-governance exhibited by a human being is different from the type of self-governance exhibited by a state—states do not consciously reason or deliberate—both can be considered to be self-governing. Thus, it is useful to distinguish between political autonomy, that is, self-rule by a nation or state, and moral autonomy, that is, self-rule by a person (Dworkin 1988).

Autonomy can be understood as a right of self-governance or as the capacity of self-governance. The capacity for self-governance is simply the ability to make well-reasoned decisions and act on them. A person who lacks the requisite cognitive abilities for sound decision-making, such as a young child or mentally disabled adult, is not autonomous. The right to autonomy entails various freedoms (or liberties), such as freedom of thought, expression, movement, association, and action (Dworkin 1988). The fact that a person, organization, or state is capable of making decisions does not imply that he/she/it has a right to autonomy. For example, immoral organizations, such as drug cartels or terrorist networks, do not have the right to self-governance. Thus, the right to autonomy requires moral or political justification, depending on whether autonomy is moral or political.[1] In this chapter, I will focus on moral justifications of autonomy.

Moral Justifications of Autonomy

There are two distinct strategies for justifying a moral right to autonomy: a deontological one and a utilitarian one. According to deontological arguments for the right to autonomy, individuals have a right to autonomy regardless of the consequences of granting that right. The right to autonomy is inherent in the very nature of the individual. One of the most influential deontological approaches to the right to autonomy has its origins in the natural rights theory posited by the 17th-century English philosopher John Locke (1632–1704). According to Locke, all human beings have rights to life, liberty (autonomy), and

---

1. I will use the words "ethical" and "moral" interchangeably.

property (Locke 2004). The main function of government is to protect individual rights, not to provide people with social services, such as education or health care. Locke's approach to rights has had a strong influence on the U.S. Constitution (1789) and various international declarations of human rights (United Nations 1948). However, one of the problems with the approach is that Locke and his followers have taken rights as a basic assumption, without explaining why human beings should have rights. What is so special about us that we should have rights? Lockeans maintain that it is part of our human nature to have rights, but what does that mean?

The 18th-century German philosopher Immanuel Kant (1724–1804) developed an ethical theory that explains the basis of a right to autonomy. According to Kant, human beings should be granted autonomy because they have the capacity to consciously develop and willingly follow moral rules: human beings are moral agents. Human beings have this capacity because they have rationality and free will (Kant 1981, 2003). An action is moral, according to Kant, if the person performs the action in order to follow a moral rule: a moral actor chooses to do his duty for duty's sake. Kant argued that a general principle, which he called the categorical imperative (CI), is the basis for all moral rules. According to one version of the CI, we should act according to a rule that could become a universal law for all people. Moral rules should apply universally. According to a different version of the CI, we should always treat human beings, including ourselves, as valuable for their own sake, not as valuable only as a means to something else. Human beings should be treated as having inherent dignity and moral worth. Both versions of the CI imply that we should respect a person's right to make choices and act on them, unless those choices violate the rules of morality (Pojman 2005). Kant's argument for autonomy does not rest on the assumption that granting individuals the right to autonomy will in some way benefit society. The right to autonomy depends on recognizing the inherent worth of individuals who have the capacity for making moral decisions (that is, moral agents), not on the consequences of granting the right to autonomy.

One of the criticisms of Kant's approach to ethics is that it does not acknowledge the importance of taking consequences into account when making moral decisions. What matters most is to follow the correct moral rule, according to Kant. The idea of following moral rules, regardless of the consequences, leads to some counterintuitive results. For example, some have argued that Kant's view implies that one should not lie to a person with murderous intent to prevent him from killing someone, since this would violate a rule against lying (Pojman 2005). Kantians have replied to this sort of objection by arguing that this problem can be avoided by clarifying the rule that might be broken. The rule is not "don't ever lie," but perhaps "don't lie, except to prevent someone with murderous intent from killing a human being." The problem with this reply is that it leads down a path where exceptions toward moral rules are made indefinitely, thus threatening the stability and usefulness of those rules. Rules with many exceptions are difficult to formulate, understand, systematize, and follow (Pojman 2005).

Utilitarian approaches to ethics, unlike deontological ones, such as Kant's view, are geared toward taking consequences into account. Utilitarian approaches to autonomy justify the right to autonomy on the basis of the consequences of granting this right. The most influential utilitarian theorist, 19th-century English philosopher and economist John Stuart Mill (1806–73), held that our primary moral obligation is to perform actions that maximize the balance of good (benefits) over bad (harms) for all people in society: we should aim to produce the greatest good for the greatest number. For Mill, happiness was the good that should be maximized, and unhappiness minimized. He referred to this idea as the greatest happiness principle (Mill 1956). Mill defended freedom of action by arguing that a greater balance of happiness/unhappiness will be produced by allowing people who are capable of self-governance to make their own choices. Interfering with the free choices of people who are capable of making choices makes those people unhappy and expends valuable resources in an attempt to control their behavior. Mill defended freedom of thought and expression by arguing that this type of freedom benefits society by promoting scientific and social progress. Solutions to problems emerge from a clash of differing opinions, and freedom of expression is important for allowing people to express different opinions. Mill also argued, however, that freedom can be restricted if the benefits of restriction outweigh the harms. The right to autonomy does not entail a right to harm other people, and freedom of expression does not imply a right to perpetrate fraud or cause a riot (Feinberg 1987, Mill 1956).

Utilitarianism has a number of different conceptual problems, but I will only mention three of them in this book.[2] The first problem is how to provide adequate protection for the rights of individuals. A very simple and naive version of utilitarianism would imply that it would be morally acceptable to kill a human being to use his organs to save five other people, because the five lives saved outweigh one life lost. Since most people would find such an action to be morally abhorrent, utilitarians must explain how to avoid this implication. The second problem with utilitarianism is to specify what is meant by "good" or "bad" consequences (Sen and Williams 1982). Mill held that happiness was the good consequence that should be maximized, but some philosophers have challenged this approach on the grounds that "happiness" is vague and poorly defined. Also, happiness may not always be good: the happiness of a bad or evil person may not be good. Other utilitarians have responded to this problem by arguing for the maximization of other types of goods, such as personal preferences, well-being, health, or economic prosperity. A third problem with utilitarianism is defining what is meant by "society." Mill held that society was limited to the people within a particular nation, but other utilitarians have argued that society should include all the people in the world, or even members of other species (Sen and Williams 1982, Singer 1999).

In this book, I will use both Kantian and utilitarian strategies to defend the autonomy of science. Since I have raised some serious objections to both of these views and I have argued that they are diametrically opposed, I owe the reader an explanation of how I will deal with these problems and weave these two disparate theories together.[3] Like Kant, I think that rules are essential for moral reasoning and decision-making. Rules play a role prospectively, when deciding what to do, and retrospectively, when justifying one's conduct to someone else (Gert 2007). Like Kant, I also think that moral rules should apply universally and should protect human dignity. A rule like "don't murder" can be justified because it applies universally and protects human dignity. Unlike Kant, I think that utilitarian considerations can be taken into account when justifying some moral rules. For example, the

2. For further discussion, see Sen and Williams (1982).

3. My approach to ethical theory is similar to views developed by Ross in 1930 (see Ross [1988]). See also Hooker (2003).

justification of a rule like "help others" is largely a function of the good consequences of following this rule (Hooker 2003).

Moral rules sometimes conflict. When this occurs, the person making a choice must decide which rule to follow. To make this decision, he or she must examine the relevant information and the available options, as well as other moral considerations, which may include (a) whether a rule protects human dignity and (b) the consequences of following different rules. Rules that protect human dignity are rules pertaining to fundamental human rights, such as the right to life, the right to autonomy, and so on. A strong burden of proof rests on those who believe the best course of action is to violate or restrict fundamental human rights. These rights can be violated or restricted only for a compelling social purpose, such as to protect other people or society from harm. Restrictions should accomplish that social purpose with the least amount of necessary burden on human rights.[4] For example, in the organ donation case mentioned earlier, the rule "don't murder" would take precedence over the rule "help others," so that one should not kill someone for his organs. Saving five people is not a compelling reason for violating one person's right to life. However, suppose a person has a deadly, infectious disease, such as tuberculosis. If he does not receive medical treatment, he may infect dozens of other people. Suppose, also, that he refuses medical treatment. It would be ethically acceptable to force him to receive medical treatment until he is no longer a threat to other people, if that option is the least burdensome one that adequately protects other people from harm. A more burdensome option, such as killing him, would not be justified, even though it would protect other people from harm.[5]

When examining the consequences of following different rules, one may consider the short-term effects on identifiable people or social institutions, as well as the long-term effects on society, including the consequences of many people following the rules. For example, lying

4. This idea is similar to the legal doctrine in U.S. constitutional law known as the strict scrutiny test. A law that restricts a fundamental right, such as free speech or due process, is constitutional only if it can pass the strict scrutiny test. To do this, the law must (a) serve a compelling government interest, (b) be narrowly tailored to serve that interest, and (c) be the least restrictive means of serving that interest (Barron and Dienes 1999).

5. See Berlin (2002) for a further discussion of freedom and human rights.

to save someone from being murdered can be justified on the grounds that the good produced by this action (for example, saving a life) will outweigh the bad. It is not likely that many people will follow this rule, because people will not often be in a position where they need to lie to murderers. However, lying to someone to help a friend acquire money may not be justified, because the good consequences of this action (for example, helping a friend acquire money) would not outweigh the bad. Many people might follow this rule because many people would be in a position to lie to help their friends.

Since utilitarian considerations are important in justifying moral rules or settling conflicts among rules, I will say a bit more about how I deal with the problems with utilitarianism I mentioned earlier. With regard to the first problem, utilitarianism aided by Kantian insights can provide adequate protection for the rights of individuals, because some of the moral rules are designed to protect human dignity and these rules receive higher priority when conflicts between rules occur. Concerning the second problem, I hold that there is no single value that should be maximized, such as happiness, but a multiplicity of values should be considered in any utilitarian calculus. My argument for this position stems from the observation that there are many things that people value, and these things cannot be compared in terms of a common metric or reduced to a single value. Some of the consequences that should be maximized include: happiness, well-being, health, justice, and economic prosperity. Some of the consequences that should be minimized include: unhappiness, disease, poverty, suffering, and injustice. Regarding the third problem, I will assume that "society" refers to the people in a particular nation, unless stated otherwise. In some situations involving international security it is important to consider people in other nations. (I will say more about national and international security in chapter 6.)

Now that I have provided some background concerning my approach to defending the autonomy of science, I will spell out my argument in more detail.

The Autonomy of Science

In arguing for science's autonomy, it will be useful to distinguish between *scientists* and *scientific organizations and institutions*. Scientific organizations and institutions include scientific disciplines, scientific associations, scholarly journals, universities, research institutes, laboratories, private companies, and other groups that conduct, support, sponsor, review, or publish scientific research. The scientists who belong to these different organizations and institutions have rights to autonomy, but the organizations and institutions do not. Organizations and institutions do not have rights because, unlike human beings, organizations and institutions cannot consciously develop and follow moral rules: organizations are not moral agents. Admittedly, organizations and institutions act like moral agents: they make decisions and adopt rules and policies pertaining to the conduct of their members. Also, organizations and institutions can be held legally and morally responsible for the decisions they make. Though it may be useful to speak of organizations and institutions as moral agents in a metaphorical sense, organizations and institutions are not literally moral agents, because they do not make conscious choices or willingly act on them. There is a moral difference between the autonomy of a human being and the autonomy of a group of human beings, such as a scientific discipline, a professional society, a private company, or a state. If only moral agents can have rights to moral autonomy, then scientific organizations and institutions do not have this right. Thus, while scientists have a right to autonomy, scientific organizations and institutions do not.[6]

The conclusion from the previous paragraph has important implications for thinking about restrictions on the autonomy of science. First, scientists have a right to autonomy, which encompasses several different

6. The autonomy I have in mind here is moral autonomy, not epistemological or metaphysical autonomy. Philosophers, such as Alexander Rosenberg (1985, 1994, 1995), have written on the epistemological and metaphysical autonomy of various sciences, such as biology and social science. For a science to be metaphysically autonomous, it must have its own independent ontology that is not reducible to some other, more basic ontology. For example, during the 19th century, biologists who accepted a theory known as vitalism held that living things have a life force or élan vital. Although few biologists accepted vitalism, many accept the idea that biology has methods of inquiry that are distinct from the methods used in the physical sciences, such as the use of teleological or functional explanations and holistic concepts (Rosenberg 1985).

rights, including freedom of expression as well as freedom of thought, freedom of religion, and freedom of association. Any restrictions on these sorts of rights must be the least burdensome means necessary to serve a compelling social purpose. For example, a restriction on a scientist's right of free expression would not be justified for political expediency or economic efficiency, but it might be justified to safeguard national security. (We will discuss national security in more depth in chapter 6.) Freedom of expression includes not only the right to publication but also the right to communicate with colleagues, students, and the public. Freedom of expression does not include the right to have one's work published by a particular journal, the right to receive public money for one's research, or even the right to employment in a publicly funded job. Freedom of association includes the right to form professional societies or associations pertaining to a particular scientific interest and the right to meet with colleagues and students to discuss scientific ideas. Freedom of association does not include the right to receive government funding for these associations. Freedom of religion includes the right to adopt any religious belief or practice, including atheism. Many countries, including the United States, have specific laws that protect the rights of scientists. The first amendment of the U.S. Constitution (1787) protects freedom of expression, association, and religion (Barron and Dienes 1999).

Second, although scientific organizations and institutions do not have rights to autonomy, some restrictions on the autonomy of scientific organizations or institutions may function as de facto restrictions on the autonomy of scientists, if scientists' autonomy is closely linked to the autonomy of the organization or institution. For example, a rule that prevented scientific journals from publishing research on a specific topic, such as bioweapons, would be a de facto restriction on the autonomy of scientists, if scientists have no other outlets for their publications on bioweapons. A law that outlawed scientific associations would be a de facto restriction on scientists' freedom of association. Therefore, when considering rules that restrict the autonomy of scientific organizations or institutions, it is also important to think about how those rules will affect individual scientists. If a restriction on an organization or institution will significantly restrict the autonomy of individual scientists, then that restriction can only be justified if it serves a compelling social purpose and is the least restrictive means of achieving that purpose.

Third, even though organizations and institutions do not have rights, there are still sound moral arguments for granting organizations or institutions autonomy within their domains. Organizations or institutions should be allowed to be self-governing so they can produce valuable benefits for society. Interfering in an organization's or institution's ability to make decisions will hamper its productivity, creativity, and efficiency and may even destroy the organization or institution (Bayles 1988). For example, consider an organization that produces valuable benefits for society, such as an electric power company. The company should be allowed to make decisions concerning its own affairs, such as choices pertaining to strategic planning, marketing, research, product development, personnel, and investments. Government restrictions on the company's ability to make decisions, such as laws or regulations, can interfere with the company's ability to operate efficiently, creatively, and productively. In extreme cases, a company may go out of business as a result of government control. Government restrictions on the autonomy of the company should not unduly interfere in its operations.

The same argument applies to scientific organizations and institutions. As argued in chapter 2, scientific organizations and institutions produce important benefits for society, such as knowledge, which leads to other social benefits, such as practical applications or policy formation. Government control of decisions made by scientific organizations and institutions can undermine their efficiency, creativity, and productivity and may even cause scientific organizations or institutions to collapse. Government control over scientific institutions and organizations can adversely affect scientists' adherence to epistemological and ethical methods, which may undermine the objectivity, reliability, and usefulness of science. Government control or interference can also stifle scientific creativity and innovation and have a negative impact on science education.[7] (I will discuss historical evidence for these points later in this chapter.)

7. Though the focus of this book is on the relationship between science and the government, there is considerable proof that science suffers when private corporations try to manipulate or control scientific research. Since the 1990s, there has been a growing body of literature demonstrating how leaders from business and industry have had an adverse effect on scientific research in pharmaceuticals and biotechnology (Krimsky 2003, Resnik 2007c). Private companies have deliberately biased research results in favor of their products through manipulating research

Although organizations and institutions that produce benefits for society should be self-governing, limits may be placed on them to protect individuals, society, or the environment from harm. The justification for restricting the autonomy of an organization or institution is utilitarian: a government may impose laws or regulations on an organization or institution if the social benefits of those restrictions outweigh the harms, including the harms to the organization or institution caused by the restrictions. Some of the reasons for imposing laws and regulations on organizations and institutions include to protect public safety, health and the environment; to ensure financial accountability and ethical integrity; and to promote equality of opportunity and fair competition. For example, there are many different laws and regulations that would apply to an electric power company, such as rules concerning emissions of pollutants into the air or water, workplace safety, financial accountability, fair employment practices, new construction of power plants, and so on.

The same argument for government control of organizations and institutions also applies to science: the government can impose restrictions on scientific organizations and institutions to promote social benefits or prevent harms. Some reasons for government regulation and control of scientific organizations and institutions include:

To ensure accountability for government funds. Many scientists are employed by government agencies or receive funding (via grants of contracts) from government agencies. The public has a right to create rules designed to ensure that its money is spent wisely and effectively. Many rules can be justified under the public accountability rationale, including regulations pertaining to financial integrity, data integrity (that is, fabrication or

---

design, spinning data analysis and interpretation, and suppressing unfavorable publications. In some areas of pharmaceutical research, over 90% of the published articles with funding from a private company favor its product (Krimsky 2003). The actions by private companies, and by investigators working for private companies, have threatened the objectivity and integrity of biomedical research (Angell 2004). To counteract the corrupting influence of money on science, journals, universities, and government organizations have developed conflict of interest policies, clinical trial registration systems, publication agreements, and other rules and procedures.

falsification), dissemination of research results (for example, publication, data sharing, and reporting), a safe workplace environment, and equality of opportunity (for example, no discrimination in hiring).

To protect the rights and welfare of human subjects. Many scientists work with human subjects. There are a variety of government regulations pertaining to research with human subjects, which address such issues as risks, benefits, informed consent, fair subject selection, and confidentiality (Shamoo and Resnik 2008).

To protect the welfare of animals. Many scientists work with animal subjects, and there are also a variety of rules, regulations, and policies to protect animals, which address such issues as pain and suffering, research methods, euthanasia, and care of animals (for example, living conditions) (Shamoo and Resnik 2008).

To protect students, staff, and others from harm. A scientific laboratory can be a dangerous workplace, and there are rules and regulations to protect people who work in the laboratory as well as people who may be affected by the laboratory. The rules address such topics as laboratory safety and the proper handling of hazardous biological, chemical, and radioactive materials.

To protect the environment. Scientific research can have environmental impacts, and there are rules and regulations concerning these as well, such as the disposal of hazardous materials.

To protect national security. There are also laws and regulations pertaining to research with implications for national security, such as classified research on nuclear weapons. (I will discuss these rules in more detail in chapter 6.)

Science and Government: Historical Case Studies

To summarize the chapter to this point, I have argued for the autonomy of scientists and the autonomy of scientific organizations and institutions. The arguments for granting scientific organizations and institutions autonomy, and for placing limitations on that autonomy, are utilitarian. The strength of these arguments depends on the evidence we have concerning the consequences of granting scientific organizations and institutions autonomy and the consequences of restricting their autonomy. Although no one has, to my knowledge, produced detailed statistical evidence on the consequences of granting scientific organizations or institutions autonomy or restricting it, there is some historical evidence that is relevant to the issues at hand. I will now describe cases from the history of science that provide evidence concerning the benefits and harms of granting scientific institutions or organizations autonomy and restricting their autonomy.

University of Padua and the Scientific Revolution   During the scientific revolution (ca. 1500–1700), many scientists encountered restrictions on their autonomy imposed by the church and the state. The Roman Catholic Church did not tolerate ideas and methods that were contrary to its teachings on the nature of the universe and man's place in it. Many of the ideas and theories discussed by scientists during the scientific revolution, such as the heliocentric (sun-centered) solar system, conflicted with the teachings of the Catholic Church. Many protestant churches, such as the Lutheran Church, also were not receptive to these new ideas. For example, Andreas Osiander (1498–1552), a cleric for the Lutheran Church, was in charge of the publication of Nicolaus Copernicus's (1473–1543) *De Revolutionibus Orbium Coelestium* (*On the Revolution of Heavenly Spheres*) in 1543. Osiander added an unsigned preface to the book, which referred to the heliocentric system described in the work as a tool useful for calendars and navigation but not as a representation of the real world. This type of administrative editing is not very different from actions taken by Bush administration officials discussed in chapter 1. During the Inquisition, Giordano Bruno (1548–1600) was burned at the stake for various heresies, including defending heliocentric astronomy. Galileo Galilei (1564–1642), a strong supporter of the heliocentric theory, used his telescope to gather observational evidence in support of the idea that the earth and planets move around the sun. The Catholic Church ordered Galileo to recant his views, but he refused, and spent the last years of his life under house arrest. The great anatomist Andreas Vesalius (1514–64) violated state and church prohibitions on dissecting the human body and was sentenced to death for grave robbing during the Inquisition. During the scientific revolution, many people who studied anatomy performed human dissections in secret to avoid trouble with the government or church (Boorstin 1983, Butterfield 1997).

The University of Padua became an intellectual center during the scientific revolution because it had a very tolerant and open environment, due in large part to the policies of the Venetian government. Many scientists and scholars went to Padua because they could freely discuss, teach, and investigate controversial ideas without fear of legal, political, or religious repercussions. The list of important scientists and scholars who spent some time at Padua includes Galileo, Vesalius, Copernicus, William Harvey (1578–1657), René Descartes (1591–1650), Paolo dal Pozzo Toscanelli (1397–1482), Gabriele Falloppio (1523–62), and Fabricius ab Aquapendente (1537–1619). They were able to conduct research that was forbidden elsewhere in Europe, such as dissections, and they were able to talk about controversial ideas, such as heliocentric astronomy and religious skepticism. Many scientists and scholars who studied at Padua spread the knowledge and ideals they learned there across Europe (Butterfield 1997). Thus, the tolerance for new ideas found at the University of Padua played an important role in the scientific revolution.

U.S. Dominance in Science and Technology   The United States is by far the leading nation in terms of scientific and technical productivity. There are many different ways to measure success in science and technology, and the United States leads in most of these measures. For example, the United States has had three times as many Nobel Prize winners in the scientific categories (physics, chemistry, physiology or medicine, and economics) than any other country. As of 2007, the countries with the most Nobel Prize winners in science include the United States (277), the United Kingdom (88), Germany (77), France (32), Switzerland (20), Sweden (20), the Netherlands (14), the Soviet Union/Russia (14), Italy (13), Canada (10), and Japan (9) (Nobel Prize Foundation 2008). Another measure of U.S. dominance in science and technology is patent awards. The United States has traditionally been one of the world's leaders in patentable inventions. In 2006, U.S. citizens registered 102,239 patents with the U.S. Patent and Trademark Office (USPTO), followed by Japan (39,411), Germany

(10,889), Taiwan (7,919), South Korea (6,509), the United Kingdom (4,328), and France (3,856) (U.S. Patent and Trademark Office 2006). One could argue that these numbers are biased because they come from the USPTO and therefore reflect commercial patenting in the United States. However, since the United States is the world's largest market, U.S. patent registration is a reliable indicator of global trends, because many businesses want to sell their products in the United States. Finally, the United States is the leading country for scientific publications. An analysis of the country of origin of papers published in 8,500 journals in the Web of Science Database during 1996–2006 found that the United States had 2.9 million papers, followed by Japan (790,510), Germany (742,917), England (660,808), France (535,629), China (422,993), Canada (394,727), Italy (369,138), Spain (263,469), Australia (248,189), and India (211,063) (King 2007).

What is the best explanation for U.S. dominance in science and technology? Some differences are due to population differences. For example, the United States has a population of 303 million, which is much higher than other science and technology leaders, such as Russia (142 million), Japan (128 million), Germany (82 million), France (64 million), and the United Kingdom (61 million). However, population differences alone do not explain all of the differences in scientific productivity, since China (1.3 billion) and India (1.2 billion) each have more than four times the population of the United States but have far fewer patents and publications and only five Nobel Prize winners among them (Nobel Prize Foundation 2008). Other countries with sizable populations, such as Indonesia (232 million), Brazil (186 million), Pakistan (163 million), and Bangladesh (159 million) lag far behind the United States and other nations. One might hypothesize that the wealth of the United States explains its leadership in scientific and technical productivity, but the United States was only the tenth leading country in per capita income in 2006 at $44,970 per year. Countries ranking ahead of the United States include Luxembourg ($76,040), Bermuda (approximately $70,000), Norway ($66,530), Liechtenstein (approximately $63,000), Channel Islands (approximately $60,000), Switzerland ($57,230), Denmark ($51,700), Iceland ($50,580), and Ireland ($44,980) (World Bank 2006). With the exception of Switzerland, none of these other countries have been among the leaders in science and technology. Additionally, explaining a country's scientific and technical success in terms of its wealth puts the cart before the horse, because scientific and technical achievements cause increases in wealth. Another possible explanation is that the United States has a racially and ethnically diverse population, which can encourage intellectual development when people encounter different world-views. Though the United States is one of the most diverse countries in the world, many countries with high diversity are not among the world's leaders in science and technology, including South Africa, Kenya, Turkey, Brazil, Venezuela, and Indonesia. Moreover, some countries with relatively homogenous populations, such as England, France, and Germany, are among the world's leaders in science and technology. Racial and ethnic diversity are important for science, but they are not the main explanation for the success of the United States.

The most likely explanation of U.S. success in science and technology is that scientists in the United States have greater autonomy than in almost any other country in the world, due to the social/political environment in the United States. Key aspects of that environment include: a tradition of social, political, and religious tolerance; strong moral values, such as honesty and a work ethic; a well-funded, high-quality higher education system; a legal regime that protects human rights and private property, including intellectual property; a government that supports science and technology; a large, diverse population; and wealth (Novak 1997). In many ways, U.S. universities are modern Paduas, because many foreigners come to U.S. universities for education and to conduct research. Universities in the United States draw students from all over the world, who are seeking not only a good education but also a climate where they have the freedom that is required for creativity, innovation, and intellectual growth. Other countries with research environments similar to the United States, such as the United Kingdom, France, and Germany, have also had success in science and technology. Thus, a social/political environment that promotes scientific autonomy, like the U.S. environment, can have a significant impact on the progress of science.

Having considered two cases that demonstrate the connection between scientific autonomy and scientific progress, I will now examine two cases that show how interfering with scientific autonomy can undermine scientific progress.

Lysenkoism in the Soviet Union The former Soviet Union is the setting for the first of these case studies. During the 1920s, biologists in the Soviet Union were debating the merits of Mendelian (or classical) genetics, the theory of inheritance based on the work of Gregor Mendel (1823–84). Mendel was an Austrian monk who performed his breeding experiments with peas in relative obscurity. Though Mendel did correspond with Charles Darwin (1809–82), Mendel's work had little impact on biology during his lifetime. At the beginning of the 20th century, Hugo de Vries (1848–1935) and Carl Correns (1864–93) rediscovered Mendel's work. Other geneticists, such as Thomas Hunt Morgan (1866–1945), refined and expanded upon Mendelian genetics. Mendel's fundamental insight was that traits can be passed from one generation to the next via discrete units of inheritance known as "factors," which were later dubbed "genes." He also held that an offspring receives half of its genes from each parent, that genes assort randomly during the genesis of sperm and ova, and that some genes tend to dominate others in the production of traits. Mendel developed three laws of inheritance to describe and explain the ratios of different traits he observed in his breeding experiments. Mendel's theory provided ancillary support for Darwin's theory of evolution by explaining the mechanism of inheritance that operates in natural selection, and classical genetics was incorporated into the evolutionary synthesis. Although modern molecular genetics has shown that Mendel's laws are rough approximations riddled with exceptions, they offer some useful predictions for many types of cases and are still taught in high school and college biology classes (Mayr 1982).

By the 1920s, most western geneticists accepted Mendel's views of inheritance, but geneticists in the Soviet Union were still trying to decide whether to accept Mendel's work or accept a theory of inheritance that gave greater weight to the environment. Many Soviet geneticists accepted Jean-Baptiste Lamarck's (1744–1829) theory of inheritance, which asserted that the traits an organism acquires during its lifetime can be inherited. During the 1920s, the All Union Communist Party (also known as the Bolsheviks) was seeking to solidify the power over Soviet society it had taken during the Russian Revolution of 1917. The party demanded that all social institutions, including science, conform to Marxist political theory. The Bolsheviks shunned sciences, such as free market economics, that they regarded as the product of bourgeois thought, and they searched for ideas that would glorify the proletariat. Trofim D. Lysenko (1889–1976) provided the Bolsheviks with the theory they were looking for. The son of a Ukrainian peasant, Lysenko performed experiments in which he soaked and chilled germinated seeds obtained from summer crops for winter planting. He claimed that this process, which he called vernalization, could improve the productivity of some crops by allowing farmers to plant seeds in the spring instead of in the fall. Although Lysenko was able to convince many scientists and politicians that his claims were true, they were, in fact, unsubstantiated. Lysenko was a poor experimenter: He did not keep good records, he did not develop detailed protocols, and he did not report negative results. What he lacked in rigor, he made up for in self-promotion (Sheehan 1993).

From 1927 to 1930, Lysenko touted his process as a way to boost agricultural productivity, and he won many converts. Soon, the Ukrainian Commissioner of Agriculture endorsed this technique and created a vernalization department at a genetics institute in Odessa (Sheehan 1993). From 1931 to 1934, Lysenko developed a theory to explain the results he claimed to have shown. He theorized that plants have different environmental needs during different stages of development, and that one can therefore change the development of a plant by altering its environment. Lysenko also cited the plant grafting experiments of Ivan Michurin to support his theory of environmental manipulation. Lysenko collaborated with I. I. Prezent, a member of the Communist Party. Lysenko and Prezent developed a new theory of heredity that rejected the existence of genes and declared that heredity results from the interaction between an organism and its environment. Although supporters of Mendelian genetics criticized Lysenko's work as unscientific and unsound, their objections were not strong enough to overcome his theory's political appeal (Hossfeld and Olsson 2002).

Lysenko's ideas, which represented a return to Lamarckianism, found many supporters in the Communist Party, who understood its political implications. Lysenkoism implied that human nature was not fixed or immutable, and that it could be changed through the appropriate environmental manipulation. Thus, it was possible to overcome human tendencies, such as greed, selfishness, and possessiveness, that might obstruct the formation of a society in which wealth is shared equally and private property is abolished, that is, the communist state (Sheehan 1993). By aligning his science with Marxist-Leninist ideology, Lysenko was able to win the support of Joseph Stalin (1878–1953), who appointed him president of the Lenin Academy for Agricultural Sciences in 1938 and then director of the Department of Genetics at the U.S.S.R. Academy of Science in 1940 (Hossfeld and Olsson 2002).

Because Lysenkoism had become the official view of the Communist Party, most Soviet geneticists stopped criticizing Lysenko's views and refrained from publicizing their endorsement of Mendel's ideas. In 1948, the Soviet government began to officially repress Mendelian genetics. Many biologists were denounced, imprisoned, exiled, declared mentally ill, and murdered for endorsing, teaching, or investigating Mendelian ideas. This period of repression lasted until the 1960s, when Soviet geneticists took advantage of the trend toward freeing Soviet science from ideological influence and openly attacked Lysenko's views (Joravsky 1986). Even though Soviet science was able to liberate itself from the shackles of Lysenkoism, the Lysenko affair was a tremendous setback for Soviet science. Before 1948, some of the world's foremost geneticists, such as Theodosius Dobzhansky (1900–75), lived in the Soviet Union. By the 1960s, Soviet genetics was decades behind its western counterpart (Joravsky 1986). Although some fields of research, such as rocketry, nuclear physics, computer science, cryptography, and aeronautics, prospered in the Soviet Union following World War II, on the whole, the repression of ideas contrary to Marxist ideology during this period had an adverse impact on science. Many different fields shouldered the burden of political repression, including not only genetics but also economics, sociology, botany, zoology, evolutionary biology, agronomy, and even mathematical logic (Sheehan 1993).

Scientists under the Nazi Regime   The second of these case studies examines events that took place in Germany under the Nazi regime. German society fell into an economic depression following its devastating defeat in World War I. The war severely damaged Germany's infrastructure, industry, and labor force. Even so, the country still retained many top-notch scientists, engineers, physicians, and technicians, and it sustained a strong academic and scholarly tradition. By the mid-1930s, the Germans had rebuilt their country and they were becoming prosperous once again. Germany had arguably the best science, technology, and industry in the world. During the first half of the 20th century, many of the great Nobel Prize–winning scientists lived, studied, or worked in Germany, including Adolph von Baeyer (1835–1917), Robert Koch (1843–1910), Albrecht Kossel (1853–1927), Paul Ehrlich (1854–1915), Max Planck (1858–1947), Albert Einstein (1879–1955), Gustav Hertz (1887–1975), Werner Heisenberg (1901–76), Erwin Schrödinger (1887–1961), and Otto Hahn (1879–1968). German physics, chemistry, engineering, and medicine were unsurpassed (Proctor 2003).

Adolf Hitler (1889–1945) was a populist leader of the National Socialist German Workers Party (Nazi Party) who was named leader and chancellor of Germany in 1934, when President Paul von Hindenburg died. Hitler's rise to power took place after his release from prison in 1924. Hitler had been imprisoned in 1921 for leading a failed coup attempt known as the Beer Hall Putsch. Hitler used a paramilitary arm of the Nazi party known as the SA (*Sturmabteilung* or "storm troopers") to distribute propaganda and intimidate opponents. Before he was named leader and chancellor, Hindenburg had appointed Hitler as chancellor in an attempt to strengthen his coalition government. Once Hitler took power, he moved quickly to secure it, disbanding the parliament and banning opposition parties. In his speeches, he blamed German's economic and social problems on the Communists; on the Treaty of Versailles, which Germany had signed at the end of World War I; and on Jewish people and other "undesirables," such as Gypsies, disabled people, and homosexuals. He asserted that the German (or Aryan) people were superior to other races, and that Germany needed to be cleansed of its racial impurities (Bullock 1962, Shirer 1990).

German anti-Semitism predated Hitler by many years. Indeed, Jews had been persecuted throughout Europe since the Middle Ages. However, the persecution of Jews took an abominable turn in Nazi Germany. It began in the 1930s through legislation restricting the civil and economic rights of Jews. By 1935, Jews were no longer recognized as German citizens and were banned from employment in government or the professions. As the anti-Semitic fervor intensified, thousands of Jews, including many scientists, engineers, and physicians, emigrated from Germany to avoid persecution and repression. Some non-Jewish scientists also emigrated to escape the repressive regime and its dictatorial science and technology policy, which emphasized research and development to help the Nazi cause and discouraged research that was contrary to Nazi ideology. The Nazis seized property belonging to Jews, destroyed Jewish businesses and temples, and required Jews to display the Star of David to indicate their race (Shirer 1990).

From 1939 to 1945, an elite unit of the Nazi party, the SS (*Schutzstaffel* or "protective squadron"), began systematically killing enemies of the state in an unprecedented act of genocide known as the Holocaust. About 11 million people died in the Holocaust, including 6 million Jews. Other victims included political opponents and members of religious resistance groups, physically or mentally handicapped people, Soviet prisoners of war, Poles, Gypsies, clergy, and psychiatric patients. People died in gas chambers, in mass executions, or from starvation in concentration camps and ghettos. The Nazis began to implement their "final solution" to the "Jewish problem" at the beginning of 1942 (Shirer 1990).

In 1939, World War II began when Germany invaded Poland. Germany soon invaded France, Belgium, the Netherlands, Denmark, Austria, and the Soviet Union, and formed a military alliance with Japan, Italy, and other countries known as the Axis. The Allied powers—the United States, the United Kingdom, the Soviet Union, and other countries—fought against the Axis nations. An estimated 62 million people died in the war, 60% of whom were civilians. After a deadlock in 1942, the Allies began to make progress against the Axis powers in 1943. The Allied forces began to reclaim territory occupied by German forces following the invasion of Normandy, France, on June 6, 1944. German and Italian forces surrendered in early May 1945, and Japan formally surrendered on September 2, 1945, after the United States dropped atomic bombs on Hiroshima and Nagasaki. American scientists, including Albert Einstein, had urged President Roosevelt to develop the atomic bomb to counter the threat posed by Nazi Germany. Toward the end of war, the leaders of the United States, the United Kingdom, and the Soviet Union—Franklin D. Roosevelt, Winston Churchill, and Joseph Stalin—entered an agreement at Yalta for dividing up postwar Europe. An effect of the agreement was that Germany became divided into East Germany and West Germany. Also, the Soviet Union was able to dominate East

Germany, Poland, Hungary, Lithuania, and other countries within its sphere of influence (Shirer 1990).

After the conflict ended, the Allies prosecuted Axis leaders and military officers for war crimes. Some scientists and physicians also were put on trial. During the Nazi era, some German physicians and scientists refused to cooperate with the party, but many did. Some provided indirect help to the Nazi cause by designing rockets, airplanes, and weapons, while others participated in killing people. In 1939, Hitler announced a decree giving German physicians the authority to kill sick and disabled infants and children. The rationale for this decree was to spare people from having to face a life "not worth living" and to purify German society. This decree later expanded to include adults and other enemies of the state, such as Jewish people. Physicians administered drugs to euthanasia victims and helped to plan mass executions. Physicians and biologists developed theories of racial supremacy that the Nazis used to justify their brand of eugenics known as racial hygiene (Proctor 2003).

Nazi physicians and scientists also conducted horrifying "medical" experiments on concentration camp prisoners. Some of the research included studies on how the human body responds to extremes of temperature, pressure, electrical stimulation, oxygen deprivation, or radiation; experiments on wound healing and infection; research on malaria and other infectious diseases; studies on changing eye color; research on sterilization; and behavioral experiments involving twins. None of the victims were willing participants and many died as a result of the experiments. Most experienced great pain and suffering. In the 1946 Nuremberg Trials following the end of World War II, sixteen German physicians were found guilty of war crimes and seven received the death penalty. To help prevent atrocities similar to these experiments, the international community adopted the world's first ethics code for research on human subjects, the Nuremberg Code, in 1947 (Spitz 2005).

A complete assessment of the impact of the Nazis on German science is beyond the scope of this book, but it is clear that the regime and its policies greatly debilitated German science. The most significant harm was that Germany lost much of its scientific labor force to emigration. Since many of the scientists who left Germany were established researchers with laboratories and students, the effect of emigration was far-reaching. Many of these émigrés resettled in the United

States and other nations outside the Axis, benefiting the Allied side of the war. Second, following the war, German scientists were isolated from the rest of the research community. Those that were not living in East Germany under Soviet domination were shunned for many years. Since the sharing of ideas and information is essential to science, being secluded from other scientists hampered German research. Third, the war itself caused tremendous destruction to Germany's economy, which affected the funding of science for many years (Deichmann 1999).

Secret Human Radiation Experiments in the United States I will now consider several cases that demonstrate the importance of placing some restrictions on scientific autonomy to protect society from harm. The United States during the cold war is the venue for the first of these case studies. After World War II, the Soviet Union and the United States emerged as the two dominant world powers. Much of U.S. foreign policy focused on containing the threat posed by Soviet expansionism and developing a defense against a Soviet attack on America or American interests. The United States and the Soviet Union began a nuclear arms race that did not slow down until the two countries reached some arms control agreements in the 1970s and 1980s. A strategy known as mutually assured destruction (MAD) helped maintain the balance of power during this period, as both countries amassed enough nuclear weapons to launch a devastating counterattack to a first strike by the other side. The U.S. military research agenda focused on developing new weapons and weapons systems, espionage and surveillance technologies, and defensive instruments and procedures. During this time, the United States took steps to prepare for the possibility of a nuclear attack, including monitoring Soviet military operations, gathering intelligence about Soviet capabilities, building bomb shelters, and developing evacuation plans. Politicians and citizens were very concerned about battling the threat of communism both abroad and at home. The peak of American paranoia came during the period of McCarthyism from the mid-1940s to the mid-1950s, when the House Committee on Un-American Activities and Senator Joseph R. McCarthy investigated American citizens suspected of being communist sympathizers (Powaski 1997).

During this era marked by America's obsession with the threat posed by the Soviet Union, the Atomic Energy Commission (AEC), a forerunner to the DOE, sponsored over four hundred secret radiation experiments involving human subjects and the environment. The primary objective of these experiments was to understand the effects of radiation on human health and the environment, so that the United States could prepare for the consequences of a nuclear attack from the Soviet Union. The experiments were treated as classified research because they were regarded as important for national security. In 1994, President Clinton declassified information pertaining to these experiments and made many records available to the public. He also established the Advisory Committee on Human Radiation Experiments (ACHRE) to review this research and determine whether it had violated ethical rules on human experimentation, such as the Nuremberg Code, the Helsinki Declaration, or the Common Rule (45 C.F.R. 46). The ACHRE found that in many of the experiments, the subjects were not informed that they were being exposed to radiation or that they were participating in a research project. In many experiments the subjects (or their offspring) suffered significant harm or discomfort (Advisory Committee on Human Radiation Experiments 1995).

There were five types of secret experiments: (a) studies that used radioactive isotopes as markers on biological compounds to follow their path through the body; (b) experiments on the uptake, retention, and excretion of radioactive isotopes; (c) the use of radioactive isotopes in diagnostic tests to calibrate equipment designed to detect radiation; (d) the use of radiation to treat diseases, such as cancer; and (e) the release of radioactive fallout clouds into the environment to follow their trajectory. The following is a sample of some of these studies (Advisory Committee on Human Radiation Experiments 1995):

- From 1945 to 1947, eighteen people were injected with plutonium at the Manhattan Engineer District Hospital in Oak Ridge, Tennessee. The investigators collected bodily excretions from the subjects to determine the rate at which plutonium was excreted.

- In 1949, the NIH, AEC, and the Quaker Oats Company fed breakfast cereal laced with radioactive materials to boys at the Fernald School for the mentally retarded in Waltham,

Massachusetts. The consent forms signed by the boys' parents did not mention the radiation experiment and only said that the boys were joining a science club.

- From 1963 to 1971, researchers at Oregon State Prison X-rayed the testicles of sixty-seven inmates to study the effects of radiation on sperm function. The inmates were not warned about the possibility of developing testicular cancer.

- From 1960 to 1971, researchers at the University of Cincinnati and Cincinnati General Hospital administered whole body radiation to eighty-eight cancer patients, many of whom were African Americans with inoperable tumors. Some of the subjects received radiation equivalent to 1,500 chest X-rays and developed nausea and bleeding. Researchers also forged some of the signatures on the consent forms.

- From the 1940s to the 1960s, 1,500 military personnel were injected with encapsulated radium to observe how it is transported in the body.

- During nuclear weapons tests in the 1940s and 1950s, over 200,000 military personnel were placed near nuclear testing sites and ordered to march through "ground zero" shortly after detonations.

- In 1949, researchers released a cloud of radioactive iodine at the Hanford Nuclear Reservation in eastern Washington to observe the effects of radioactive fallout.

One of the painful ironies of the human radiation experiments is that they took place in the United States, a country which had helped to draft the Nuremberg Code as a way of ensuring that the atrocities committed by Nazi researchers would never happen again. Although the victims of these secret experiments were not prisoners in concentration camps, they were often desperately ill or socially or economically disadvantaged. Many of the victims were military personnel who were following orders. In many instances, the subjects did not give their informed consent and suffered considerable harm. These experiments took place in secret, without the benefit of public knowledge or oversight. It is likely that many of these experiments would never have taken place if they had not been treated as classified research (Advisory Committee on Human Radiation Experiments 1995).

Biological Weapons   The final case I will examine is the development of biological weapons. Although we tend to think of biological weapons as a modern scourge, they have been used in warfare for centuries. The Romans contaminated the water supplies of their enemies by dumping dead animal bodies into their wells (Mayer 2006). In 1346, the Tartars mounted a siege on the Kaffa (Feodosia), a walled city located in the Crimean region of the Ukraine. The Tartars, who lived in Crimea, were of Greek, Turkish, Scythian, and Mongolian origin, and they spoke a Turkish dialect. To weaken their enemy, the Tartars catapulted the bodies of plague victims over the walls. The resulting infestation forced residents of Kaffa to surrender and flee their city, triggering the bubonic plague of 1347–51, which killed 25 million people (Lewis 2001). During the French and Indian War in the 1700s, the British gave blankets contaminated with smallpox to the Indians, who were holding Fort Carillon. The weapon weakened the Indians' defenses by causing a smallpox epidemic. The British took over the fort and renamed it Fort Ticonderoga (Mayer 2006). The British also used smallpox as a weapon on rebel forces during the American Revolutionary War, but this strategy was not very effective, as the Americans quarantined smallpox victims (Lewis 2001). In the American Civil War, Confederate soldiers used the Roman tactic of water supply contamination against the Union army (Mayer 2006).

In World War I, the Germans attempted to infect their enemies' livestock with anthrax and other diseases, but this campaign was not very successful (Lewis 2001). Chemical weapons, such as chlorine, phosgene, and mustard gas, had a far greater impact on military strategy and tactics during World War I than biological weapons. Both sides of the conflict used chemical weapons, which killed an estimated 92,000 soldiers and civilians. The horrors of chemical warfare prompted over a hundred nations to adopt the Geneva Protocol in 1929, which bans the use of chemical and biological weapons during warfare, but not research on biological weapons (Lewis 2001).

Between World War I and World War II, the British and the Japanese conducted research on biological weapons, but only the Japanese tested and used biological weapons during World War II. In Manchuria, the Japanese used Chinese prisoners as human subjects for experiments with various disease agents, including anthrax, the plague, typhoid, and cholera, killing an estimated ten thousand people. The Japanese launched attacks against Chinese civilians, including contamination of food and water dispersal of fleas infected with the plague. At the end of World War II, leaders of Japan's Imperial Army Unit 731 destroyed records of their biological weapons research and deployment, but they reached a deal with U.S. forces to provide information about their activities in exchange for immunity from prosecution for war crimes (Lewis 2001). Although the Japanese used biological weapons to inflict great harm on the Chinese people during World War II, these weapons did not have a significant effect on the outcome of the war. Nuclear weapons, however, did play a key role in the outcome of the war. As noted earlier, the Japanese surrendered after the United States dropped atomic bombs on Hiroshima and Nagasaki. At least 214,000 people, mostly civilians, died from the initial impact of the bombs or their aftereffects (Harris and Paxman 2002).

During the cold war, the United States and the Soviet Union conducted research on biological weapons. In 1969, President Richard Nixon ordered the U.S. military to discontinue its research on offensive biological weapons and focus exclusively on defenses against biological weapons. In 1972, 118 nations, including the United States and the Soviet Union, signed the Biological and Toxin Weapons Convention (BTWC), a treaty by which signatory countries agree to refrain from producing, stockpiling, acquiring, or deploying biological weapons. The only research permitted under the BTWC is research on defense against biological weapons. Even though the United States had discontinued its offensive weapons research, the Soviet Union continued to conduct secret biological weapons research (Lewis 2001). The Soviets studied a variety of pathogens including the plague, anthrax, and the Ebola and Marburg viruses. They also perfected methods for delivering biological weapons via missiles and were interested in developing "superbugs" to overcome the human immune system and existing vaccines and antibiotics (Mayer 2006). An outbreak of anthrax, which killed seventy people in Sverdlovsk, may have been an accidental contamination from Soviet research. This secret biological weapons program began to wane in the 1990s, following the end of the cold war and the breakup of the Soviet Union (Lewis 2001).

In 1985, the former leader of Iraq, Saddam Hussein, began to take steps to develop and acquire biological, chemical, and nuclear weapons. Though Iraq denied the existence of these weapons, at the conclusion of the Persian Gulf War in 1991, a team of weapons inspectors from the UN Special Commission (UNSCOM) determined that Iraq had acquired and developed several different agents, including anthrax, botulinum toxin, and aflatoxin, and had prepared SCUD missiles to deliver biological and chemical weapons. The inspectors did not actually locate Iraq's stockpiles, but they concluded that Iraq had an active biological and chemical weapons program before the war began (Mayer 2006). Iraqi officials admitted that they were conducting research on biological and chemical weapons. Iraq used chemical weapons on Iran during the Iran-Iraq war and to quash a Kurdish rebellion. Over 20,000 Iranians died from the initial use of chemical weapons, and thousands are still receiving medical treatment. Five thousand Kurds died from exposure to mustard gas, sarin, tabun, or VX (Atkinson 1994, Pitt and Ritter 2002).

During the 1980s, terrorist groups began to develop and use biological and chemical weapons. Members of a religious cult led by Indian guru Bagwan Shree Rajneesh put *Salmonella* bacteria on salad bars in rural Oregon, causing 750 people to develop food poisoning. Although no people died, forty-five required hospitalization. The CDC had initially determined that the outbreak of food poisoning was a natural event, but an independent police investigation concluded that it resulted from a terrorist attack. Between 1993 and 1995, the Japanese religious cult Aum Shinrikyo released botulinum toxin and anthrax in the Tokyo subway system at least ten times without producing any harmful effects. One possible explanation for the failure of these attacks is that the anthrax used by the group had not been weaponized sufficiently, that is, the particles released were not small enough to enter the lungs easily. In 1995, however, the group released a chemical weapon, sarin gas, in a Tokyo subway, killing twelve people and sickening thousands (Lewis 2001).

Shortly after the al-Qaeda skyjacking attacks of September 11, 2001, which destroyed the World Trade Center buildings in New York City and killed almost 3,000 people, letters containing anthrax spores were sent to Tom Brokaw of NBC News in New York, the offices of the *New York Post*, and Senator Tom Daschle (D-SD) in Washington, DC. Eighteen people contracted anthrax, five people died from the disease, and thousands of people took antibiotics as a prophylactic measure. Although the anthrax letters did not kill many people, they caused considerable disruption to work routines, anxiety, and hysteria. In July 2008, the FBI produced evidence linking Bruce Ivins to these crimes. Ivins, who was a microbiologist working at a U.S. Army research lab in Fort Detrick, Maryland, committed suicide before he could be apprehended.

Terrorist groups, such as al-Qaeda, have declared their intentions to acquire biological, chemical, and nuclear weapons. Osama bin Laden, al-Qaeda's leader, has stated that it is a religious duty to acquire these weapons. The *Encyclopedia of Afghanistan Resistance*, discovered by U.S. forces at an al-Qaeda camp near Jalalabad during Operation Enduring Freedom, contained instructions for making biological and chemical weapons (Boureston 2002).

Scientific Scandals   Many of the rules governing research in the United States have arisen as a result of scandals in science that have drawn the attention of politicians and laypeople. For example, a congressional investigation of the Tuskegee Syphilis Study and other unethical studies involving human experimentation led to the adoption of the National Research Act in 1974, which authorized federal agencies to develop regulations for research involving human subjects. The Tuskegee Syphilis Study was an observational study (1932–72), sponsored by the U.S. government, involving 400 black men with advanced syphilis in Tuskegee, Alabama. The goal of the study was to follow the natural progression of untreated syphilis to learn more about its clinical manifestations. The men were not told that they were participating in a research study or that they were not receiving treatment for syphilis. They were led to believe they were receiving treatment for "bad blood" when in reality all they were receiving were physical exams and routine medical care. In the 1940s, penicillin became available as a treatment for syphilis, but the researchers did not tell the subjects about this treatment or make it available to them. The U.S. government reached a $10 million dollar out-of-court settlement with research subjects and their families, but did not issue an official apology until 1997 (Shamoo and Resnik 2008).

In the 1980s, a congressional investigation into alleged data fabrication and falsification by Thereza Imanishi-Kari, a scientist at the

Whitehead Institute at the Massachusetts Institute of Technology, helped to prompt the development of federal regulations concerning misconduct in scientific research, the formation of federal agencies to deal with research misconduct and other ethical issues, and required education in the responsible conduct of research for graduate students receiving NIH funding. Imanishi-Kari coauthored a paper published in the journal *Cell* in 1986 with Nobel laureate David Baltimore and four other authors. A postdoctoral student, Margot O'Toole, accused Imanishi-Kari of data fabrication and falsification when she was unable to reproduce the experimental results from the paper and she could not reconcile Imanishi-Kari's lab notebooks with the data reported in the paper. The investigation, which Baltimore described as a "witch hunt," made national headlines for ten years. An NIH appeals panel absolved Imanishi-Kari of any wrongdoing in 1996 (Resnik 2003a).

During 2003–5, congressional committees investigated violations of conflict of interest rules by scientists and senior officials at the NIH. Forty-four researchers in the NIH's intramural program accepted thousands of dollars in consulting fees and stock from pharmaceutical companies without disclosing their arrangements to their supervisors or obtaining prior approvals. In some cases, the violations of conflict of interest rules were serious enough to warrant researchers' dismissal from the NIH and criminal charges (Kaiser 2005). A senior researcher at the National Institute of Mental Health, Trey Sunderland, earned over $585,000 for sharing tissue samples and consulting with Pfizer. Sunderland did not obtain prior approval for his relationship with Pfizer (Weiss 2006). In response to the congressional inquiry, the NIH revised its policies concerning outside activities, gifts, and conflicts of interest.

Lessons from the Case Studies   These cases illustrate several important points that were discussed earlier in this chapter. First, granting scientists and scientific organizations and institutions autonomy promotes progress and innovation in science and technology. Science has flourished in settings where scientists have been able to communicate freely and openly, test new ideas, challenge old ones, and establish their rules, methods, and agendas. Second, government control of science can have many detrimental effects, such as inhibiting creativity, innovation, and progress, and biasing research. In the Soviet Union, the Communist Party's acceptance of Lysenkoism and its repressive policies stifled progress in many areas of science. Political considerations dictated which research problems could be studied, which courses could be taught in universities, and which articles or books could be published. In Germany, the Nazi Party's quest for racial hygiene forced Jewish and non-Jewish researchers to leave the country to find a safe and productive work environment. This emigration impaired German research for many years. Additionally, the Nazis, like the Soviets, imposed an ideological agenda on research. Although scientists in the United States and other industrialized nations do not currently face threats similar to what researchers faced in the Soviet Union or Nazi Germany, there is evidence that scientists in industrialized nations face significant political pressures concerning the content of their research. A study by Kempner and colleagues (2005) found that many scientists have had to deal with the political ramifications of their research and sometimes engage in self-censorship to avoid controversy. Furthermore, many scientists today are living in countries with totalitarian regimes, such as Iran and North Korea, and they suffer under the yoke of political repression and persecution (Amnesty International 2006).

Third, while it is important for scientists, scientific organizations, and institutions to have autonomy, governments can and should impose some limitations on science to safeguard moral and social values, such as human health and safety, human rights, national security, environmental protection, and so on. The violations of human rights and welfare that occurred during the secret human radiation experiments demonstrate the importance of government oversight and public knowledge of scientific research. Although members of the executive branch of government knew about the experiments, the experiments took place without oversight from the legislative or judicial branches of government. If these experiments had not been kept secret, it is likely that the public outcry would have forced researchers to refrain from conducting these experiments or to modify them to protect the subjects' rights and welfare. Additionally, the history of biological warfare demonstrates that it is important to keep the results of some types of research out of the hands of people who would use them to harm individuals, society, or the environment. Societies need to have ways of managing the results of research, including restrictions on publication, collaboration, and the sharing of data, materials, and methods.

Appropriate Oversight of Science

The arguments and evidence presented in this chapter support the general conclusion that science should be permitted to be self-governing but that its autonomy should not be absolute: scientific freedom needs to be tethered by government oversight and authority. The government may impose ethical and legal requirements on research to protect human rights, public health, and other important values (Guston 2000, Kitcher 2001, Shamoo and Resnik 2008). I have used both ethical theories and historical case studies to support this thesis. I suspect that few people would disagree with this proposal. However, difficult and controversial questions arise when we try to decide how to balance scientific autonomy and government control. Granting science too much autonomy can produce harmful consequences for society, but excessive government control of scientific decision-making can have a negative impact on science and, ultimately, society. Government oversight of science should be appropriately balanced, carefully measured, and fair.

In thinking about government oversight of science, it will be useful to make several key distinctions. The first distinction is one we are already familiar with: the distinction between scientists and scientific organizations or institutions. As argued earlier, restrictions on the autonomy of scientists are morally different from restrictions on the autonomy of scientific organizations or institutions. Since scientists have moral rights, restrictions on the autonomy of scientists are justified only if they serve a compelling social purpose and are the least burdensome means necessary to achieve that purpose. Restrictions on the autonomy of scientific organizations or institutions can be justified if the social benefits of those restrictions outweigh the harms. (Table 3.1 lists the different types of restrictions on scientific autonomy, the justification that is required, and some examples.)

The second distinction relevant to our discussion is a distinction between restrictions on the *content* of science and restrictions on the *process* of science. Restrictions on the content of science are restrictions on the subject matter of scientific inquiry, debate, education, or publication. They are restrictions on what science is about. For example, the Soviet Union's suppression of all science that

Table 3.1. Restrictions on the autonomy of science

Type of restriction	Justification required	Examples
Autonomy of scientists	Compelling social purpose	Rules for research with human subjects Laboratory safety
Autonomy of scientific organizations/ institutions	Social benefits outweigh harms	Rules for accounting for research grant funds Hiring and promotion in universities
Content restrictions	Compelling social purpose	Government funding of research Censorship
Process restrictions	Social benefits outweigh harms	Conflict of interest rules for service on government committees Intellectual property laws
Oversight	Social benefits outweigh harms	Minimizing risk with human subjects Protecting the welfare of laboratory animals
Micromanagement	Compelling social purpose	Rules for submitting grants Informed consent requirements

Note: The examples (far right column) are not necessarily justified restrictions on autonomy.

contradicted Lysenkoism was a restriction on the content of science. The Catholic Church's opposition to heliocentric astronomy was another restriction on the content of science. Restrictions on the content of science are potentially the most intrusive and damaging form of government control, because they undermine the core values of science: intellectual freedom, openness, and honesty. Content-based restrictions can also adversely affect scientific creativity, innovation, discovery, objectivity, and progress. Because they can have such a negative impact on science, content restrictions should be implemented with great care and used only for compelling social purposes, such as to protect against threats to national security or to ensure public accountability. Moreover, content restrictions should be the least burdensome means necessary to achieve compelling social purposes.

Process restrictions are limitations on the methods, techniques, procedures, tools, and resources used to conduct research. They are restrictions not on what science is about but on how science is conducted. For example, prohibitions against human dissection in medieval and Renaissance Europe were restrictions on the process of research. Other process restrictions include rules concerning the use of human or animal subjects in research, laboratory safety rules, prohibitions against data fabrication or falsification, and the funding of research. Because they do not address the content of science, process restrictions tend to be less intrusive and less damaging than content restrictions. Accordingly, process restrictions do not require as much justification as content restrictions: process restrictions can be imposed when the benefits of restrictions to society outweigh the harms. Process restrictions sometimes function as de facto content restrictions when they prevent researchers from developing some types of knowledge. For example, as discussed in chapter 1, the Traditional Values Coalition tried to convince Congress to stop funding for 198 NIH grants for research on human sexuality. This restriction on the process of funding research was clearly aimed at stopping research on human sexuality. Thus, it is important to pay careful attention to proposed process restrictions to ensure that they are not functioning as restrictions on content. If they are, then they should be evaluated as such.

The final distinction worth using is a distinction between *oversight* and *micromanagement*. An overseer is someone who supervises the work of another but does not become enmeshed in the details of that work. A micromanager is someone who supervises the work of another but attempts to control the details of that work. For example, an employer who tells his employees to plan a Christmas

party for the first Friday afternoon in December, with music, decorations, and food, and a budget of no more than $400, would be
overseeing the party. If the employer who gave these instructions
also planned the menu, ordered the food, and selected the music
and decorations, he would be doing more than just supervising the
party: he would be micromanaging it. Micromanagement in a business organization can have many negative effects. It leaves little
room for employees to take their own initiative, be responsible, or
make mistakes. Micromanagement treats employees like children, not
like responsible (autonomous) adults. Employees who are micro-
managed may grow to resent and distrust their managers. Micromanagement can also waste valuable time and resources, because
it reduces the delegation of authority in a business organization
(Chambers 2004).

Micromanagement by a government can have several detrimental effects on science. First, micromanagement can inhibit scientific
creativity and innovation by constraining the practice of science. To
be creative or innovative, a person must be able to "think out of the
box" and challenge the status quo, but it is difficult to do this when
one is constrained by various rules. Second, micromanagement can
introduce bias or error into science by imposing the judgments of
nonscientists on the practice of science. Nonscientists are usually
not qualified to make judgments relating to matters of scientific
practice, such as research design, methodology, analysis of data, or
the evaluation of research proposals. Third, micromanagement can
increase the administrative costs and burdens of research. While
some administrative oversight is necessary to protect the public and
ensure the integrity and accountability of research, too much red
tape can cause research to grind to a halt. Fourth, micromanagement can undermine freedom and openness. If politicians or members of the public frequently have input into microlevel decisions,
then researchers may begin to fear that their decisions will be sec-
ond-guessed. They may adopt strategies to avoid outside criticism,
such as carefully guarding information, avoiding controversial projects that are likely to draw the public's attention, rewriting publications and reports to avoid offending political interest groups, and
choosing conservative theories, methods, and research designs.
Researchers who are constantly watching out for the threat of

outside scrutiny of their work may grow to resent the public, and become frustrated, which can lead to low morale and interfere with communication and trust.[8] The pork-barrel science projects and the cancellation of the CHEERS study, discussed in chapter 1, are examples of how government micromanagement can have negative impacts on science.

Because micromanagement can have such negative impacts on science, it should be avoided, unless there is a compelling social purpose and it is necessary for achieving that purpose. For example, holding scientists and scientific institutions or organizations financially accountable for the money they receive from the government is a compelling social purpose that is accomplished by spelling out detailed rules concerning how that money should be applied for, spent, and accounted for. Ensuring that researchers obtain informed consent from human subjects or their representatives is another compelling social purpose that is accomplished by federal regulations concerning informed consent (45 C.F.R. 46.116), which includes fourteen required elements of consent and two major exceptions.

In contrast to micromanagement, oversight does not usually have detrimental effects on science, unless is also involves restrictions on content or restrictions on the autonomy of individual scientists. One way that the government can oversee science without micromanaging it is to establish general rules (policies or guidelines) pertaining to research and education. General rules do not spell out every detail and leave some leeway for interpretation and application. For example, the federal regulation (45 C.F.R. 46.111) that requires researchers to minimize risks to human research subjects is highly general, because it allows scientists to decide what procedures they will use to minimize risks and how they will implement those procedures. Another general rule is the prohibition against fabricating research data on grants funded

8. Problems with micromanagement are not unique to science, since politicians and the public are also not qualified to make microlevel decisions concerning national defense, law enforcement, air traffic control, food quality assurance, and many other activities. If politicians and citizens have no business deciding the flight plan of a commercial jet or the number of soldiers needed to defend a city, then they also should refrain from micromanaging scientists.

by the Public Health Service (42 *C.F.R.* 93.103). Although the rule has a specific definition of data fabrication, scientists must still decide how to interpret and apply the definition in a specific case. Qualified scientists, not politicians or members of the public, decide whether there is sufficient evidence to prove an allegation of data fabrication. One of the strengths of general restrictions is that they allow for public oversight without excessive intrusion into the practice of science. A weakness of such rules is that they may be too vague to be useful. To avoid vagueness, general restrictions should be clearly defined.

Putting these three distinctions together, an inquiry concerning the appropriateness of a particular form of government restriction on the autonomy of science can be framed in terms of three questions:

1. Is the restriction aimed at controlling the autonomy of individual scientists, scientific organizations/institutions, or both?

2. Does the restriction affect the content of science, the process of science, or both?

3. Does the restriction involve oversight or micromanagement?

Restrictions that require a high level of justification are those that are aimed at controlling individual scientists, that affect the content of science, or that are a type of micromanagement of science. Restrictions that require less justification are those that are aimed at controlling scientific organizations/institutions, that affect only the process of science, or that are not micromanagement.

Conclusion

In this chapter, I have used ethical theories and historical case studies to argue for the autonomy of science within limits. I have argued for the autonomy of scientists based on their human rights. The autonomy of scientists should be restricted only for a compelling social purpose and the restriction should be the minimum necessary to achieve this purpose. I have argued for the autonomy of scientific organizations and institutions based on the utility (benefits/harms) of allowing scientific organizations and institutions to be self-governing. To produce useful results for society, such as knowledge with practical applications and policy implications, scientists should be allowed to make decisions within their domain of expertise, free from outside interference and control. However, the autonomy of scientific organizations may be restricted if the social benefits of restriction outweigh the harms. There are a variety of legitimate reasons for restricting the autonomy of scientific organizations and institutions, including promoting health and safety, protecting the environment, ensuring financial accountability, promoting research integrity, protecting human and animal research subjects, and establishing fair employment practices.

The government should enact restrictions that benefit society while doing minimal damage to science. Government oversight of science should be appropriately balanced, well measured, and fair. To help achieve this result, I have distinguished between different types of restrictions on scientific autonomy, including restrictions on the autonomy of scientists versus restrictions on the autonomy of scientific organizations/institutions, content restrictions versus process restrictions, and oversight versus micromanagement. I have argued that restrictions on the autonomy of individual scientists and restrictions on the content of science can only be justified for compelling social purposes, whereas restrictions on scientific organizations/institutions or scientific processes can be justified if the benefits outweigh the harms. I have also argued that a government should avoid micromanaging science, unless micromanagement is necessary to accomplish a compelling social purpose.

In the remainder of the book, I will apply the framework developed in this chapter and the previous one to questions concerning science and politics, including government science advice, government funding of research, national security, research with human subjects, and science education.

4

Government Science Advice

Good advice is always certain to be ignored, but that's no reason not to give it.

—Agatha Christie

In the previous two chapters I developed a foundation for thinking about the relationship between science and politics. I will now apply this framework to different problems relating to science policy, beginning with government science advice.

★★★

Reliable information and expert advice are essential to making good decisions at all levels of government. Scientists, engineers, and technicians provide numerous types of information and expertise to many different branches of government, in areas such as food and drug safety, environmental protection, urban planning, public health, national defense, meteorology, disaster preparedness, forensics, highway construction, air traffic control, energy production, and telecommunications. Scientists work for many different government agencies, serve on government advisory boards, give testimony to congressional committees, and provide advice to governors, mayors, and the president. Scientists help to enforce health and safety regulations, launch rockets into space, design bridges and dams, prevent airplanes from crashing, monitor electric power grids, prepare for disasters, investigate disease epidemics, and manage natural resources. Scientific experts serve on advisory committees at the NIH, EPA, FDA, USDA, NASA, NSF, CDC, and many other U.S. federal agencies. It is hard to imagine how a modern government could function without science advice (Jasanoff 1990).

It wasn't always this way. Before the scientific revolution, science played only a minor role in government decision-making. Science was an interesting hobby for many, but not something that kings depended on. The age of exploration had a major impact on the relationship between science and the government. The great naval powers of Europe, England, France, Spain, and Portugal, were interested in conquering and colonizing the new world. They sought new trade routes, gold, spices, and other resources. To make long voyages across the oceans, ship captains needed accurate maps of the stars, because they could not use visible landmarks, such as the coastline, for navigation. Using a compass, sextant, clock, and star chart, a good navigator could determine his position on the earth relative to celestial landmarks. England, France, and other countries understood that they needed to build observatories to develop accurate star charts. The first of these national observatories was built in Greenwich, England, in 1675. These observatories were built to provide governments with information they needed to sail military ships, but the information could also be used for sailing merchant ships. Astronomers traveled on government ships to gather more information for star charts. Many ships also included naturalists, who gathered information about the plants, animals, minerals, weather, and geology of new lands. This information was also useful in exploration, colonization, and trade. Charles Darwin, for example, was a naturalist aboard the H.M.S. *Beagle* during 1831–36 (Burke 1995).

An Idealized Model of Government Science Advice

To help clarify our thinking about government science advice, I will develop a model of how advice would occur under ideal conditions. Although real world science advising may often fail to satisfy these conditions, the model will be useful for evaluating and critiquing government science advice in order to bring it up to ideal standards. To set the stage for the model, let's consider another type of expert decision-making familiar to most readers: medical decision-making. Suppose that a patient makes an appointment with his physician because he has had dizziness, nausea, and headaches. The physician takes the patient's blood pressure and finds that it is elevated. The physician explains to the patient what high blood pressure is, what causes it, and how it can adversely affect his health. The physician also discusses treatment options, including blood pressure medications, exercise, and dietary modifications. In this encounter, there are several different roles the physician can play. The physician could serve as a mere technician, providing the patient with information and options, but not providing any advice, such as a recommendation for treatment. The problem with this approach is that most patients would like more than information: they would also like some advice and help with making decisions. They want to know which medication they should take, if any. Conversely, the physician could play a domineering role in decision-making, providing the patient not only with information and advice but also making strong recommendations and giving the patient very little choice about what to do. The physician could tell the patient what he thinks the patient ought to do, with little room for discussion or debate. The physician might even manipulate the information to ensure that the patient makes the "best" choice. This approach errs in the opposite direction by involving the physician too much in medical decision-making and not leaving enough room for the patient's preferences and choices. The model is paternalistic and manipulative. In between these two extremes is a third option. The physician could be an advocate for the patient's autonomous decision-making, giving the patient the information he needs to make wise choices, but also helping the patient to evaluate these choices for himself. The physician could provide information, advice, and medical opinion in a way that affirms the patient's right to make his own choices (Emanuel and Emanuel 1992, Pellegrino and Thomasma 1981). Though I think this is the best approach to medical decision-making, one difficulty is that it requires the physician to walk a fine line between being merely technical/informative and demonstrating a paternalistic or manipulative attitude. Most people would prefer this shared decision-making approach to medical decisions. They want physicians to provide information, advice, and recommendations, but they still want to make their own choices.

If we apply this shared decision-making approach to public policy, it suggests that scientists can play the following roles:

1. Providing information relevant to the decisions to be made
2. Helping laypeople to understand the information
3. Describing different policy options, and the likely consequences of each
4. Evaluating the options in light of the information

I think expert scientific advice should be similar to expert medical advice. Scientific experts should do more than just provide information and technical assistance: they should help laypeople to understand, interpret, and apply that information to policy issues. Scientists can also help to evaluate different options and make recommendations (Pielke 2007). Though scientists should help to inform public policy, they should refrain from attempting to manipulate or control public decision-making. They should present information, options, and recommendations without manipulating or distorting the evidence. This approach, like the medical decision-making approach described above, requires scientists to walk a fine line between technical advice and advocacy. Scientists must be careful to maintain their neutrality and to avoid even the appearance of bias. Although scientists may render an opinion on a policy option, the opinion should be based on an honest and open assessment of the evidence. This is not an easy path to follow: scientists who engage in policy debates are often accused of bias, even when they make a concerted effort to avoid bias. Nevertheless, this path is worth following.

To see how this model could apply to a particular case, consider a decision about whether to approve a new drug. Suppose that the drug has completed rigorous preclinical and clinical testing and there is now extensive data on its safety and efficacy. The FDA appoints a panel of experts to make a recommendation concerning the new drug. The panel's role is purely advisory: the final decision rests with FDA administrators. The role of the experts is to help the agency understand and interpret scientific evidence, to help the agency consider different policy options and the consequences of those options, to weigh risks and benefits, and to make a recommendation. (This is the process that was followed in the Plan B emergency contraception case discussed in chapter 1.) It is perfectly acceptable for experts on the panel to do more than just present information: they can also help to interpret the information, weigh risks and benefits, and so on. However, it is important for members of the panel to refrain from advocacy or manipulation and to avoid even the appearance of bias, because this can undermine the panel's integrity, objectivity, and trustworthiness. For example, if one of the experts has a financial interest related to the drug being evaluated, then people may regard her advice as biased, and they may not trust her recommendations. Likewise, if one of the experts has a political axe to grind concerning the drug, this could render his advice questionable (Krimsky 2003, Resnik 2007c). Ideally, all of the experts on the panel should be disinterested parties, only concerned with making the best decision for society.

Having described the ideal approach to government science advice and how it might apply in a particular case, I will describe some ways that the real world often differs from the model and the sample case. First, not all government policies are made by a single agency on the advice of a single expert panel. Sometimes different agencies and branches of government (executive, legislative) are involved in policy-making. For example, many different agencies and branches of govern-ment are involved in complex issues like global climate change and health care inequalities. Second, the government also receives input from other sources besides expert panels, such as private industry, polit-ical interest groups, lobbyists, and citizens. These groups may hire their own experts to present their opinions to the government. For example, many different groups have expressed their views about global climate change to the government. Expert advice often plays a major role in policy formation, but there are many other players with power and influence (Jasanoff 1990). Third, as noted in chapter 2, the scientific expertise is rarely purely objective: it may be strongly influenced by the political, social, financial, or other interests of the people conducting or sponsoring the research (Jasanoff 1990). For example, scientific studies sponsored by a pesticide company may be biased in favor of its product, while studies sponsored by an environmental group may be biased against the pesticide. Even though steps can be taken to minimize the impacts of financial, political, or other interests on expert advice, expert opinion may be tainted by money, ideology, and other biases. Accord-ing to an expert on expertise, Bruce Bimber: "The conclusion to be drawn is that 'objectivity' should be approached as a matter of degree. Experts can be more or less objective, more or less neutral, more or less credible as experts rather than simply advocates. . . . Much of the politics of expertise is played out in this terrain between the inherently inter-ested process of advocacy at one end, and the ideal notion of disinter-ested expertise on the other" (Bimber 1996, 14).

Thus, the real world is much more complex than the model described here. Even so, the model is not worthless, since we can use the model to understand how government decisions involving science deviate from this model. The model can also be used to evaluate and criticize those decisions and to formulate some ways to try to avoid bad decisions. Our main concern will be to consider the types of problems that can undermine the objectivity of scientific expertise in government decision-making and what to do about them. Problems can occur at various stages of scientific research relating to government decisions, from funding, to research design, to interpretation of data, to the selection of experts, to publication and dissemination of knowledge.

Selection of Experts

If experts were completely unbiased, who is selected to serve as an expert on a committee or government panel would make no difference. The experts would offer information and advice to the government, unaffected by their political, moral, or religious views or financial interests. But, as we have already seen, experts are not completely unbiased. As human beings, they often allow their personal opinions, views, and interests to sway their scientific judgment. To be sure, some experts are more objective than others. Bimber (1996) uses the term "degree of politicization" to describe the extent to which experts are affected by politics. Experts range from objective experts, with a low degree of politicization, to informed advocates with a high degree of politicization (Bimber 1996). As noted in chapter 2, Pielke (2007) distinguishes between different models of expertise, ranging from pure scientist to issue advocate. Research institutions also exhibit degrees of politicization. Most universities and some think tanks aspire to be apolitical, but others have particular political allegiances. For example, the American Civil Liberties Union and the Institute for Policy Studies are politically left-of-center, while the American Enterprise Institute and the Heritage Foundation are right-of-center. The University of California at Berkeley has a reputation for supporting liberal causes, while Southern Methodist University has a reputation for promoting conservative ones.

Because biases can affect expertise, the political composition of a committee that provides scientific advice to the government can have a significant impact on the committee's findings. For example, if a committee is composed entirely of people with conservative political allegiances, the committee will probably develop recommendations that support conservative causes (Bimber 1996). It is possible, therefore, to virtually predetermine the outcome of a committee's deliberations by stacking the committee with members who have particular political views. Intellectually, stacking a committee is similar to a breach of research ethics known as "cooking" the data (Shamoo and Resnik 2008). In cooking the data, one designs an experiment to achieve a predetermined outcome: the experiment is not a genuine test of a hypothesis.

Since it is probably not possible to eliminate potential biases from government advisory committees, one strategy for promoting objectivity is to allow biases to counteract each other. Committees should be politically balanced and diverse. Indeed, the Federal Advisory Committee Act requires balance and diversity, as well as openness and accountability (Federal Advisory Committee Act 1972). These four qualities can minimize bias and improve and enhance credibility (Jasanoff 1990). Citizens are more likely to trust the recommendations of a bipartisan committee than one composed entirely of people from a particular ideological persuasion. Citizens are also more likely to trust the deliberations of a committee that is open to the public and gives a public account of its decisions, rather than one that does not. When biases cannot be eliminated or reduced, objectivity and reliability in science can sometimes emerge from playing biases against each other in an open forum (Solomon 2007).

Although common sense, respect for science, and a commitment to democracy all favor political balance on government advisory committees, this goal is often ignored. Many politicians have attempted to stack the deck, but one of the most ignominious instances of this practice occurred when President George W. Bush appointed the President's Council on Bioethics (or PCB), which we previously mentioned in chapter 1. Bush's decision to severely limit the use of government funds on embryonic stem cell research was influenced by his own religious faith and his alliance with conservative Christian groups, who helped him win the 2000 presidential election. Conservative Christians are opposed to embryonic stem cell research because current methods of deriving stem cells from human embryos involve the destruction of the embryo, which conservative Christians regard as equivalent to murdering a human being. Liberals and moderates support embryonic stem cell research because they believe that it may lead to therapies for diseases that result from malfunctioning or dead tissue, such as paralysis, diabetes, heart failure, or Alzheimer's disease (Green 2001).

President Bush announced his intention to form the PCB on the same day that he announced his "prolife" stem cell policy. The PCB was officially established on November 28, 2001, by Executive Order 13237. Its mission is to:

> [A]dvise the President on bioethical issues that may emerge as a consequence of advances in biomedical science and technology. In connection with its advisory role, the mission of the Council includes the following functions:
>
> 1. To undertake fundamental inquiry into the human and moral significance of developments in biomedical and behavioral science and technology;
> 2. To explore specific ethical and policy questions related to these developments;
> 3. To provide a forum for a national discussion of bioethical issues;
> 4. To facilitate a greater understanding of bioethical issues; and
> 5. To explore possibilities for useful international collaboration on bioethical issues. (Bush 2001)

Although the mission of the PCB is not purely scientific, it was authorized to deal with many different questions concerning biomedical science and technology. The Executive Order stated that the Council "shall be composed of not more than 18 members appointed by the President from among individuals who are not officers or employees of the Federal Government," and "shall include members drawn from the fields of science and medicine, law and government, philosophy and theology, and other areas of the humanities and social sciences" (Bush 2001).

As I have argued above, to deal effectively with the scientific, ethical. and policy issues, a committee like the PCB should have balance and diversity. It should include members who are conservative and liberal, antitechnology and protechnology, laypeople and scientists, and so on. From its inception, it was clear that the PCB would not be well balanced (Mooney 2005). As mentioned in chapter 1, Bush appointed one of the most conservative bioethicists in the country, Leon Kass, to chair the PCB. Other well-known conservatives appointed to the PCB included Francis Fukuyama, a professor of political economy at Johns Hopkins University; Robert George, a professor of jurisprudence at Princeton University; Mary Ann Glendon, a professor of law at Harvard University; Alfonso Gomez-Lobo, a professor of moral philosophy at Georgetown University; William Hurlbut, a consulting professor of human biology at Stanford University; Charles Krauthammer, a national columnist; and Gilbert Meilaender, a professor of Christian ethics at Valparaiso University. For "balance" Bush added Elizabeth Blackburn, a professor of biophysics and biochemistry at the University of California, Berkeley; William May, a professor of ethics at Southern Methodist University; Janet Rowley, a professor of cell and molecular biology at the University of Chicago; and James Q. Wilson, a professor of management and public policy at the University of California at Los Angeles. The PCB initially included four law professors, three professors of politics or government, four science professors, four physicians, and three professors of ethics, philosophy, or theology, for a total of eight people from the sciences and ten from the humanities (White House press release 2002). The committee only included two people, Kass and Rebecca Dresser, a professor of law at Washington University, with established reputations as bioethicists. Other than Kass, the PCB did not include any bioethicists with peer-reviewed publications on human cloning or embryonic stem cells.

The PCB released its first report, *Human Cloning and Human Dignity: An Ethical Inquiry*, in July 2002. The report distinguished between cloning to reproduce children and cloning for biomedical research (President's Council on Bioethics 2002). Both types of cloning use nuclear transfer techniques to transfer the nucleus from a donor cell into a fertilized egg that has had its nucleus removed. The egg containing the new nucleus is an embryo capable of developing into a human child. In cloning to produce children, the embryo would be transferred into a woman's womb, so that a child may develop and grow. In cloning for research, embryonic stem cells would be harvested from the embryo, and the embryo would be destroyed. The PCB report discussed arguments for and against both types of cloning but ultimately came out against them. A majority of the members of the PCB recommended a permanent ban on cloning to produce children and a four-year moratorium on cloning for research, to allow for additional scientific investigation and ethical debate about the issue. A minority of the PCB recommended a ban on cloning to produce children and the regulation of cloning for research. The minority opinion was endorsed by Blackburn, May, Wilson, Rowley, Michael Sandel (a professor of government at Harvard University), and four others. Kass, Krauthammer, Meilaender, Hurlbut, Dresser, Glendon, Gomez-Lobo, Fukuyama, George, and Paul McCue, a professor of psychiatry at Johns Hopkins University, supported the majority position. Given the composition of the PCB and its leadership, there was never any serious doubt that it would recommend bans on various forms of cloning. President Bush got the result he wanted.

As noted in chapter 1, the White House asked Blackburn to resign in February 2004. Although she received no official explanation for this request, it is safe to assume that the decision was political (Mooney 2005). Blackburn had been an outspoken proponent of human embryonic stem cell research. She was arguably the most highly esteemed scientist on the panel: she discovered teleomerase, an enzyme that lengthens structures at the tip of chromosomes known as teleomeres. This discovery alone may earn her the Nobel Prize in Medicine someday. She is a member of the Institute of Medicine and the National Academy of Sciences. Conservative think tanks, such as the Family Research Council, applauded Blackburn's dismissal, while 170 bioethicists signed a statement protesting her ouster. Rowley decried Blackburn's dismissal as destructive (Mooney 2005). As noted in chapter 1, Blackburn wrote a commentary on this incident published in the *New England Journal of Medicine*.

Blackburn was concerned not just about the policies that the PCB had adopted but also about the distortion and obfuscation of stem cell science (Mooney 2005). One of the important scientific issues related to human embryonic stem cell research is whether adult stem cells, umbilical cord stems, or placental stem cells can be effective in treating diseases. Most scientists regard embryonic stems as having the greatest potential for treating diseases, but some scientists also believe that it may be possible to achieve many medical breakthroughs with other types of stem cells. Bone marrow stem cell transplants have been used successfully for many years to treat leukemia, for example. The PCB had commissioned papers and reports touting the potential of adult stem cells for treating diseases. Blackburn was concerned that the PCB had overstated the usefulness of other types of stem cells and understated the potential of embryonic stem cells (Blackburn and Rowley 2004).

William Hurlbut, a PCB member who favors a ban on research cloning, has suggested that it might be possible to create pluripotent embryonic stem cell lines from nonviable embryos. Hurlbut argues that experiments with mice suggest that it may be possible to introduce a mutation into a human embryo that makes it impossible for the embryo to develop. Stem cells could be derived from these nonviable embryos. Killing nonviable embryos should be less morally controversial than killing embryos, according to Hurlbut, because nonviable embryos lack human potentiality (Hurlbut, George, and Grompe 2006). However, some scientists have questioned the technical feasibility of Hurlbut's proposal (Melton, Daley, and Jennings 2004). Some scientists and ethicists have argued that the proposal creates its own ethical problems, since a nonviable embryo would still have moral status and one would need to destroy many viable embryos to create nonviable embryos. So, people who oppose embryonic stem cell research on the grounds that it destroys human embryos may not be pleased with Hurlbut's proposal (Byrnes 2005).

To be fair to President George W. Bush, many other presidents and congressmen have stacked special commissions (Jasanoff 1990). Perhaps the most famous attempt to stack the deck was perpetrated in 1937 by a Democrat, President Franklin D. Roosevelt. Frustrated by a Supreme Court that had ruled against several of his New Deal proposals, Roosevelt came up with a scheme to increase the number of judges on the court from nine to as many as fifteen. Fortunately, Roosevelt's plan died in a congressional committee (Supreme Court Historical Society 2006). Also, the PCB is just one committee out of dozens appointed by Bush in his tenure in office. It may be the case that other committees have had more balance and diversity than the PCB.

According to Mooney (2005) and Shulman (2007), however, Bush has stacked other federal advisory committees. Another incident of committee stacking occurred when three highly qualified ergonomics experts were dismissed from a peer review panel at the National Institute for Occupational Health and Safety (NIOSH). Although peer review panel appointments are usually apolitical, in this case they may not have been. According to Shulman (2007), the three members were asked to leave the committee because they supported workplace ergonomics standards, a policy opposed by the Bush administration. Shulman (2007) also reports that the Bush administration has asked many prospective committee members about their political views during the appointment process, which is contrary to the intent of the Federal Advisory Committee Act.

Another episode of committee manipulation occurred when the Bush administration dismissed Deborah Rice from an EPA advisory panel that was reviewing a report on ondecabrominated diphenyl ether (deca-BDE), a flame retardant used in carpeting, furniture, and electronics products. The report, which recommended a ban of the chemical, had been delayed by the Bush administration. Rice, who is one of the top toxicologists in the United States, had published research showing that deca-BDE can affect brain development in animals. The American Chemistry Council put pressure on the Bush administration to remove Rice from the panel because it claimed that she was biased (Vestag 2008).

In response to concerns expressed by scientists and engineers that the Bush administration was politicizing federal advisory committees, Congress asked the Government Accounting Office (GAO) to put together a report on ensuring balance and independence on federal advisory committees. The report commented on detrimental effects that bias and politicalization can have on such committees:

> For federal advisory committees to be successful, the members must be independent and the committees balanced—that is, they must be able to provide, and be perceived as providing, credible and balanced advice. A spectrum of scientists and other experts perceive recent appointments to some science and technical committees as being influenced more by ideology than expertise. Independent of the facts and specific issues involved, this perception alone is problematic. The perception of the federal advisory committee system as politicized can jeopardize

the value of an individual committee's work; discourage the participation of scientists, experts, and other potential members on future advisory committees; and call into question the integrity of the federal advisory committee system itself. Because allegations of conflict of interest and bias can undermine the work of otherwise credible and competent committees and threaten the integrity of the federal advisory committee system, the best interests of the government are served by government-wide guidance and agency-level policies and procedures for addressing potential conflicts of interest and ensuring that committees are, and are perceived as being, balanced. (Government Accounting Office 2004, 50)

The events surrounding Blackburn's dismissal from the PCB vividly illustrate some of the problems that can occur when politicians use the appointment process to manipulate the deliberations of a government advisory committee. What options are there for avoiding these problems? One option is to provide additional guidance for federal advisory committees, which is what the GAO report does. The GAO report included the following recommendations:

OGE [Office of Government Ethics] guidance on representative appointments can be strengthened to better ensure that agencies are appropriately appointing committee members. Unless certain ambiguities in the guidance are clarified, some agencies may continue to appoint members providing advice on behalf of the government as representatives and not conduct reviews of potential conflicts, thereby leaving the specific committees and the federal advisory committee system itself vulnerable to potential criticism if potential conflicts of interest are identified. . . .

GSA [General Services Administration] could provide guidance that would assist agencies in identifying the kinds of information they should systematically collect in order to determine the viewpoints of prospective committee members for the purpose of ensuring that committees are, and are perceived as being, balanced. . . .

[A]lternative procedures used to create and manage advisory
committees at some federal agencies and the National
Academies constitute promising practices that can better ensure
independence and balance. Procedures such as obtaining
nominations for committee members from the public, reviewing
more pertinent information regarding members' points of view,
and prescreening prospective members using a structured
interview would help agencies establish more systematic and
consistent methods of achieving independent and balanced
committees. (Government Accounting Office 2004, 50–51)

While these are all fine recommendations, they do not address one
of the most important factors in politicalization: the concentration of
too much power in the executive branch pertaining to science and
technology advice. The authors of the U.S. Constitution (1787)
intended the government to be a system of checks and balances, to
avoid the accumulation of too much power in a single person or a
single branch of government. The legislative, executive, and judicial
branches of government each have different powers and functions
(Hamilton and Madison 1788). The drafters of the Constitution were
especially concerned about giving too much authority to the president, and they included provisions in the government to limit presidential power (Hamilton 1788). For example, a two-thirds majority of
both houses of Congress can override a presidential veto of legislation,
and presidential appointments to cabinet positions, ambassadorships,
and the federal judiciary must be approved by Congress. Currently, the
president has the power to make federal advisory committee appointments or influence those appointments by conveying his wishes to
agency heads. An argument can be made that this arrangement gives
the president too much authority over science advice and that this
power should be diluted. When the Constitution was adopted over
220 years ago, science did not play nearly the role that it plays today in
policy formation. If science had played a larger role in government
decision-making when the Constitution was drafted, it is likely that
the founding fathers would not have given the president so much
authority over scientific advisory committees and scientific agencies.

How might this presidential power be diluted? The Constitution
already includes provisions for congressional approval of some executive

branch appointments. One could argue that congressional approval should be required for some key scientific appointments, such as appointments to science agencies, for example, the FDA and NIH, and appointments to federal advisory committees that deal with scientific issues. However, since there are over 950 federal advisory committees with over 62,000 members, it would be wasteful and time-consuming to require congressional approval for all of these appointments. One way to promote efficiency would be to restrict congressional approval to a limited number of committees, such as thirty, and to only require a congressional subcommittee, such as the Committee on Science and Technology, to approve the appointments, not the entire Congress. The PCB should be included on the list of thirty committees requiring congressional approval. Congressional approval would help to dilute the power of the executive branch in the arena of government science advice, because it would introduce accountability and oversight into the appointment process. Congress already has the authority to pass legislation that would require congressional approval of appointments to scientific advisory committees. According to the U.S. Constitution, the president shall have the authority to nominate and appoint "other public ministers and consuls, judges of the Supreme Court, and all other officers of the United States, whose appointments are not herein otherwise provided for, and which shall be established by law: but the Congress may by law vest the appointment of such inferior officers, as they think proper, in the President alone, in the courts of law, or in the heads of departments" (U.S. Constitution [1787], Article II, Section 2). This passage says that Congress may vest the appointment of inferior officers, such as scientific advisors, to the president or heads of departments. Congress has vested a great deal of appointing power in the president and department heads; perhaps it should take some back.

Ignoring the Experts

As discussed earlier in this chapter, expert advice is just that, advice. Hence, the public has the authority to follow or ignore expert opinion. The purpose of expert opinion is to give the public information and advice to be used in making policy decisions. Society should be governed by the people, not by the experts. So, politicians, as elected representatives of the public, should have the ultimate control over scientific research and its applications. The role of experts in public decision-making is similar to the role of experts in private decision-making: a doctor may give a patient an expert opinion about his medical condition, but the patient should be free to decide whether to follow that advice. This ethical and legal doctrine, known as informed consent, should be adhered to in medicine, unless a patient's decision to ignore medical advice endangers other people. For example, a patient with active tuberculosis does not have a right to refuse to take medication for his condition, because he may give other people the deadly disease if he does not (Resnik 2005).

There have been many well-known cases where politicians have ignored expert opinion. The FDA's handling of Plan B emergency contraception, discussed in chapter 1, is a classic study of a political decision to ignore expert advice. The FDA ignored the advice of its expert committee and several professional associations. While the FDA cited concerns about young women's health in its decision to not approve Plan B, it is abundantly clear that the agency was also responding to pressure from the Bush administration related to its prolife agenda (Mooney 2005). Religious conservatives, who had helped to shape Bush's stem cell policy, also influenced the FDA's decision-making. Another example of ignoring expert opinion is the EPA's decision to terminate the CHEERS study, discussed in chapter 1. In this case, the EPA, facing pressure from congressional Democrats and environmental groups, decided to cancel a study that had been approved by its own advisory panels and three IRBs. The study was being re-reviewed when it was cancelled. As also mentioned in chapter 1, the Bush administration has largely ignored scientific advice on global warming. The Bush administration ignored the advice of the Intergovernmental Report on Climate Change and a National Academy of Sciences 2001 study on climate science, which both concluded that greenhouse gases related to human activity are causing global temperatures to rise (Mooney 2005). Finally, the EPA recently went against the unanimous advice of its scientific advisory council when it chose only a modest tightening of the smog standards, as opposed to a more stringent tightening recommended by the council (Wald 2008).

Even though politicians are free to ignore expert opinion, there are several reasons why this is usually not a good idea. First, ignoring expert advice can lead to uninformed or imprudent decisions. The whole point of soliciting expert opinion is to get good information and advice. The politician who ignores experts is like the automobile owner who drives a car even though his mechanic has told him his brakes need replacing: he risks harming himself or others. Second, ignoring the advice of expert committees can undermine support for those committees among experts who may serve on them in the future. Scientists put considerable time and effort into serving on advisory committees. Committee work takes time away from other obligations, such as teaching, research, family, and so forth. Committee members may be disinclined to work for an agency again if their advice is ignored. Other potential committee members may also take a dim view of the agency. Third, ignoring the advice of experts can undermine the morale within an agency. As mentioned in chapter 1, Susan Wood resigned her position as director of women's health at the FDA when the agency ignored the recommendation to approve Plan B. The FDA's decision had an impact far beyond Wood's resignation, however (Mooney 2005). The morale at the EPA's human subjects program was also adversely affected by the CHEERS episode. Finally, ignoring expert advice can undermine the public's confidence in an agency, since it may lead the public to believe the agency's leaders are incompetent, biased, or both (Shulman 2007).

The space shuttle Challenger disaster illustrates vividly the dangers of ignoring expert opinion. This tragedy is familiar to many readers, though it bears repeating here. Roger Boisjoly was a rocket engineer employed by Morton Thiokol, which manufactures and services the space shuttle for NASA. He had over twenty-five years of experience as a rocket engineer. In July 1985, he wrote a memo to his supervisors discussing design flaws with the O-rings in the shuttle. O-rings are two pieces of rubber that connect two solid rocket boosters. According to Boisjoly, one of the O-rings had failed to seal during a previous shuttle mission, due to cold weather. If both O-rings had failed, the result would have been disastrous. The shuttle Challenger was scheduled for launch on January 28, 1986. The overnight temperature was expected to be −1 degrees centigrade, colder than any previous launch. Boisjoly informed the management at Morton Thiokol about the problem and asked them to delay the launch until the weather warmed. Morton Thiokol agreed that the problem was serious enough that they should delay the launch and they called NASA managers. In the middle of the telephone conference, Morton Thiokol managers decided to tell NASA that the data were inconclusive, so the launch could go forward. Since NASA had committed itself to an ambitious schedule of shuttle missions, it did not want to delay the launch. Unfortunately, Boisjoly's assessment of the situation was correct: the O-rings failed in the cold temperatures and the Challenger exploded after seventy-three seconds of flight, killing all seven passengers (Online Ethics Center 2005).

Since ignoring expert advice is fraught with peril, the burden of proof falls on those who intend to ignore expert advice. Politicians who propose to ignore the advice of scientific advisory committees should have a strong argument for doing so.

Distorting Expert Opinion

Sometimes politicians do not completely ignore expert opinion but they decide to distort or misinterpret it a way that suits a particular viewpoint. For example, the way in which conservative members of Congress and the Bush administration have responded to the threat of global warming illustrates how politicians may acknowledge expert opinion but interpret it for their own purposes. Since the 1980s, climatologists, geologists, ecologists, and other environmental scientists have formed a solid consensus concerning the role of human activity in global climate change. An overwhelming majority of environmental scientists now accept the following five general statements (National Academy of Sciences 2006):

1. The earth has grown warmer in the last 500 years: the last century has been the warmest on record.

2. Greenhouse gases produced by human activity, such as carbon dioxide, methane, and ozone, have been increasing since the Industrial Revolution.

3. Increases in greenhouse gases cause global temperatures to rise.

4. Human activity has therefore been at least partly responsible for rising global temperatures.

5. Global temperatures will continue to rise unless human beings take steps to limit the production of greenhouse gases.

In response to this scientific consensus, many organizations have recommended that all nations take steps to limit the production of greenhouse gases, such as reduction of automobile and factory emissions, use of clean fuels, and so forth. The Kyoto Protocol, mentioned in chapter 1, outlines some steps the signatories can take to limit the production of greenhouse gases.

Though the United States signed the agreement under the Clinton administration, the Bush administration refused to ratify the agreement because it wanted more time to study the problem before taking any action that could have adverse economic impacts (Vedantam 2005). The Bush administration and many conservative members of Congress have emphasized the scientific uncertainties concerning climate change. It is true that there are still many areas of scientific disagreement concerning specific details related to climate change, such as the rate of change, the degree of human influence on the climate, the significance of processes that counteract human activities (removal of greenhouse gases by plants), models of climate change, and the changes in global temperatures that are likely to occur in the future and their impact on society. However, these areas of disagreement concerning specific details do not in any way dispel the areas of agreement concerning the generalities listed above. Uncertainty and disagreement are part of the nature of science, and climate science is no exception. Prudence requires societies to take precautionary measures to prevent serious threats even when those threats are uncertain (Goklany 2001, Resnik 2003b). For example, the citizens of California have enacted laws requiring buildings to be able to withstand earthquakes, even though there is a great deal of uncertainty over when an earthquake will hit California again, where it will occur, how powerful it will be, and so on. Nevertheless, it would be foolish to design and build new buildings without preparing for the possibility of an earthquake. By emphasizing the uncertainties related to climate change as a reason to take no action, politicians have misinterpreted scientific information and opinion and spurned common sense.

Since the public has final authority over the governance of society, politicians are free to interpret expert opinion, just as they are also free to ignore expert opinion. The political interpretation of expert opinion is an essential part of the policy-making process (Jasanoff 1990). People need to receive information and advice and decide how to act on it. But just as it is foolish to ignore expert opinion, it is also unwise to misinterpret expert opinion. Misinterpretations of expert opinion cannot be rationally justified. For example, suppose a physician tells a patient that he has advanced lung cancer and has only a 5% chance of living more than a year. It would be unreasonable for the patient to believe that he has a very good chance of living more than a year and that he has no need to make preparations for his death, such as drafting a will. The patient may hope that he lives longer than a year, but he should still prepare for the fact that he will not.

In some cases, it may seem like there is little difference between ignoring expert opinion and misinterpreting it. For example, one might argue that the Bush administration did not misinterpret expert opinion at all: it simply ignored it. Although the Bush administration's stance on global climate change looks like a case of ignoring expert opinion, there are reasons to say that it is still a case of misinterpreting expert opinion. The administration responded to reports by the NAS; it did not simply ignore them (Mooney 2005). The administration decided to focus on the scientific disagreement mentioned briefly in the reports rather than on the scientific consensus discussed at length. Without a doubt, the decision to focus on the scientific disagreement was motivated by political objectives, but it was still a decision to address expert opinion rather than to ignore it.

Censorship

Censorship is the most problematic response that politicians can make to government science advice. If stacking a committee is similar to cooking research data, then censorship is similar to fabricating, falsifying, or suppressing data. Censorship can have detrimental impacts on the objectivity, reliability, and integrity of science; the quality of government science advice; and the morale of scientists who lend their expertise to the government. As discussed in chapter 1, the Bush administration censored government reports prepared by the EPA, CDC, AHRQ, and other agencies to promote its political agenda (Mooney 2005).

As noted in chapter 3, censorship is a form of content-restriction on science. As such, censorship creates significant problems for the autonomy of science and can only be justified for a compelling social purpose, and even then, the censorship must be the minimal amount needed to achieve that social purpose. Censorship that is aimed at individual scientists, such as in the case of Hansen, poses additional problems and concerns, which I will discuss in chapters 5 and 6. For now, I will focus on the censorship of government reports prepared by scientific panels, committees, or organizations.

Our preliminary inquiry concerning censorship should be: "Does censorship of government reports ever serve a compelling social purpose?" The answer to the question depends on the facts of the case, but it is conceivable that in some instances censorship would serve a compelling social purpose. For example, if a government report contains information whose disclosure could compromise national security or criminal investigations, or if it includes confidential medical, business, or personnel information, then some form of censorship would be warranted. Even when censorship is justified, the minimal amount of censorship should be used. For example, if a government report contains classified information, then the information could be redacted from the report without altering the rest of the document.

None of the cases discussed in chapter 1 appear to meet the requirement that censorship serve a compelling social purpose. In each case it appears that individuals censored documents and reports for narrow, political purposes. In many of the cases, censorship was carried out to promote a particular policy on climate change. Although politicians are free to express their disagreements with government science reports, the proper way to do this is to publish a memo or paper criticizing or objecting to the report; censorship should not be an option. Politicians should help to assure that government science reports are published in a timely fashion, free from the threat of censorship, intimidation, or harassment. Politicians should respect and support openness, freedom, and truthfulness in government science reports.

If an administration censors scientific reports without a compelling social purpose, what can be done about this? In the United States, Congress has the authority to challenge presidential power. For example, Congress can investigate allegations of censorship by government agencies, and Congress can require government agencies to produce the original, uncensored documents. Indeed, Congress took some steps to respond to allegations of improper conduct relating to federal advisory committees when it asked the GAO to examine the selection of experts on federal advisory committees. Scientists should also take some action by forming groups to monitor government science advice and make their concerns known to Congress.

Funding Problems

As noted earlier in this chapter, the government receives information from sources other than advisory committees, such as private companies. For example, pharmaceutical companies submit evidence to the FDA from clinical trials when they apply to have a new drug approved, and pesticide companies submit data to the EPA for approval of their products. Problems can arise when the government uses evidence submitted by private companies pertaining to regulatory decisions without having enough evidence from independent sources, because the evidence submitted by those companies may be biased (Resnik 2007c).

A growing body of scholarship supports the existence of funding effects in industry-sponsored research. For example, a study by Ridker and Torres (2006) of 349 randomized clinical trials related to cardiovascular disease found that 67% of trials funded by industry favored the new treatment over the standard of care as compared to 49% of trials funded by nonprofit organizations. Ridker and Torres also found that 82% of industry-funded clinical trials of medical devices favored the new device as compared to 50% of trials funded by nonprofit organizations. Friedberg and colleagues (1999) found that 95% of industry-sponsored articles on drugs used in cancer treatment favored the drug, as opposed to 62% sponsored by nonprofit research. A study by Cho and Bero (1996) showed that 98% of drug studies published in symposium proceedings sponsored by a company favored the company's products.

There are several different ways that sponsors can influence the outcome of studies. First, the sponsor may manipulate the research design so that the study is likely to demonstrate (or not demonstrate) a particular result. For example, if a study does not have sufficient statistical power to demonstrate a particular effect, such as a toxic reaction to a drug, then it will not demonstrate the effect. Second, since there is usually more than one way to analyze a data set, a sponsor may select a method of data analysis that is favorable to its product. Third, a sponsor may also interpret the data in a way that puts a favorable "spin" on its research results. For example, a drug company could emphasize the benefits of its medication and deemphasize the risks and side effects. Fourth, a company could suppress the publication of unfavorable results. For example, there is evidence that Merck knew that its drug Vioxx could cause cardiovascular problems, but that the company chose to delay publication of this data, pending further analysis. Finally, the most serious problem that can occur is that a sponsor may put pressure on researchers to fabricate or falsify data (Resnik 2007c).

Although there is evidence that shows that sponsors can, and often do, influence the outcome of research, it is important to realize that this does not always happen. Indeed, many sponsors promote ethical, sound science. However, since financial interests can bias research results, it is wise for government agencies that review data submitted by private companies to adopt strategies to minimize or counteract these effects. Some of these include (a) disclosure and management of financial conflicts of interest, (b) independent review of research designs and methods, (c) routine audits of data and research records, (d) reanalysis of data, (e) strict adherence to good research practices, and, last but not least, (f) independent research and analysis (Krimsky 2003, Resnik 2007c, Shamoo and Resnik 2008). Federal agencies that review data submitted by private companies already practice the first five strategies, but not the last (independent research and analysis). In an ideal world, a federal agency would review research submitted by a private company and research submitted by an independent research group, but this often does not happen. Frequently, agencies must rely only on data submitted by companies that are facing regulatory decisions.

The EPA reviews reams of data submitted by private companies facing regulatory decisions. The EPA has the authority, under various statutes, to develop and enforce regulations concerning air and water pollution, pesticides, endangered species, and industrial chemicals. The EPA employs over 18,000 people, over half of whom are scientists, engineers, or policy analysts (Environmental Protection Agency 2006). Many different companies submit information to the EPA pertaining to the impact of their operations and products on the environment. The EPA also sponsors its own environmental research, but the EPA's science budget has not fared well under the administration of President George W. Bush and a Republican-controlled Congress (Stokstad 2004). The EPA's budget for scientific research (extramural and intramural) has dwindled from over $700 million to $572 million (National Science Foundation 2006). Although other agencies, such as the NIH and NSF, also fund environmental research, the amount of money that the U.S. government spends on environmental research is far less than industry spends on R & D related to products with an impact on the environment. This imbalance of funding can affect the information and advice that the EPA uses to make regulatory decisions. If 80% of the environmental studies pertaining to a particular chemical are funded by a company that manufactures the chemical, then it is likely that most of the studies that the EPA examines will be favorable to the chemical.

A similar type of funding problem occurs with the FDA's evaluation of the safety and efficacy of new drugs. The pharmaceutical industry spends over $51 billion per year on R & D for basic research, drug discovery, and drug development (Pharmaceutical Research and Manufacturing Association 2006). The main counterweight to the pharmaceutical industry in the United States is the NIH, with a budget of over $28 billion a year. Although the NIH spends billions of dollars each year on clinical trials, most of its budget goes toward basic research in the biomedical sciences. Thus, most of the data that the FDA examines in making decisions concerning the regulation of drugs has been generated by private industry (Resnik 2007c). Although privately funded research is often well designed, well executed, and highly reliable, it can sometimes be biased. As noted earlier, many studies have shown that there is a strong funding effect in industry-sponsored research. (For review, see Krimsky 2003, Resnik 2007c.)

Another funding problem with the FDA is that a significant proportion of the agency's budget comes from application fees from drug companies. The FDA collects over $140 million per year in user fees and spends most of that money on employee salaries and benefits. Since the FDA's total budget for salaries and benefits is about $1 billion, about 14% of this budget is supported by fees from industry. This type of financial relationship between the FDA and the pharmaceutical industry may encourage the agency to take a sanguine approach toward drug companies. Because the FDA depends on fees from drug companies, it may give them a break when it comes to regulatory decisions and the enforcement of rules. According to some commentators, the FDA's financial interests related to the very industry that it regulates constitute a conflict of interest that affects the objectivity, integrity, and trustworthiness of the agency (Krimsky 2003).

Many other federal agencies review research submitted by private companies, including the Occupational Safety and Health Administration (OSHA), the USDA, the Federal Communications Commission (FCC), the U.S. Nuclear Regulatory Commission (USNRC), and the Federal Trade Commission (FTC). The federal government should have a strong commitment to sponsoring research with implications for regulatory decisions and government policy, so that agencies that make regulatory decisions have sources of information and advice that are independent from the parties that are regulated.

Finally, it is worth mentioning that the demise of the Office of Technology Assessment (OTA) represents another serious type of funding problem. During the 1990s, members of Congress, led by Representative Newt Gingrich (R-GA), became frustrated with what they perceived as a political bias at the OTA. The OTA had issued several reports that were highly critical of Republican ideas, such as President Ronald Reagan's Strategic Defense Initiative, also known as "Star Wars" (Bimber 1996). Although the FDA and EPA have been underfunded, they have not been eliminated. Congress created the OTA in 1972 to provide it with independent science advice, and Congress terminated the organization in 1995 when it determined that its advice was no longer needed. Ironically, the OTA's neutrality, a scientific virtue, may have been its ultimate undoing (Bimber 1996). If the organization had been allied with a particular political constituency, such as environmental or public health advocacy groups, then it might have had enough political support to withstand the budget cuts that Congress made in the 1990s. As I shall argue in the last chapter of this book, there needs to be a political coalition or group that supports the kind of independent advice offered by the OTA.

Conclusion

I began this chapter by reflecting on the importance of expert, scientific opinion in government decision-making and describing an ideal model of the role of expertise in government. I then described some problems that can occur with government science advice, including stacking of government committees or panels, ignoring expert opinion, misinterpreting expert opinion, censoring expert opinion, and funding problems. To avoid these problems it is important for the government to take steps to secure scientific advice that is independent, open, and adequately funded. One way to secure such advice is for the government to increase its utilization of nonpartisan organizations, such as the NAS or organizations that would replace the OTA. When the government relies on advice from special panels or committees, it is important to ensure that appointments are based on scientific qualifications, not on politics or ideology. While it is almost impossible to avoid politics or ideology in the appointment process, an effort should be made to ensure that committees or panels have bipartisan, diverse representation. The deliberations of scientific organizations and panels that provide advice to the government should be open to the public, so that people can understand their arguments, deliberations, and assumptions. Politicians and government officials should not ignore, misinterpret, or censor scientific advice. To ensure that these recommendations are followed, it may be necessary to develop strategies, such as congressional oversight, for government decisions involving expert, scientific advice. I will discuss this option in the last chapter of this book.

5

Government Funding of Science

A billion here, a billion there, pretty soon you're talking about real money.

—Attributed to U.S. senator Everett McKinley
Dirksen (R-IL)

The previous chapter considered the role that politics generally plays in government science advice. This chapter will look at a particular area of science advice: decisions concerning the funding of research by the government. I will first describe the U.S. system for allocating federal research and development (or, as earlier, R & D) funds. The system is similar to those used by other industrialized nations, such as Canada, the United Kingdom, Japan, and members of the European Union. I will also describe the political process for earmarking R & D dollars. Subsequently I will discuss the best way to balance political and scientific participation in R & D funding decisions.

Government Funding of R & D
in the United States

Although U.S. R & D funding seems minuscule when compared to the hundreds of billions of dollars per year spent on national defense or entitlements, such as Medicare or Medicaid, it is still a huge amount of money. The U.S. government's investment in R & D has risen steadily since World War II (Greenberg 2001). Some states, such as California and New Jersey, have also made significant investments in biomedical R & D, but most of the government-sponsored research in the United States is funded by the federal government. In 2007, the U.S. federal government spent $138 billion on R & D (American Association for the Advancement of Science 2006) or roughly 5% of the $2.8 trillion federal budget. From 1952 to 1976, the federal government spent more than private industry on R & D, but since 1980, the private sector has spent more than the public sector on R & D, as a result of increased investments by the pharmaceutical, biotechnology, and information technology industries (Greenberg 2001). Approximately 60% of all R & D in the United States is sponsored by private industry (Resnik 2007c). Figure 5.1 shows the federal R & D investment in R & D since 1952. Most government-sponsored R & D in the United States is funded through different federal agencies, such as the DOD, the NIH, the NSF, and NASA. Table 5.1 shows the allocation of federal government spending on R & D in 2007. More than half of all federal R & D funding ($75.2 billion) was allocated to the DOD, which sponsors research related to national defense. The NIH, which sponsors biomedical research, was next highest on the list at $28.8 billion, followed by NASA at $16.8 billion.

Most of the federally funded R & D is sponsored by a particular agency, although there are some interagency projects, such as the Human Genome Project and the National Nanotechnology Initiative (Human Genome Project 2005, National Nanotechnology Initiative 2006). The chief administrators of federal departments and agencies are nominated by the president and confirmed by Congress. Some other upper-level agency

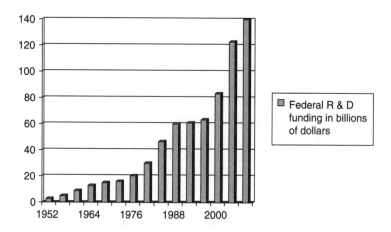

Figure 5.1. Federal funding of R & D, 1952–2008 (est.), based on Resnik (2007c).

Table 5.1. U.S. government R & D spending in 2007

Agency	Estimated funding in billions of dollars
Department of Defense	75.2
National Institutes of Health	28.8
National Aeronautics and Space Administration	16.8
National Science Foundation	6.0
Department of Energy	4.1
Department of Agriculture	2.3
Other	4.8
Total	138

Source: Based on American Association for the Advancement of Science (2006) and Kintisch and Mervis (2006).

administrators are also political appointees. The directors of all the different institutes within the NIH are appointed by the president. The director of the NIH is also a presidential appointee, who is confirmed by Congress. The director of the NIH reports to the secretary of the DHHS, who is appointed by the president and approved by Congress. The DHHS secretary reports to the president. Although the president has oversight authority over federal agencies, Congress can wield considerable influence over these agencies, since Congress drafts the legislation authorizing the agencies to spend money. Congressional committees frequently ask agency leaders to give testimony about particular issues, problems, or concerns, and Congress sometimes passes legislation that controls how government agencies allocate their R & D funds. For example, Senator Boxer's amendment (discussed in chapter 1) places limits on EPA-funded research. Since the 1990s, Congress has prohibited the NIH from funding research that destroys human embryos (Resnik 2007c).

Peer Review of Funding

Most of the civilian research funded by the government is allocated on the basis of peer review. Under the peer review process for R & D funding, a government agency will rely on recommendations from a panels of experts to set funding priorities within the agency and decide which research proposals should be funded. The chief administrator of any agency has the final authority over all funding decisions, but he or she will usually accept the recommendations of experts. To understand how the peer review process works, it will be useful to explore the NIH's system, which is similar to those used by other agencies. The NIH consists of twenty-seven different institutes and centers, most of which are located on campus in Bethesda, Maryland. Over 18,000 people are employed by the NIH. The NIH's intramural program supports research that is conducted at NIH facilities by NIH scientists, who are employees of the government. Only about 20% of the NIH's funds support intramural research (National Institutes of Health 2006a). Though intramural research is peer reviewed, I will not discuss the mechanisms for reviewing NIH intramural research in this book. Many other intramural programs have significant intramural research programs, including those of NASA, the DOE, and the EPA.

About 80% of the NIH's budget supports the extramural program, which sponsors research conducted at different locations across the United States and the world (National Institutes of Health 2006a). Most of the NIH's extramural research is funded via peer-reviewed grants, though a small percentage of this research is funded by means of special contracts. The different NIH institutes and centers solicit research grant proposals through requests for applications (RFAs) or program announcements (PAs) listed in the NIH *Guide to Grants and Contracts* (National Institutes of Health 2006b). Grants are reviewed by a panel of fifteen to twenty experts in a particular discipline known as a study section. To be appointed to a study section, a researcher must be an expert in the field, be (or have been) a principal investigator (PI) on a project similar to those being reviewed, and be dedicated to quality and fairness in the review process. Also, the NIH seeks geographic, ethnic, racial, and gender diversity in study sections (National Institutes of Health 2006b). Study sections that review clinical research often include some members of the public known as consumer reviewers. These reviewers supplement the scientific review process by providing the panel with information about the feasibility and relevance of a proposed project, its prospects for recruiting patients, and informed consent issues related to the project. Consumer reviewers are not expected to contribute to the review of scientific research design (National Institutes of Health 2006b).

All study section members are expected to read all of the proposals to be reviewed at a particular meeting, and each proposal is assigned a primary and a secondary reviewer. The primary reviewer's job is to summarize and evaluate the proposal in a presentation before the group. Other members of the group also comment on the proposal and rate it. The NIH study sections rank proposals on the basis of eight criteria, including (a) scientific significance, (b) methodology, (c) qualifications of the principal investigators and other scientists, (d) preliminary data or prior research, (e) institutional support and available resources, (f) budget, (g) compliance with federal laws and regulations, and (h) social impact (Resnik 2001, 2007c).

After the proposals have been ranked, they are sent to one of the NIH's national advisory committees (NACs) for a final assessment. The NACs each consist of about fifteen members, including scientists and public representatives. The purpose of the NACs is to ensure that the NIH receives advice from a cross-section of the research community and the public (National Institutes of Health 2006b). The NACs decide which of the most highly ranked proposals should be funded. Different institutes within the NIH act on the recommendations of the NACs and fund as many projects as they can, within their budgets. The director of the NIH has final approval over any funding decision. Research funding for NIH proposals is highly competitive, as only about 24% of proposals are funded (National Institutes of Health 2006b). Other agencies have funding rates that are similar or lower.

The NIH's use of public representatives on the NACs and on peer review committees can be very useful for the agency and for its researchers. The public's perspective can help researchers learn more about their work, including an increased understanding of the social, political, and moral significance of their work; public understanding and interpretation of research; issues that can affect recruitment of research subjects and the informed consent process; and the feasibility of conducting some types of studies. The NIH did not always include public members on peer review committees or advisory committees. For many years, funding decisions were made by scientists and administrators. The NIH changed its approach to funding decisions in the 1980s and 1990s, due to intense political pressure from advocacy groups representing people with various diseases, especially breast and ovarian cancer and HIV/AIDS (Dresser 2001). These groups lobbied for more input into the NIH's allocation decisions, arguing that their health problems were being ignored.

Although the peer review system for funding research functions fairly well, it is far from perfect (Lenard 2006). First, the system tends to favor well-established researchers over neophytes, because the well-established researchers have usually served on peer review panels. They know what the reviewers are looking for, know many of the reviewers personally, and have well-established research portfolios. Although some types of conflicts of interest are prohibited in peer review, it is impossible to convene panels where none of the reviewers know the applicants. Thus, something like an old boy network exists in some disciplines, and it can be difficult for newcomers and outsiders to enter these groups (Shamoo and Resnik 2008). Second, although sexual, racial, and ethnic discrimination are prohibited in peer review, since most of the well-established researchers are white males, the system tends to disproportionately favor white males (Shamoo and Resnik 2008).

Third, the system also tends to favor applicants from top-tier research universities over applicants from smaller, lesser-known institutions. The top universities have many advantages over other institutions, such as better facilities, equipment, and technical support; more highly qualified researchers; and more prestige. Because the top research universities tend to be concentrated in specific geographic areas, such as Boston, New York, San Francisco, Chicago, Houston, and Los Angeles, the geographical distribution of research funds is also inequitable (Resnik 2007c). Fourth, peer review often fails to fund highly innovative research, due to the conservatism inherent in the system (Shamoo and Resnik 2008). Reviewers can be biased against highly innovative research because it may challenge their own work and established theories and assumptions in the field. Many researchers prefer to avoid funding research that may threaten their professional interests. Fifth, interdisciplinary research also presents a challenge to the peer review system, since reviewers from different disciplines may have fundamental disagreements about how to evaluate proposals due to different research methods, goals, and assumptions.

Despite these flaws, most scientists and commentators agree that peer review is the best way to evaluate research proposals for government funding, because it utilizes scientific decision-making and embodies scientific values. Although biases can affect the outcome of peer review, the system does not fall too short of fulfilling the goals of objectivity and fairness. Moreover, funding agencies are taking steps to deal with the problems with peer review, such as developing special programs for beginning investigators or racial or ethnic minorities; seeking geographic diversity among the applicants' institutions; and instituting programs for highly innovative or interdisciplinary research. Thus, peer review may not be perfect, but it is preferable to any alternative system. Without peer review, scientific research proposals would be subject to the whims of the political process.

Earmarked Funding

In contrast to peer review, earmarking is a highly political method for making decisions about scientific research proposals. Earmarking bypasses the usual mechanisms that federal agencies have established for allocating funds. In the United States, earmarking occurs when Congress passes legislation that designates money for particular projects. Federal agencies are obligated to allocate funds according to the congressional mandate. Any debate concerning an earmarked project takes place in a congressional committee or at a congressional session, rather than in a peer review panel. Although Congress usually seeks advice from experts when earmarking funds for special projects, the experts do not make any decisions: all authority rests with the politicians (Greenberg 2001).

Earmarking is not always an imprudent way of making decisions concerning scientific funding, since some projects are so expensive, innovative, or interdisciplinary that they are difficult to fund through normal channels. Since World War II, the United States has used earmarking to fund a variety of important science projects including the Hubble Space Telescope, the Human Genome Project, Space Station Freedom, and the National Nanotechnology Initiative (Resnik 2007c). Earmarked funding also supports federal laboratories and posts in Los Alamos, New Mexico; Oak Ridge, Tennessee; Antarctica; and other places. However, earmarking often results in half-baked decisions that pander to political interests and waste taxpayer dollars. Many scientific studies funded by the government are pork-barrel projects. A pork-barrel project can be defined as an appropriation that is requested by only one member of Congress to serve a particular political or local interest with no congressional debate, competitive bidding, or review by experts (Citizens against Government Waste 2006). Pork-barrel projects are usually tacked on to an appropriations bill at the last minute. Although there are no procedures that prevent congressional debate about these special projects, members of Congress have an unspoken agreement not to criticize each other's pork. The phrase "I'll scratch your back, you scratch mine" applies here. Some examples of scientific pork in 2006 include compact laser sensors at Montana State University ($1,250,000), space radiation research at Loma Linda University ($4,000,000), development of high-efficiency free piston sterling converters at Auburn University ($3,500,000), a fiber optic project at Oak Ridge National Laboratory ($2,100,000), and the Geospatial Science Laboratory at Coppin State University ($200,000) (Citizens against Government Waste 2006). As mentioned in chapter 1, Congress spent over $2 billion on pork-barrel science projects in 2006.

Pork-barrel spending on science projects is a clear example of the politicalization of research funding. The problems with pork-barrel science projects, though painfully obvious to government watchdog groups, bear repeating here. First, pork-barrel funding is inherently unfair, since funding is based on political influence rather than merit or geographic equity. Interest groups and constituencies with a great deal of money and influence can get their projects funded, while those with less money and influence are not as successful. Second, pork-barrel funding of science is wasteful because it allows funding for projects that would probably not have been approved by a peer review committee. For example, it is doubtful that an NIH study section would have approved the $15 million Gulf War illness project mentioned in chapter 1. Third, pork-barrel funding can take away money from worthwhile projects that have been or would be approved by a peer review committee. Although politicians spend money as if it grew on trees, there is not an unlimited amount of money to spend on scientific research in the federal budget. The $2 billion that is spent on pork-barrel projects could be spent on more peer-reviewed research at the NIH, NSF, or DOE. Fourth, pork-barrel funding of science is undemocratic. As noted earlier, there is often little or no debate about pork-barrel projects. Most citizens are not aware of how much money Congress allocates to pork-barrel projects or how they are approved. Even most members of Congress are caught off-guard by special projects slipped into appropriations bills at the last minute, during the wee hours of the morning.

Balancing Political versus Scientific Decision-Making

As one can see from this brief overview of federal extramural R & D funding in the United States, political and scientific considerations both play a role in the allocation of money, which raises the question, "What is the proper place of politics in the allocation of government extramural R & D funds?" There are good arguments for scientific and public input on funding decisions (Resnik 2001). The main argument for scientific input is rather obvious: Scientists are best-qualified to evaluate research within their domain of expertise. Only scientists are qualified to evaluate such matters as the originality, scientific merit, and feasibility of a project; the qualifications of the investigators; and the proposed methodology. Politicians and the public should defer to scientific experts concerning scientific judgments about research proposals. However, politicians and the public are qualified to evaluate the moral, social, and legal implications of research projects. Politicians and the public can provide input into the social worth or impact of a proposed project, ethical issues relating to the use of human subjects or animals in research, and conflicts of interest or other matters relating to research integrity.

To decide how to balance scientific and political considerations in government funding of R & D, it will be helpful to make use of some of the distinctions discussed in chapter 3. First, funding decisions generally do not impinge on the autonomy of individual scientists, since someone who does not receive funding from a federal agency could still obtain funding from another source. The denial of funding is different from censorship of a publication. Funding decisions normally impact scientific institutions or organizations, such as universities. Second, funding decisions, by their very nature, address the content of science. Judgments about the originality and the scientific and social significance of research play a large role in deciding whether to fund a grant proposal or contract. These judgments evaluate what the science is about. Decisions concerning how to allocate funding among different research programs, disciplines, or areas also involve judgments about the content of science. In chapter 3 I argued that restrictions on the content of science can be justified only if they serve a compelling social purpose and they use the least burdensome means necessary to accomplish that purpose. Content restrictions on funding can be justified so that the government can be publicly accountable for its allocation of R & D funds. Public accountability is one of the most important characteristics of government: A government should represent the interests and wishes of its people. To do this, it must be accountable for how it makes decisions, spends money, administers justice, and so on (Gutmann and Thompson 1996). The government should enlist the aid of experts in deciding how to allocate R & D funds, as it would use experts in making any other important funding decision, such as allocating funds to the military, public works, education, and the like.

Micromanagement

Although content-based restrictions on the funding of R & D are ethically justified, the methods used by the government may not always be the least burdensome means of accomplishing this task since they may lead to the micromanagement of science. Several of the cases discussed in chapter 1, including the Traditional Values Coalition's attempt to stop 198 NIH grants related to human sexuality, Senator Hutchison's earmarked money for research on Gulf War illness and her opposition to social science funding by the NSF, and the termination of the CHEERS study, are troubling examples of political micromanagement of the scientific peer review process. In these cases, politicians and interest groups tried to subvert scientific peer review for political goals, and in some cases they were successful. What is troubling about these cases is that politicians tried to overturn the peer review process or evade it, substituting their own judgment for the judgment of expert panels and scientific advisory councils, both of which included some public representatives. Actions like these can undermine the progress, integrity, and objectivity of science, and can have demoralizing effects on the scientists whose research is threatened or on the experts who are asked to evaluate research.

Micromanagement may be justified in some rare cases when the peer review system breaks down. Peer review is by no means perfect, and it is possible for errors, biases, and omissions to slip through (Shamoo and Resnik 2008). As mentioned in chapter 3, some unethical studies have slipped through the peer review system, such as the Tuskegee Syphilis Study.[1] Also, there have been numerous high-profile episodes of fabrication or falsification of research data using federal funds that have drawn the attention of Congress (Shamoo and Resnik 2008). When the system breaks down, politicians are justified in getting involved in the details of scientific R & D and holding researchers and administrators accountable. Some might argue that this is what senators Boxer and Nelson were doing when they demanded that EPA administrator Stephen Johnson terminate the CHEERS project. This project was very different from the Tuskegee study, however; CHEERS had some ethical problems, but these probably could have been fixed if the study had been revised appropriately. Indeed, the EPA had suspended the study and was in the process of rereviewing it when Boxer and Nelson intervened (Resnik and Wing 2007). The appropriate response to ethical concerns about the study would have been to express those concerns to the committee that was rereviewing the study, instead of playing hardball politics with the study. Senators Boxer and Nelson set a dangerous precedent in the way they handled the study, and they opened the door for politicians on the other side of the ideological divide to play politics with different studies for different reasons.

Micromanagement may also be justified when there are worthwhile projects that cannot be adequately evaluated by the peer review system due to their size, scope, cost, or controversial nature. For example, the Human Genome Project, the Hubble Space Telescope, and the Space Station Freedom were approved outside the normal peer review process. Scientific input is still important even when this occurs, because political leaders need expert advice to help them understand the strengths and weaknesses of these projects so they can decide whether they merit funding (Resnik 2007c). To avoid pork-barrel R & D funding, Congress

1. For more on the Tuskegee Syphilis Study, see Jones (1993).

should actively solicit expert advice from independent scientists when earmarking funds. Ideally, an independent body could review and evaluate different projects. At one time the Office of Technology Assessment (OTA) was able to serve this function, but, as mentioned in chapter 4, it was terminated in 1995 by a Republican-led Congress.

To best way to avoid micromanagement is to maintain a well-functioning peer review system that allows for public/political input at various stages, which will relieve some of the pressure to micromanage and politicize government R & D funding. The peer review system established by the NIH, in which scientists and members of the public both have some input into funding decisions, seems an appropriate way to balance government oversight and scientific expertise. Although the NIH has established a variety of rules that grant recipients must abide by to receive money, the agency does not manage the day-to-day affairs of scientists. Once a grant is approved, investigators are free to conduct their research with little or no outside interference from the agency or politicians. For the most part, NIH grantees are shielded from Washington's politics.

While the NIH's system minimizes micromanagement by politicians, it still allows for ample political input at a very general level, since members of Congress and the president both have oversight authority of the agency. The president appoints the director of the NIH and the directors of the different NIH institutes (Resnik 2007c). The president and Congress both have the authority to influence and control the NIH's funding priorities and its research focus, and they have exerted this authority on several memorable occasions. For example, in 1971 President Richard Nixon declared a "war on cancer" and made cancer research a top priority. In the late 1980s, HIV/AIDS activists successfully argued for spending more money on HIV/AIDS research. In the early 1990s, feminist activists and members of Congress, such as Pat Schroeder (D-CO), convinced the NIH to spend more money on women's health research (Dresser 2001).

Specific Funding Restrictions

Congress and the president have, at times, placed restrictions on the use of government funds to support specific types of research. As noted in chapter 1, in 2001 President Bush signed an order that prevents the NIH from funding human embryonic stem cell research. In 2005, Congress passed an amendment that prohibits the EPA from funding intentional exposure studies on pregnant women and children (Resnik 2007b). During the 1980s, President Reagan prohibited the federal government from funding research on human embryos. In 1993, President Clinton lifted the Reagan ban on embryo research, but then Congress enacted a ban on embryo research in 1995 (Green 2001).

While specific funding restrictions are justified, in principle, as a way of holding the government accountable for the money it spends on research, they can still cause problems for the progress of scientific research. While the public has a right to refuse to allow the government to support projects that are widely viewed as unethical, such as the Tuskegee Syphilis Study, there are very few projects like this. There are many projects that have a great deal of scientific value but are ethically controversial, such as research on human embryonic stem cells, human sexuality, or environmental exposure studies involving children. If the government bans funding of research that is merely controversial, as opposed to widely regarded as unethical, this sets a dangerous precedent that could lead to additional funding bans, because a great deal of scientific research is ethically controversial. For example, if Christian conservative groups succeed in banning research on human embryonic stem cells, what's to stop environmental groups from lobbying to ban research on the safety of offshore oil drilling, or agricultural interest groups from trying to ban research on the risks of pesticides? When different interest groups succeed in banning government funding of the research they oppose, science loses. To prevent the proliferation of specific funding restrictions, it is important to set a high bar for imposing such restrictions. The government may impose specific funding restrictions only if an overwhelming majority (67% or greater) of the citizens in a nation oppose funding the research.

Another problem with specific funding restrictions is that it can be difficult to anticipate how science will develop and what will be needed for future research funding. As a result, a specific funding restriction may have the unintended consequence of preventing the government from paying for research that has scientific merit and would be considered ethical by many. For example, Senator Boxer's amendment was intended to prevent the EPA from sponsoring dangerous research on children and pregnant women, such as studies that expose them to pesticides. An unintended consequence of this ban is that it also prevents the EPA from funding research that most people would regarded as morally legitimate, such as research on products that children commonly use, such as sunscreen or insect repellent (Resnik 2007a). The ban also prevents the EPA from collaborating with the NIH or private industry on clinical trials of new drugs in pediatric populations. Most people would probably support this type of research, but the EPA ban forbids it. While it is nearly impossible to avoid unintended consequences when enacting legislation, one can minimize their impact by including sunset clauses, which require the legislation to be renewed after a period of time. When legislation is up for renewal, politicians and the public will have a better understanding of the impact of the legislation, which will help them to decide whether the legislation should be renewed or revised. If the legislation is not renewed, it expires. Thus, I would recommend that government rules that ban specific types of R & D funding have sunset clauses.

As I have just argued, specific funding restrictions are justified only when (a) they have widespread popular support, and (b) they have a sunset clause. The Bush administration's decision in 2001 to restrict NIH funding of human embryonic stem cell research had neither. As an executive order with no expiration date, it can only be overturned by another executive order or congressional legislation. Polls in the United States have consistently shown that an overwhelming majority of the public favors government support for human embryonic stem cell research (ABC News 2004, Harris Interactive 2004). In July 2006, the House and the Senate passed a bill that would allow the NIH to fund some human embryonic stem cell research, but Bush vetoed the measure (Babington 2006). Many scientists contend that Bush's policy has had a detrimental effect on embryonic stem cell research in the United States and has threatened America's leadership in this new area of biomedical science (Daley 2004). Although private companies, private foundations, and some states, such as California and New Jersey, have funded human embryonic stem cell research, federal leadership and money are still essential to progress in this area of science (Holden 2006).

Intramural Research

The last topic I would like to address in this chapter concerns restrictions on the autonomy of intramural researchers, that is, scientists who work for particular government agencies, such as the NIH, CDC, EPA, or NASA. The Bush administration's effort to stop NASA scientist James Hansen from speaking out on global warming, discussed in chapter 1, illustrates the problems that some intramural researchers have faced. Using the analytical tools developed in chapter 3, we can say that censorship of an intramural researcher would (a) constitute a restriction on the autonomy of an individual and (b) be a content-based restriction. Both of these restrictions require the highest level of moral justification, that is, a compelling social purpose. What would constitute a compelling social purpose for restricting the autonomy of an intramural researcher, and did the Bush administration have one?

As we have discussed in this book, there are many problems with restricting the autonomy of individual scientists or imposing content restrictions on science. It makes little difference whether that scientist works for the government or a university. In both settings, the goal of science is to advance human knowledge, and the scientist should be treated as an independent researcher with a right to free inquiry (Resnik 2008). Even though scientists who work for the government, like their academic counterparts, have a right to autonomy, there are legitimate reasons for the government to have some control over how intramural researchers communicate with colleagues and the public, and these reasons rise to the level of compelling social purposes. First, the government has a legitimate interest in ensuring that research published by intramural scientists meets standards of quality and integrity, since incompetent research can reflect poorly on the government and undermine the public's trust in government science. Second, the executive branch of the government has a legitimate interest in promoting consistency and clarity in its public policies. If a government scientist speaks to the media on a matter relating to a particular policy issue, such as global warming, politicians, the media, and the public may regard that scientist as representing the executive branch's official position, when he may not (Resnik 2008).

Although these are good reasons for government to have some control over intramural researchers' communications with colleagues and the public, the government should still impose the least burdensome means necessary to achieve these goals. Restrictions on intramural researchers' autonomy should be nominal and fair. To ensure that government research meets standards of quality and integrity, government science agencies may require their researchers to submit their publications for internal peer review. A publication to be submitted to a journal, for example, may be reviewed internally beforehand (Resnik 2008). Internal peer review should not be used to suppress research for political reasons: Peer review evaluations and decisions should be based on scientific rather than political considerations. To ensure that the executive branch can communicate clear and consistent public policy, the government may review and monitor government scientists' communications with the media. However, the government should not prevent government scientists from talking to the media or use media review as a form of harassment or intimidation. Government agencies can also require government scientists to include appropriate disclaimers in their communications with colleagues and the public, that is, stating that their opinions are their own and do not represent the views of the government or one of its agencies. To ascertain that the government meets its obligations to ensure freedom of speech for its scientists, an independent group, such as the American Association for the Advancement of Science, should periodically review the government's treatment of its intramural researchers and should serve as a conduit for complaints (Resnik 2008).

Conclusion

In this chapter I have considered the role of political and scientific considerations in making decisions about government-funded R & D. I have argued that while public input and scientific input are both important, there must be a proper balance of each. On the one hand, scientists need to heed the advice of politicians and concerned citizens so they will not ignore areas of research that are important to the public, and also so that they will fulfill their responsibilities to society. On the other hand, political influences on funding decisions can hinder scientific progress and objectivity. The best way for the government to exert some control over funding decisions is through general oversight and guidance, not micromanagement. Micromanagement of funding decisions should be avoided, except in rare cases in which unethical (or incompetent) research slips through the peer review system. Wherever possible, all science projects, including those receiving earmarked money, should undergo some form of peer review. Pork-barrel science should be avoided. Special restrictions on the use of government funds should be imposed only when a clear majority favors such restrictions and the restrictions have a sunset clause. Scientists who work for the government, like their academic colleagues, have rights to free speech that should be protected. However, the government may impose minimal restrictions on the rights of government scientists to promote quality and integrity in research and clear and consistent public policy communications.

6

Science and National Security

*Security is mostly a superstition. It does not exist in nature, nor
do the children of men as a whole experience it. Avoiding danger
is no safer in the long run than outright exposure. Life is either
a daring adventure, or nothing.*

—Helen Keller

As noted earlier in this book, science and technology have come to
play an increasingly important role in national defense, aiding in the
development of military intelligence, weapons systems, strategies,
and so forth. Because knowledge often has military applications,
governments attempt to control information and technology with
national (and international) security implications. However, this
desire to control information and technology can undermine the
objectivity, reliability, and autonomy of science. This chapter will
examine some of the political and ethical questions that arise at the
intersection of science, technology, and security. Since national security plays an important role in these issues, it will be useful to say
more about this concept first.

National Security

By "national security" I have in mind the protection of a nation, that is,
its citizens, national interests, government, or institutions, from military
threats, including terrorism. By implication, international security is the
protection of nations from military threats. Thirty years ago, national
security mainly involved protecting a nation from aggression by another
nation. For example, during the cold war, the United States considered
an attack from the Soviet Union to be its primary national security

threat. Accordingly, U.S. national security strategies focused on deterring, preventing, or responding to an attack from the Soviet Union. Today, the world is much more complicated, as many of the threats to national security come not from nations but from terrorist organizations or individuals, located inside or outside of the country. Terrorist organizations may have economic, political, philosophical, or religious motivations (Hoffman 2006). Depending on how a threat transpires, it may be classified as warfare, terrorism, or crime. Since the boundaries defining crime, terrorism, and warfare have become murky in recent years, I will not attempt to distinguish between these types of behavior in this book.

It may seem obvious to most people that protecting national security is a morally worthwhile goal, but is it? What is the moral basis for national security? To think clearly about this question, it will be useful to distinguish between protecting the security of *people* living within a nation and protecting the security of a *nation*. Consider the destruction of the World Trade Center buildings that occurred on September 11, 2001, killing over 2,000 people. Efforts to prevent these terrorist attacks would have been justified as a means of saving human lives, if for no other reason. The attacks harmed people living within the United States. But the attacks also harmed the United States as a nation. The September 11 attacks helped to inspire other terrorists to take arms against the United States and had a significant impact on U.S. economic, strategic, and political interests. Someone who opposes the U.S. government and its policies could condemn the killing of innocent people caused by the attacks even if they welcome their adverse impact on security in the United States.

If national security is different from the security of people living within a nation, then what justifies national security? For the pursuit of national security to be a worthy goal, the nation whose security is protected must have moral and political legitimacy. What makes a nation morally and politically legitimate? This is a complex issue in moral and political philosophy that I cannot discuss in adequate detail here, so I will only sketch a brief answer and refer the reader to other sources for a deeper exploration of the topic.[1] A nation is more than a geographic territory: it is a group of people living in a geographic

---

1. See Rawls (2001, 2005).

territory, over time, under a government. For a nation to have legitimacy, the government must be legitimate (Beitz 1999). The legitimacy
of a government can be considered from an internal or external point
of view. A nation has external legitimacy insofar as it is at peace with
other nations, does not threaten other nations, does not meddle in the
affairs of other nations, and recognizes international laws and treaties.
External legitimacy has to do with a government's international relations (Rawls 2001). A nation has internal legitimacy insofar as the
government respects that dignity, rights, and welfare of its own people.
Internal legitimacy has to do with a government's relations with its
own people (Beitz 1999, Rawls 2005).

Which nations are legitimate? This is not an easy question to
answer, because all governments have problems involving relationships
with their own people and other nations: no nation has perfect external or internal legitimacy. External and internal legitimacy are best
viewed as ideal standards that we can use to judge governments. Some
governments (and nations) have more legitimacy than others. The bottom line, as far as national security is concerned, is whether a nation
has enough legitimacy that its national security deserves to be protected. I will assume that most nations in the world, including the
United States, have enough legitimacy that they are warranted in taking reasonable steps to protect their own security. While some may
disagree with this assumption, there cannot be much discussion about
national security without it.

One of the problems with using national security as a justification
for government actions or policies is that there are so many different
ways of threatening a nation's security. Some of these potential threats
include:

- Military aggression
- Terrorism
- Organized crime
- Economic instability
- Public health emergencies, including epidemics and bioweapons
- Food and water contamination
- Political or strategic alliances

- Damaging the infrastructure, including electrical grids,
  computer networks, telecommunications, nuclear power plants,
  and bridges

Because there are so many different ways of threatening a nation, there are many different ways of protecting its security. If national security is not clearly defined, almost any government action or policy could be justified under the guise of national security. If the national security justification is not carefully restricted, it may lead to totalitarianism and a police state. In the 20th century, the Soviet Union, Cuba, and the People's Republic of China repressed dissidents, spied on citizens, censored the media, and controlled public education in the name of national security. In the 21st century, North Korea has taken the same path. Some argue that U.S. presidents, such as Richard Nixon and George W. Bush, have misused the national security justification (Woodward 2004). To avoid these problems, the national security justification must be clearly defined and limited in scope (Jordan, Taylor, and Mazarr 1998).

With these preliminary remarks in mind, let us now consider some of the ways that national security may have an impact on scientific research.

Control of Information

One of the government's basic strategies for protecting national security is to control the flow of information to nations, organizations, or individuals who may use that information to threaten national security. Some obvious examples of information that could damage national security if publicly disseminated include: locations of troops, weapons, and supplies during a war; weapon systems designs and capabilities; intelligence sources and methods; and vulnerabilities of bridges, nuclear power plants, and computer networks. Some of this information is generated by people who work for the government, such as military leaders, military scientists, intelligence officials, and so on. However, some of this information may be generated by people who work outside the government sector, including journalists, scientists, and scholars. Governments have different methods at their disposal to deal with these various sources of information.

Classified Research   In the United States and many other countries, if information with national security implications is generated by someone who is working for the government as an employee, contractor, or special volunteer, the government may control that information by classifying it.[2] In the United States, government agencies, such as the DOD, National Security Agency (NSA), Federal Bureau of Investigation (FBI), DHS, DOE, and DHHS, have the authority to classify information that would harm national security if disseminated. This information may include the results of scientific research, whether conducted in a government laboratory or on a university campus. Classified research ranges from basic research in nuclear engineering, combinatorial mathematics, and jet propulsion to applied research on particular weapons, tactics, strategies, and defensive weaknesses. It encompasses disciplines such as physics and chemistry, medicine, toxicology, computer science, rocketry, aeronautics, cryptography, forensic science, foreign intelligence, international relations, and psychology. Research on nuclear weapons is automatically classified and does not require an action by an agency to be treated as such (American Association of University Professors 2003).

Classified information is distributed on a need-to-know basis. To have access to classified information, a person must require the information to perform his or her job for the government. The U.S. government has established three levels of classification based on the sensitivity of the information. The more that unauthorized disclosure of an item of information could damage national security, the more sensitive it is. The most sensitive information is categorized as "top secret," and the next most sensitive is "secret," followed by "confidential" (Shulsky and Schmitt 2002). To gain access to classified information, one must also have a security clearance, which can be obtained if one passes a thorough background check. Classified information may include information related to intelligence activities, weapons research and development, weapons capabilities, troop deployments, computer security measures, defensive and surveillance systems, diplomatic

2. Other governments also have laws and policies related to classified information, but I will focus on the United States for the purposes of this book. Historically, the United States has been much less restrictive than other countries, such as the Soviet Union or China.

efforts, and much more. According to official policies and laws, government officials should not classify information for political purposes, but they often violate this requirement (Shulsky and Schmitt 2002).

Government secrecy presents a fundamental dilemma for democratic societies. On the one hand, some secrecy (or confidentiality) is necessary for many government activities, including personnel decisions, medical treatment, criminal investigations, legal counseling, and military operations. On the other hand, secrecy is antithetical to a democracy. In a democracy, citizens and politicians must have access to as much information as they need to make decisions. Citizens also cannot effectively petition, criticize, or protest the government if they lack important information about the government's activities (Gutmann and Thompson 1996). Furthermore, government officials may classify information to manipulate political debates and public opinion. Critics argued that President Richard M. Nixon routinely classified information for political reasons while he was in office, and some have argued that President George W. Bush has done the same (Moynihan 1999, Woodward 2004).

In addition to interfering with democratic decision-making, secrecy can undermine the accountability of the government (Moynihan 1999). For the public to hold government officials accountable for their actions, people need to know what officials are doing and they also need to know what they know. To be accountable, government must be open. By interfering with openness, classification can reduce accountability and enable government officials to abuse their power. Throughout history, governments, including the U.S. government, have used secrecy to hide scandals, illegal actions, unpopular policies, and mistakes. As noted in chapter 3, the U.S. government used secrecy to hide unethical human radiation experiments from the public. President Nixon used secrecy to prevent the public from learning about the illegal bombing of Cambodia during the Vietnam War and the Watergate scandal (Jordan, Taylor, and Mazarr 1998).[3]

3. The Freedom of Information Act, which Congress passed in 1966, is one of the most important pieces of legislation for promoting openness in the federal government. This legislation requires that all government documents be available to the public. Nevertheless, FOIA has a number of exceptions, including one for national security (Freedom of Information Act 1996).

While government secrecy is contrary to democracy, it is also bad for science. Openness is one of science's core values, because it is essential for collaboration and criticism in research. New ideas are usually not accepted until they have undergone rigorous testing, criticism, and external review. For peer review to be effective, it is important for reviewers and researchers to be independent from each other. Reviewers and researchers should have different financial, institutional, and intellectual interests. For example, in order to avoid a conflict of interest, a scientific paper should not be reviewed by someone in the same laboratory or institution as the person submitting the paper (Shamoo and Resnik 2008). It is also important for the scientific community to include people from diverse backgrounds with diverse viewpoints and interests, because diversity enhances the clash of ideas that is necessary for rigorous criticism (Longino 1990). Independence and diversity may be lacking when research is classified, due to the small size of the community of scientists with access to the research. In most scientific fields, researchers in different institutions may receive criticism, help, and advice from colleagues all over the world. But this cannot happen when research is classified, because only a handful of scientists in a single institution may have access to the information. This intellectual inbreeding can encourage dogma, bias, and closed-mindedness, which can lead to bad science and bad public policy based on that science.

If we think about classified research using the analytical tools developed in chapter 3, we can view the classification of research as a type of content restriction on science, because research is classified by its subject matter. Classification also impacts the autonomy of individual scientists because it prevents scientists from sharing their work with the public. Thus, classification of research can only be justified for a compelling social purpose, such as national security. Moreover, the government should use the least burdensome means necessary to achieve this purpose. The government should promote open science and classify scientific research only when necessary. A decision to classify research should be based on a clearly defined national security interest, not on political expediency or a poorly defined interest. Research should be declassified when classification is no longer necessary (Shulsky and Schmitt 2002).

Open science policies, if adopted by governments, would be good for democracy and good for science. Unfortunately, it is very difficult to enforce these policies because one cannot know whether a government is pursuing an open science policy unless one has access to information that the government is keeping secret, and one cannot get access to this information if the government is violating the open science policy. This is a catch-22 of the highest order. From time to time, the media and advocacy groups help to defend the public's right to know by exposing research that should not have been classified, but for the most part, citizens must place their trust in political leaders to promote openness in government. Some leaders do a better job of promoting openness than others. Critics of President George W. Bush have argued that he been more secretive than any president other than Nixon (Shulman 2007, Woodward 2004). Regardless of whether these accusations are true, all leaders face the temptation of secrecy. We must trust—and hope—that our leaders will make wise choices in these matters.

Government Censorship   While classification may allow the government to control research with national security implications that is conducted by government employees, classification does not apply outside the government arena. The government does not have the authority to classify research sponsored by a private company or a university, for example. When the government cannot control research by classifying it, what alternatives remain? One possibility is that the government could co-opt the research by inviting scientists who are doing research with national security implications to work for the government, which would allow the research to become classified. This has happened quite a few times in the United States, especially in the field of cryptography (Resnik 1998).

But suppose that scientists do not want to work for the government and that they want to publish their research, despite its potential threat to national security. The government's option at this point would be to engage in some form of censorship. We have already discussed censorship in chapters 4 and 5, in connection with the censorship of government reports and the censorship of government scientists. Censorship of science that has not been sponsored by the government is legally problematic. In the United States and other countries with legal traditions that recognize the right to free speech, government censorship of science may violate scientists' legal rights

(Robertson 1977). Scientific research in the United States is constitutionally protected speech. In the United States, there is a solid constitutional tradition against prior restraint of speech by the government. Prior restraint is stopping the publication of information rather than punishing someone after the fact. The reason that prior restraint is regarded as highly questionable is that it can have a tremendous chilling effect on free speech in general. The government may stop the publication of information only in exceptional cases where national security is clearly threatened (*New York Times Co. v. the United States* 1971). The publication must pose a grave and irreparable danger to national security, such as publishing the positions of troops or weapons during warfare (*Dennis v. United States* 1951). It is likely that very few scientific publications would meet this stringent standard, because scientific publications almost never include information that is directly applicable to a military action or terrorism.

There are also ethical problems with government censorship of unclassified research. Using the analytical tools from chapter 3, we can say that censorship is a form of content restriction that affects the autonomy of individual scientists. So, it can only be justified if it serves a compelling social purpose and it is the least burdensome means necessary to achieve that purpose. While protecting national security is a compelling social purpose, censorship may not be the least burdensome means of achieving this purpose, because even a nominal amount of censorship could have a significant impact on scientific freedom. Government censorship of scientific publications can have a chilling effect on scientific communication and information exchange. For censorship to be effective, the government would have to employ many people to monitor scientific research, so that publications that threaten national security could be stopped in time. Since thousands of new scientific papers are published each week, it would take an enormous taskforce of government agents (spies) to identify publications that threaten national security. The free and open exchange of scientific information would be severely hampered if scientists knew that "Big Brother" was watching them (Miller and Selgelid 2007).

Another problem with censorship is that government censoring of scientific research would be subject to political manipulation. As we have seen in this book time and again, political leaders have censored government science for political reasons. It is likely that the temptation to censor scientific research for political reasons would be just as strong or stronger if the government made a deliberate effort to control non-governmental information with national security implications. Even if the government adopted policies and procedures to protect the censorship of science from political manipulation, it is likely that political manipulation would still occur. Finally, there are many practical problems with having the government take an active role in the censorship of unclassified scientific research, including lack of expertise, knowledge, money, and resources.

For these reasons, the government should avoid censoring non-classified scientific research. Indeed, this is currently the U.S. official policy. Since 1985, the U.S. government has affirmed a commitment to ensuring that fundamental research results will be shared freely with the scientific community, to the maximum extent possible. "Fundamental" research includes basic or applied research that is ordinarily published and shared freely with the academic community (American Association of University Professors 2003).

Self-Censorship   If the government refrains from censoring unclassified research, it is still the case that there may be unclassified research that could threaten national security, and scientists will need to decide whether to publish that research. In the absence of government censorship, some form of self-censorship may be appropriate. In between the categories of classified and unclassified research there lies a grey area sometimes referred to as "sensitive but unclassified" (SBU). Although this category currently has no legal standing in the United States, there is a growing recognition among scientists, citizens, and politicians that some types of unclassified research deserve careful scrutiny and special handling (Bhattacharjee 2006). Several times since 2001, scientists have published articles that could be of great value to terrorists. Concerned citizens, government agencies, and members of Congress have questioned whether the following studies should have been published:

- An article published in the *Journal of Virology*, which described a method to increase the virulence of a mousepox virus (Jackson et al. 2001)

- An article published in the *Proceedings of the National Academy of Sciences (PNAS)*, which demonstrated how to overcome the human immune system's defense against smallpox (Rosengard et al. 2002)
- An article published in the journal *Science*, which showed how to make a poliovirus through ordering DNA by mail from a private company (Cello, Paul, and Wimmer 2002)
- An article published in *PNAS*, which developed a mathematical model for the minimum amount of botulinum toxin needed to contaminate the milk supply (Wein and Liu 2005)

Several members of Congress introduced a resolution objecting to the publication of the articles by Rosengard and colleagues (2002) and Cello, Paul, and Wimmer (2002) (Resnik and Shamoo 2005). The DHHS learned about the article by Wein and Liu (2005) prior to its publication and asked *PNAS* to not publish the article. Members of the *PNAS* editorial staff met with officials from the DHHS concerning the publication of the article, but they decided to publish it, because in their judgment the information contained in the article was valuable for biodefense (Alberts 2005, Resnik 2006b).

In January 2003, the National Academy of Sciences (NAS) and the Center for Strategic and International Studies, urged by the American Society of Microbiology, cohosted a workshop to explore the national security issues raised by biological research. The workshop was attended by publishers, scientists, security experts, and government officials. Members of the workshop issued the following statement, published in *PNAS*:

FIRST: The scientific information published in peer-reviewed research journals carries special status and confers unique responsibilities on editors and authors. We must protect the integrity of the scientific process by publishing manuscripts of high quality, in sufficient detail to permit reproducibility. Without independent verification, a requirement for scientific progress, we can neither advance biomedical research nor provide the knowledge base for building strong biodefense systems.

SECOND: We recognize that the prospect of bioterrorism has raised legitimate concerns about the potential abuse of published information, but also recognize that research in the very same fields will be critical to society in meeting the challenges of defense. We are committed to dealing responsibly and effectively with safety and security issues that may be raised by papers submitted for publication, and to increasing our capacity to identify such issues as they arise.

THIRD: Scientists and their journals should consider the appropriate level and design of processes to accomplish effective review of papers that raise such security issues. Journals in disciplines that have attracted numbers of such papers have already devised procedures that might be employed as models in considering process design. Some of us represent some of those journals; others among us are committed to the timely implementation of such processes, about which we will notify our readers and authors.

FOURTH: We recognize that on occasion an editor may conclude that the potential harm of publication outweighs the potential societal benefits. Under such circumstances, the paper should be modified or not be published. Scientific information is also communicated by other means: seminars, meetings, electronic posting, etc. Journals and scientific societies can play an important role in encouraging investigators to communicate results of research in ways that maximize public benefits and minimize risks of misuse. (Journal Editors and Authors Group 2003)

Later in 2003, the National Research Council (NRC), a branch of the NAS, released an influential report, *Biotechnology Research in the Age of Terrorism: Confronting the Dual Use Dilemma* (National Research Council 2003). The report discussed the basic dilemma involved in dual use research, that is, scientific freedom and openness versus national security. The report recommended that scientists should give special scrutiny to articles that raise national security issues, and that the United States should form a national board to provide scientists with advice on how to handle potentially dangerous research. It did not recommend creating a new category of research, "sensitive but unclassified," however. In 2004, the DHHS followed some of the report's recommendations and formed the National Science Advisory Board for Biosecurity (NSABB) (Alberts 2005). The charge of the NSABB is to help develop:

- A system of institutional and federal research review that allows for fulfillment of important research objectives while addressing national security concerns;
- Guidelines for the identification and conduct of research that may require special attention and security surveillance;
- Professional codes of conduct for scientists and laboratory workers that can be adopted by professional organizations and institutions engaged in life science research;
- Materials and resources to educate the research community about effective biosecurity; and
- Strategies for fostering international collaboration for the effective oversight of dual use biological research. (National Science Advisory Board for Biosecurity 2005)

The NSABB does not have the authority to prevent the publication of potentially dangerous research. It plays a supportive role by providing information and advice to scientists.

If we consider how scientists could censor themselves, there are several opportunities to make decisions to refrain from publishing research. Individuals can evaluate their own work and decide whether they should share it with the rest of the scientific community or keep it secret, laboratory chiefs can evaluate research conducted by people working with the lab, and department heads can evaluate research by department members. And, of course, scientific journals can evaluate research when they receive submitted articles. One problem with encouraging individuals to decide whether to disseminate their research is that they may not have a sufficient understanding of the risks of publishing their work. They may benefit from the input of other researchers with additional information and a different perspective. This problem—lack of enough information and expertise—can occur at other decision points as well. The best place to make decisions concerning dissemination is at the level of the scientific journal or conference, where editors or conference organizers may have access to experts who can provide information and advice concerning the risks of scientific papers or presentations. However, even they may not have enough information or expertise. Hence, there is a real need for support from an organization such as the NSABB.

If journal editors or conference organizers should be the primary gatekeepers for scientific information with national security implications, how should they make their decisions? Since openness is very important in science, the burden of proof falls on those who propose to limit the sharing of scientific information. To meet this burden of proof, decision makers must carefully consider the following factors (National Research Council 2003, Resnik and Shamoo 2005):

1. *Potential benefits to science and society of disseminating the information.* These benefits may include: contributions to scientific knowledge, the applications of scientific knowledge to new medicines or other products, and the use of scientific knowledge to prepare for a defense against a threat to society. For example, the information contained in the article by Wein and Liu (2005) may be useful in helping researchers gain a better understanding of food safety, developing food safety products or devices, or preparing strategies for protecting the food supply against an attack. The same piece of information could be used for terrorism or counterterrorism, crime or the prevention of crime, warfare or defense against warfare. However, even though information may have beneficial uses, there may be a time lag between the harms produced by disseminating information and its benefits. For example, suppose that it would take an investment of billions of dollars and many years of work to protect the milk supply but that a quick and inexpensive act of terrorism could contaminate it. If this were the case, prudence would suggest that dissemination of information about the vulnerability of the milk supply should be delayed long enough to put researchers and public health agencies on alert about the need to protect the milk supply. If the information will eventually be made public, there is no need to give terrorists (or other people with nefarious motives) a head start.

2. *Potential harms to society of disseminating the information.* In assessing potential harms (risks), the first step is to identify the different types of harms that may occur. The harms may include uses of the information by criminals, terrorist groups, or rogue nations to inflict damage on people, institutions, infrastructure, government, or the economy. To identify potential harms to society, it may be necessary to enlist many different experts with various backgrounds, including people with knowledge about the research under scrutiny and also people with some knowledge about particular terrorist groups or others with an interest in the research. For example, if the potentially dangerous research involves methods for mutating anthrax, experts used to assess risks might include microbiologists, immunologists, geneticists, physicians, biochemists, and toxicologists, and also political scientists, sociologists, economists, or psychologists. It may also be essential to use information gained from intelligence agencies about the hostile intents of particular groups or countries, if they are willing to share it with researchers. After harms have been identified, the next step is to estimate the probability that different harms will occur. Again, advice from a variety of experts will be needed to perform this step.

3. *Different options for disseminating the information.* There may be many different ways of controlling the dissemination of the research short of completely blocking its public presentation or publication. If the research is reported in a scientific article, for example, one option might be to publish part of the article but not the complete article. Access to the full article could be granted to responsible scientists with legitimate interests in research. Another option would be to distribute the entire article to a select group of researchers. A third option would be to delay publication of the article to allow for a more comprehensive assessment of its benefits and risks (National Science Advisory Board for Biosecurity 2006).

When deciding whether to place restrictions on the dissemination of research, journal editors and conference organizers should assess and balance the potential benefits and the potential harms (or risks) of dissemination in light of the available options. In theory, one could apply the risk management approach to decisions concerning the dissemination of scientific information. Many government agencies use this approach to make important decisions relating to public health and safety. Under this approach, decision makers identify and assess benefits and risks, then attempt to maximize benefits and minimize risks. For example, panels convened by the FDA assess the benefits and risks of new drugs. Approval of a new drug is based on a careful balancing of its potential benefits and harms, based on data from clinical trials and review of the relevant literature. Review panels can use the information they have about new drugs to estimate the probability that a particular person will benefit the drug, how much they will benefit, and whether they will have an adverse reaction. (Risk management is similar to the utilitarian approach to ethics discussed in chapter 3.)

There is a difficulty with applying the risk management strategy to decisions related to the dissemination of scientific information, since it may be impossible to make objective estimates of the probability of various harms that may occur as the result of dissemination. To make an objective estimate of the probability of an event, one needs data from either (a) the observed frequency of the event or (b) a causal analysis of the event (Howson and Urbach 2005). For example, one can estimate the probability that a black woman will develop breast cancer from observing the breast cancer rate among black women. If it is not possible to measure the frequency of the event, it may be possible to estimate the probability that an event will occur by analyzing the different factors that contribute to it. For example, to estimate the probability that a bridge will collapse when bearing a particular weight, one can analyze this problem in terms of various factors that may lead to a collapse, such as the design of the bridge, the materials used to build it, wear and tear on the bridge, and so forth.

Two problems make it difficult to assign objective probability estimates to acts of terrorism (and many other events involving war or violence): rarity and uniqueness. For example, while the potential harm of hijacked commercial airplanes crashing into the World Trade Center had been identified prior to September 11, 2001, there were no good estimates of the probability that this event would occur. Terrorists had hijacked airplanes many times before September 11, 2001, but terrorists had never hijacked airplanes with the intent of crashing them into skyscrapers. Since the type of event that led to the destruction of the World Trade Center had never occurred before, there were no data on the frequency of its occurrence. Thus, the probability of this event occurring could not have been based on observed frequencies. Since the event was unlike any other previous act of terrorism, many of the different factors contributing to its occurrence were not known. Thus, it was also not possible to develop a probability estimate based on a causal analysis of the event. The best that decision makers could do, prior to September 11, 2001, was to make a best guess concerning the probability that this act of terrorism would occur. This type of probability estimate, also known as a subjective probability, has many difficulties. Perhaps the most significant one is that subjective probabilities are inherently biased: a best guess is always a guess based on a set of assumptions, beliefs, or theories, which may vary considerably from one person to the next. Because subjective probabilities are inherently biased, many scientists and scholars hold that probability estimates used in science should be objective, not subjective (Earman 1992).

Because it is usually not possible to assign objective probabilities to the potential harms related to a decision to disseminate scientific information, the risk management approach is not an appropriate strategy for making such a decision. An approach based on precaution, rather than risk management, is more apt. In the last two decades, the precautionary principle (PP) has played an important role in debates about environmental and public health risks (Goklany 2001). Although the principle has been criticized as vague and politicized, clearly defined versions of the principle can play an important role in making decisions when scientific evidence is lacking. According to a version of the PP that I have defended in print elsewhere, one should take reasonable precautions to address threats that are plausible and serious (Resnik 2003). A precaution is reasonable if helps to prevent, minimize, or mitigate a threat without excessive costs to individuals or society. A threat is plausible if there is substantial evidence that the threat may materialize, even though there may not enough evidence to assign a probability estimate to the threat. A threat is serious if it may cause significant harm to individuals or society.

How would the PP apply to decisions about disseminating scientific information? Suppose that two researchers have studied the electric power grid in the eastern United States and identified its weakest points. They plan to publish an article in a scientific journal. Publication would give terrorists all the information they need to disrupt the grid. The first question we should ask is: Is the threat plausible? Let's assume that it is, since terrorists are interested in inflicting economic damage on the United States and a complete failure of the power grid would cause significant economic damage. The next question should ask is: What is a reasonable precaution we can take to avert the threat? One option would be to tell the authors that they cannot publish the article. This option would probably incur too many costs on science and society, since it is important for people who manage power grids to have that information. Another option would be to publish the article, but this would also seem to be unreasonable because this would place the information in the public domain without doing anything to avert the potential harm. Perhaps the most reasonable solution in a situation like this would be to publish part of the article, or distribute the whole article to a select group of researchers and policy makers who can use the information to strengthen the power grid and make it less susceptible to terrorism.

Obviously, decisions about disseminating knowledge with national security implications are very complex and challenging. Decision makers should make use of all the resources that are available to them, such as the NSABB, and they should clearly articulate their reasons for disseminating (or refusing to disseminate) scientific research, so that scientists, politicians, and the public can be assured that decisions that are made are fair, consistent, and responsible. To aid decision makers, the NSABB has developed a list of what it considers some types of biotechnology research that deserve careful scrutiny (see box 6.1). However, this list does not include many important threats that deserve careful scrutiny, such as contamination of the food supply, disruption of the electric power grids, interference with the Internet and telecommunications, and bombing of bridges, tunnels, ports, stadiums, and nuclear power plants. This is understandable, since the NSABB focuses on threats related to biotechnology. Since there are many different areas of science that may have an impact on national security, it would be wise to expand the NSABB to include all areas of science. It could be renamed the NSSAB (National Science Security Advisory Board).

Box 6.1. Dual use research of concern

Careful consideration should be given to knowledge, products, or technologies that:

- Enhance the harmful consequences of a biological agent or toxin
- Disrupt the immunity or the effectiveness of immunization without clinical and/or agricultural justification
- Confer to a biological agent or toxin resistance to clinically and/or agriculturally useful prophylactic or therapeutic interventions against the agent or toxin, or facilitate the ability to evade detection methodologies
- Increase the stability, transmissibility, or the ability to disseminate a biological agent or toxin
- Alter the host range or tropism of a biological agent or toxin
- Enhance the susceptibility of the host population
- Generate a novel pathogenic agent or toxin, or reconstitute an eradicated or extinct biological agent

Source: Based on National Science Advisory Board for Biosecurity (2006).

Before concluding this section I would like to make a few remarks about the government's proper role in scientists' decisions concerning the publication of research with national security implications. Though the government should refrain from censoring nonclassified research, it may encourage scientists, scientific organizations, and scientific institutions to become more aware of the national security implications of research and to assess and review publications that merit extra scrutiny. The government should provide financial, material, logistical, and technical support for scientists' efforts to deal with this sensitive research. The government can also support conferences, workshops, and educational activities related to science and security. It may also be important for the government to share classified information, such as intelligence, with scientists who are involved in these decisions, if the information is vital to understanding the nature of a potential threat to national security. Government agencies, scientists, research institutions, and national security specialists should work together to deal with the issues in a way that protects national security without undermining freedom and openness in science.

Control of Technology, Materials, and Access

Another strategy for protecting national security is to control the flow of technology and materials outside of the nation and to restrict access within. For many years, the U.S. government has had the authority to control the export of weapons, weapons-related technologies, and some materials that could be used to make weapons, such as dangerous chemical, biological, or nuclear materials. The U.S. government has also had the authority to restrict access to dangerous materials, such as uranium, toxic chemicals, and deadly pathogens. Following the attacks of September 11, 2001, and the anthrax attacks that killed five people and sickened many more during the fall of 2001, Congress passed the Uniting and Strengthening America by Providing Appropriate Tools Required to Intercept and Obstruct Terrorism (USA PATRIOT) Act (also known as the Patriot Act), which makes it a crime to possess or transfer a biological agent, toxin, or delivery system in a quantity that would not be reasonably used for a peaceful purpose (Resnik and Shamoo 2005). The Patriot Act bars restricted persons from having access to a list of select biological and chemical agents, that is, pathogens and toxic compounds. Congress also passed the Public Health Security and Bioterrorism Preparedness and Response Act, which requires institutions possessing select agents to develop an inventory of these agents and to take steps to improve security. Congress passed other laws that require institutions to keep an inventory of select agents, to conduct background checks on personnel who are granted access to select agents, and to keep track of who has access to select agents (Resnik and Shamoo 2005).

If we apply the analytical tools developed in chapter 3 to government restrictions on technology and materials, we can see that these restrictions affect the process of science, not the content of science. The restrictions are concerned with how research is conducted, not with what research is about. The restrictions also tend to have more of an impact on scientific organizations and institutions, such as universities and laboratories, rather than on individuals. Thus, the restrictions do not raise major concerns for individual autonomy. Restrictions on technology and materials are justified, then, if the benefits of those restrictions outweigh the harms. The benefits of these restrictions are that they can help protect national security as well as public health and safety. It is a good idea to control access to a dangerous microbe, such as smallpox, to protect public health and safety and to prevent bioterrorism. The risks of these restrictions are that they can interfere with scientific research. These restrictions can make it difficult for researchers to gain access to materials they need for research, and they can increase administrative costs and difficulties related to research. Researchers who are categorized as a security risk will be unable to work with select agents, which could lead to discrimination based on nationality or ethnicity. Politicians, government agencies, and research institutions must carefully consider these risks—and how to manage them—when developing and implementing policies that control technologies and materials.

Manipulation of Military Intelligence

The last topic I would like to discuss before concluding this chapter is the manipulation of classified research, specifically military intelligence research. Military intelligence is the gathering, analyzing, and interpretation of classified information related to national security, such as information about the weapons possessed by a rival nation or a terrorist organization; the locations of weapons, troops, or facilities; vulnerabilities; and a rival nation's intelligence capabilities. Military intelligence may be gathered by people working in the field, such as spies or informants, or by sophisticated instruments, such as satellites, spy planes, hidden microphones, and seismometers. People working in government agencies, such as the NSA and DOD, analyze and interpret military intelligence and make this information available to military leaders and politicians with the appropriate security clearance. Because many important political decisions are based on military intelligence, military intelligence should emulate the goals and methods of science (Pielke 2007). It would be folly to launch an attack or to ignore a potential threat, based on erroneous intelligence. To achieve reliability and objectivity, it is important for intelligence agents and analysts to adopt many of the epistemological and ethical standards that govern science, such as empirical support, testability, consistency, precision, and honesty. Agents should honestly report their information.

Intelligence analysts should assemble the best evidence available for their hypotheses and theories and subject them to rigorous tests. Analysts should consider alternative hypotheses and theories, question their own assumptions, and be open to new or different ideas (Shulsky and Schmitt 2002). And last but not least, intelligence should be shielded from political manipulation, because political manipulation undermines the reliability, objectivity, and integrity of intelligence.

Critics of President George W. Bush have charged that his administration manipulated intelligence concerning Iraq's biological, chemical, and nuclear weapons programs to justify the March 2003 invasion of that country (Shulman 2007, Woodward 2004).[4] One of the Bush administration's justifications for the invasion of Iraq was to make the nation comply with UN Security Council resolutions concerning its biological, chemical, and nuclear weapons programs. The resolutions required Iraq to provide access to UN weapons inspectors and provide an accounting of the biological and chemical weapons that it claimed to have destroyed after the first Gulf War in 1991. The Bush administration argued that Iraq was not complying with the resolutions, that it still had biological and chemical weapons, that it was seeking to develop nuclear weapons, and that it posed an imminent threat to the United States and the rest of the world. The administration argued that it was justified in going to war with Iraq under the strategic doctrine of preemption. According to this doctrine, a country is justified in going to war if it faces a growing threat to its national interests. The administration argued that Iraq's weapons of mass destruction (WMDs) in the hands of Iraq's brutal dictator Saddam Hussein constituted such a threat and that it would be better to go war than wait until he used them against the United States. The doctrine of preemption is similar to the precautionary principle (discussed earlier) in that it recommends taking preventative measures to avoid grave harms (Pielke 2007). It

---

4. I understand that questions about the Bush administration's decision to invade Iraq are highly contentious, and that there are other opinions of how the administration handled this situation. For a pro-Bush perspective on the invasion, see the Bush administration's press releases related to the Iraq invasion at www.whitehouse.gov (accessed July 16, 2008).

is a controversial strategic doctrine because it justifies acts of war prior to an imminent threat or active aggression. It justifies wars to prevent wars.

The Bush administration's factual case for going to war was built on its claims concerning Iraq's WMDs. The administration argued that it had ample intelligence information concerning Iraq's chemical, biological, and nuclear weapons programs. It further argued that Iraq was linked to terrorist groups, and that Iraq might give these weapons to terrorists. In February 2003, Bush's secretary of state, Colin Powell, gave a lengthy speech to the UN, partly excerpted here, in which he defended military action against Iraq:

> For more than 20 years, by word and by deed Saddam Hussein has pursued his ambition to dominate Iraq and the broader Middle East using the only means he knows, intimidation, coercion and annihilation of all those who might stand in his way. For Saddam Hussein, possession of the world's most deadly weapons is the ultimate trump card, the one he must hold to fulfill his ambition. We know that Saddam Hussein is determined to keep his weapons of mass destruction; he's determined to make more. Given Saddam Hussein's history of aggression, given what we know of his grandiose plans, given what we know of his terrorist associations and given his determination to exact revenge on those who oppose him, should we take the risk that he will not some day use these weapons at a time and the place and in the manner of his choosing at a time when the world is in a much weaker position to respond? The United States will not and cannot run that risk to the American people. Leaving Saddam Hussein in possession of weapons of mass destruction for a few more months or years is not an option, not in a post–September 11th world. My colleagues, over three months ago this council recognized that Iraq continued to pose a threat to international peace and security, and that Iraq had been and remained in material breach of its disarmament obligations. Today Iraq still poses a threat and Iraq still remains in material breach. Indeed, by its failure to seize on its one last opportunity to come clean and disarm, Iraq has

put itself in deeper material breach and closer to the day
when it will face serious consequences for its continued
defiance of this council. (Powell 2003)

Prior to Powell's speech, the administration had not publicly shared
its intelligence concerning Iraq's weapons of mass destruction. It
had only shared the intelligence with some leaders of Congress and
allied nations, such as the United Kingdom. The administration
realized, however, that it must be forthcoming with its intelligence
to convince the world of the danger posed by Iraq. During his
speech, Powell (2003) discussed many different intelligence claims,
including:

- Iraq was hiding equipment from UN inspectors
- Iraq was thwarting UN inspections
- Iraq was denying inspectors access to its scientists
- Iraq had not accounted for all of the chemical and biological
  weapons it had produced in the early 1990s and was supposed to
  destroy under UN resolutions
- Iraq had mobile bioweapons laboratories mounted on trucks
  and trailers
- Iraq was seeking to restart its nuclear weapons programs and
  was attempting to acquire aluminum tubes used for building
  uranium enrichment equipment
- Iraq possessed SCUD missiles with a range of up to 600 miles,
  which were prohibited under UN resolutions
- Iraq had ties to a1-Qaeda, the terrorist group responsible for the
  September 11 attacks (Powell 2003)

Following the invasion of Iraq in the spring of 2003, the U.S.
military made a diligent effort to find the weapons of mass destruction that were the basis for the war. To date, none have been found.
What happened to the WMDs? Though some people speculate that
Saddam Hussein destroyed the WMDs just prior to the invasion or
smuggled them into another country, such as Syria, the most likely
explanation is that they never existed at all or they never existed in

as large a quantity as the U.S. government had assumed. So what went wrong with the U.S. military intelligence? Why were the top leaders of the United States and many other countries convinced that Iraq had WMDs?

One possible explanation of what went wrong is that the intelligence was based on unreliable sources, such as dissidents who had fled Iraq, defectors, or exiles with ambitions of overthrowing the government (Pielke 2007). Intelligence analysts are trained to consider the reliability of sources when assessing intelligence, and to discount intelligence from unreliable resources. It is possible that analysts failed to question the reliability of the intelligence sources, or, more likely, that any doubts they expressed were ignored. A second explanation for the intelligence failure was that the Bush administration had restructured the U.S. intelligence operations so that information could go straight to the top (that is, the president and a small group of advisors), with little intervening dissent or debate. This restructuring included the dissolution of committees that had opposed some of the administration's military policies (Pielke 2007). As noted earlier, debate and dissension are very important for the formation or reliable and objective intelligence. A third explanation is that the administration deliberately selected pieces of intelligence that fit its Iraq policy and ignored others. The administration had decided as early as 2001 to invade Iraq, and sought out military intelligence to justify this plan (Woodward 2004). It got the intelligence it wanted (Rampton and Stauber 2003, Shulman 2007). A fourth explanation is that some of the intelligence was actually faked (Shulman 2007).

We will probably never have a complete and accurate explanation of what went wrong with the U.S. assessment of Iraq prior to the invasion in 2003, because much of the essential information is classified. Since I am not privy to this information, and I am not an intelligence expert, I will not claim that the Bush administration lied, fabricated, falsified, or manipulated data. It entirely plausible that the intelligence failures were due to human error, an inept intelligence organization, lack of dissension and debate, and a single-minded focus on removing Saddam Hussein from power. This may all be true. I would like to look beyond this unfortunate episode to the lessons it offers for science and politics.

The main lesson to draw from these intelligence failures is the importance of allowing intelligence agencies and analysts to make independent judgments, free from political manipulation, intimidation, or control. Though military intelligence may not be considered a science, many of the points about the autonomy of science apply to intelligence gathering, analysis, and interpretation. The nation's intelligence operations should be structured to allow for plenty of room for debate, dissension, and the consideration of alternative points of view. Many of the epistemological and ethical values of science can play an important role in intelligence operations.

Conclusion

In this chapter I have examined conflicts between science and national security. Though the protection of national security represents a legitimate reason for restricting the autonomy of scientists, scientific organizations, and scientific institutions, this rationale should be applied with care to protect the rights of individual scientists and to protect the reliability and objectivity of science. For classification of government-sponsored research to be justified, there must be a clearly defined national security interest at stake. Classification should be used only when necessary and should be withdrawn when no longer needed. Research should never be classified for purely political reasons. Because censorship of nongovernment science represents such a grave threat to scientific progress, creativity, and innovation, the government should avoided censorship of nonclassified research. The best way to restrict the publication of research with national security implications is for scientists to police themselves. Journal editors and other gatekeepers must carefully consider the benefits, risks, and options concerning dissemination. Since restrictions on the dissemination of information can cause significant harm to scientific progress, the burden of proof falls on those who propose to prevent the dissemination of scientific information. The threat to national security must be more than a fanciful scenario: it must be a plausible threat based on sound evidence. If scientists identify plausible threats, they should take reasonable measures to prevent those threats from materializing. The government should play a supportive role in scientists' assessments of research with national security implications. To avoid the politicalization of military intelligence, intelligence analysts and agencies should be shielded from political pressure and should be able arrive at independent judgments. Intelligence should not be manipulated toward political ends.

7

Protecting Human Subjects in Research

> *Three basic principles, among those generally accepted in our cultural tradition, are particularly relevant to the ethics of research involving human subjects: the principles of respect of persons, beneficence and justice.*
>
> —The Belmont Report

Research that involves human subjects is a very controversial area of science because it pits the good of the individual versus the good of society, which is among the most difficult dilemmas in ethical theory or practice. On the one hand, it is important to conduct research with human subjects to learn more about human physiology, pathology, health, psychology, and behavior in the development of new therapies and interventions. Research involving human subjects can benefit society by leading to advances in science and medicine. On the other hand, human beings are different from other experimental subjects because they have inherent moral value (or dignity) that must be respected. Researchers have moral obligations to protect the rights and welfare of human subjects (Shamoo and Resnik 2008). This clash of values can create many different ethical dilemmas in research because it may not be possible to maximize the protections of human subjects and the progress of science and medicine at the same time. Society must balance the advancement of science and medicine and the need to protect human subjects. People often disagree on how trade-offs among these values should be made. Some believe strongly in a proresearch framework, while others champion human rights above all else (Shamoo and Resnik 2008). This chapter will consider how society can maintain adequate oversight of research with human subjects without adversely impacting the autonomy of science.

Balancing Progress of Science versus Protection of Human Subjects

The conflict between protecting human subjects and promoting scientific research manifests itself in many different controversies related to research with human subjects. Some of these are as follows:

- *Risks and benefits.* What degree of risk can human subjects be exposed to in research? Can human subjects participate in risky research when they may receive substantial medical benefits from participation? Are experiments that may cause death or permanent damage ever justified? What is a reasonable balance of risks and benefits in research? Should there be differences in risk exposure based on the category of subjects (for example, healthy adults, children, pregnant women, or prisoners)? Can children participate in risky research when they are not likely to benefit from their participation? When is it ethical to enroll pregnant women or prisoners in research studies? What are some ways to minimize risks in research? Should researchers minimize risks to third parties who are not participating in research? Should researchers protect communities from harm?

- *Research design issues.* Is it ever ethical to give research subjects placebos? Is it ethical to randomize subjects to different treatment groups? When should a research study be stopped early to benefit subjects or prevent harm to subjects? Is it ethical to conduct a study that is statistically underpowered or overpowered? Can clinical researchers individualize their interventions based on the needs of the patient/subject or should they stick to the research protocol?

- *Consent issues.* Should researchers always obtain consent from research subjects or their representatives? Should consent always be documented? What should subjects be informed about when they participate in research? Are cultural or social variations in the informed consent process acceptable? Should communities be consulted about research projects that affect them? Is it ever ethical to deceive subjects about the nature of the research study? How can one prevent coercion or undue inducement in research? Can money be an undue inducement to participate in research?

- *Confidentiality issues.* How should confidentiality be protected in research? Should personal identifiers be removed from the data to protect confidentiality? Should demographic information be removed from data if this is necessary to protect confidentiality? Who should have access to research data?
- *Justice issues.* How should the benefits and risks of research be distributed? Should researchers and sponsors share the benefits of research with populations or communities? How should benefits be shared? Do research subjects have the right to share in the benefits of the commercialization of research? Should researchers make special efforts to ensure that racial and ethnic minorities are represented in research studies?

In these and other issues, society often faces the basic dilemma of protecting the rights and welfare of research subjects versus promoting science and medicine. Different solutions to these problems offer more (or less) protection to human subjects and help (or hinder) research. I will not discuss these dilemmas in this book, but I will refer the reader to other sources (see Amdur 2003, Coleman et al. 2005, Emanuel et al. 2004, Shamoo and Resnik 2008). Instead, I will discuss some of the regulations and guidelines that apply to the situations that create these dilemmas. In creating these regulations and guidelines, society has attempted to strike a balance between protecting human subjects and advancing science.

Ethics Regulations and Guidelines

As noted in chapter 3, the first international ethics guidance for research with human subjects, the Nuremberg Code, was adopted in 1947, in response to the atrocities committed by Nazi researchers. The Nuremberg Code emphasizes many points that are still recognized as important for research with human subjects, including the following (Nuremberg Code 1949):

- Informed consent
- Subjects free to withdraw at any time
- Research has social benefits

- Sound research design
- Qualified personnel
- Minimization of risks and discomfort or pain
- Risks justified by the benefits or importance of the research

Another important ethics code, the World Medical Association's Helsinki Declaration, was adopted in 1964. The Helsinki Declaration has been revised many times, most recently in 2004 (World Medical Association 2004). The Helsinki Declaration emphasizes many of the points made by the Nuremberg Code and adds some more, such as (World Medical Association 2004):

- Protection of privacy and confidentiality
- Proxy consent for incompetent research subjects
- Protection of vulnerable subjects
- Rules for the use of placebos in research
- Access to treatments after the study is completed
- Disclosure of conflicts of interest
- Publication of results

Although these two codes marked an important step in the oversight of research with human subjects, they were only ethical guidelines, without substantial legal power. Since researchers were not legally required to follow these rules, they often did not. As also noted in chapter 3, during the 1940s, 1950s, and 1960s, the U.S. government conducted secret radiation experiments on human subjects that violated informed consent, an ethical standard stated in the Nuremberg Code and the Helsinki Declaration. In 1966, Henry Beecher (1966) published an article in the *New England Journal of Medicine* describing twenty-two studies that he contended violated ethical guidelines. Three of these studies have since become infamous: the Willowbrook Hepatitis Experiments, the Jewish Chronic Disease Study, and the Tuskegee Syphilis Study (Shamoo and Resnik 2008).

The congressional investigation into the Tuskegee study (mentioned in chapter 3) and other ethically questionable studies resulted in the adoption of the National Research Act in 1974, which authorized U.S. federal agencies to develop regulations for research with human subjects. In 1977, President Jimmy Carter appointed the National Commission for the Protection of Human Subjects of Biomedical and Behavioral Research, which published the *Belmont Report* in 1979. The *Belmont Report* provided a moral and conceptual framework for a major revision of federal research regulations in 1981. Three moral principles described in the report are (a) respect for persons, which requires researchers to obtain informed consent and protect confidentiality; (b) beneficence, which requires researchers to minimize risks to subjects and conduct research only when the benefits outweigh the harms; and (c) justice, which requires researchers to protect vulnerable subjects and distribute the benefits and risks of research fairly. The *Belmont Report* provided a moral foundation for a revision of the federal research regulations in 1981, and it plays a key role in interpreting and applying research regulations (Amdur 2003, Shamoo and Resnik 2008).

The two main federal regulations are the Department of Health and Human Services (DHHS) regulations (also known as the "Common Rule"), which have been adopted by seventeen federal agencies, and the FDA regulations. The DHHS regulations apply to research conducted or sponsored by the DHHS, including NIH research. The FDA regulations apply to research conducted or sponsored by organizations (usually private companies) who are submitting data to support an application for approval of a new drug or a biological or medical device to the FDA. The DHHS regulations and FDA regulations are very similar, and the FDA has adopted some parts of the DHHS regulations (Shamoo and Resnik 2008).[1]

The federal research regulations establish a system for the oversight of research with human subjects. The focal point of this system is an ethics committee known as an institutional review board for research with human subjects (or IRB).[2] An IRB is responsible for reviewing research

1. Many other countries have also adopted regulations governing the conduct of research with human subjects. Most of these rules are similar to the federal research regulations. In this chapter, I will focus on the U.S. federal research regulations. See Office of Human Research Protections (2007b).

2. Other countries have similar committees known by different names, such as research ethics committees or research ethics boards.

with human subjects. It has the power to approve or disapprove proposed research studies (or protocols), to conduct continuing reviews of research, and to monitor research (Department of Health and Human Services 2005). The IRB also provides investigators with education, information, and advice concerning research projects (Amdur 2003). A simple majority of the IRB is required to approve research protocols. The IRB chairperson (or designee) may review IRB actions that qualify for expedited review, such as approval of minor changes to protocols that have already been reviewed, or approval of new protocols that pose only a minimal risk to subjects. An IRB may be associated with a particular research institution, such as a university or hospital, or it may be independent. Pharmaceutical companies often use independent, for-profit IRBs to review clinical trials that are conducted at medical clinics instead of universities or hospitals (Lemmens and Thompson 2001).

The federal regulations require that an IRB have at least five members from varying professional, educational, and cultural backgrounds. An IRB should include people who are from different races, genders, or professions; members who are competent to review the scientific, ethical, and legal issues; and scientists as well as nonscientists. The IRB should also include at least one community member, that is, someone who is not associated with the institution. The boards may solicit the help of outside experts to assist in the review of research. Members of IRBs should not vote on any protocol that they have a direct interest in. The chair should not vote, except to break a tie. If an IRB reviews research involving vulnerable populations, such as children or fetuses, prisoners, mentally disabled adults, or economically disadvantaged people, then it should include members who have knowledge or experience concerning the needs of those populations (45 C.F.R. 46).

An IRB may approve a research protocol only if it determines that the following requirements have been met (45 C.F.R. 46):

1. Risks have been minimized
2. Risks are reasonable in relation to the anticipated benefits to the subjects or society (the knowledge gained)
3. Subject selection is equitable
4. Informed consent will be sought and properly documented

5. There are provisions in place for data and safety monitoring, if appropriate

6. There are provisions for protecting privacy and confidentiality

7. There are additional safeguards for protecting vulnerable subjects, if appropriate

In addition to applying these seven criteria for approval to protocols, most IRBs also evaluate the research design of protocols, since it is unethical to use research subjects in studies that are poorly designed. If a study is poorly designed, it may not yield any useful knowledge, and therefore the risks to the subjects may not be justified (Emanuel, Wendler, and Grady 2000). The federal regulations also state a number of other rules for research with human subjects, such as informed consent requirements (and exceptions); documentation of consent requirements (and exceptions); special protections for children and fetuses, pregnant women, and prisoners; standard operating procedures for IRBs; IRB records and minutes; and responsibilities of research institutions (45 C.F.R. 46).

In addition to the federal research regulations, the privacy rules that are part of the Healthcare Insurance Portability and Accountability Act (HIPAA) apply to medical research. These rules state conditions for disclosure, access to, and protection of personal health information (PHI). They give patients the right to view or amend their medical records and to know who has had access to them. The rules also include some specific rules for medical research, such as rules for recruiting patients into clinical trials, using anonymous data, and reviewing research records (National Institutes of Health 2008). Finally, there are also state laws that pertain to biomedical research. For example, California has its own human research rules (State of California 2007).

Balancing Scientific Autonomy and Government Control

If we apply the analytical tools developed in chapter 3 to the regulation of research with human subjects, we can view these rules as restrictions on the autonomy of scientists, because they prevent scientists from performing some types of research with human subjects. They also restrict the autonomy of scientific institutions and organizations because they prevent institutions or organizations from conducting or sponsoring some types of research. Because the rules address the way in which research is conducted, not what research is about, they restrict the process of scientific research, not the content of scientific research. Since the restrictions limit the autonomy of scientists, to be justified they must serve a compelling social purpose and be the least burdensome means necessary to achieve this purpose. Without a doubt, protecting the rights and welfare of human beings is a compelling social purpose. But are the current regulations the proper amount of government control of research? Are they excessively burdensome or are they too lax? Do they represent too much or too little government control of research?

To answer these questions, one must examine a particular system of rules to see how the rules impact research and human subjects. Since I have been focusing on the U.S. federal regulations in this chapter, I will continue to do so. However, most of the points I make in my discussion will probably also apply to other nations. For several years, U.S. researchers have complained that the research regulations are excessively burdensome. Others have argued that the regulations do not go far enough. Complaints have focused on some problems with current regulations and their implementation. The complaints, listed below, are numbered for convenience only, not in order of importance.

1. *Bureaucracy and red tape.* Some critics of the current system of regulations have argued that the rules impose a heavy regulatory burden on researchers and IRBs because of the sheer volume of paperwork and red tape relating to the review of human subjects research (Institute of Medicine 2002). Researchers must submit protocols and other documents (such as consent forms) to the IRB; respond to required changes; submit amendments to the IRB when they plan to change the protocol or other documents; report protocol deviations or violations to the IRB; inform the IRB about unanticipated problems and adverse events; and submit applications to have their research renewed when its approval period expires. The IRBs must record meeting minutes, make sure that researchers make required changes to protocols, follow standard operating procedures, keep records, develop policies, audit research, communicate with researchers, deal with reports of adverse events and noncompliance with regulations, provide advice to researchers, and many other tasks. All of these activities take time and effort, and require signatures, letters, and approvals. Though the federal regulations allow the IRB chair (or a designee) to handle many IRB actions on an expedited basis without involving the full IRB, the sheer volume of work can be enormous. The agencies that oversee IRBs, such as the Office of Human Research Protections (OHRP) and the FDA, have added to this paperwork by emphasizing administrative issues, such as recordkeeping, standard operating procedures, and IRB meeting minutes, during IRB inspections and audits. One might argue that all parties (researchers, subjects, and IRB members) could benefit by reducing the bureaucracy involved in research with human subjects, since this would free up more time and energy to focus on important ethical concerns rather than on administrative ones (Fost and Levine 2007).

2. *Overworked and undersupported IRBs.* Several studies have found that IRBs are overworked and undersupported, lacking adequate administrative staff, resources, and training (Department of Health and Human Services 1998, Emanuel et al. 2004, Institute of Medicine 2002). When IRB members are overworked, the quality and efficiency of IRB review can decline. University-based IRB members are faculty who volunteer their time and energy to IRB work, and perform this service in addition to their teaching, administrative, and research responsibilities. Because IRB work is often not adequately rewarded, it is also difficult to recruit and retain talented faculty members. When IRB administrative staff members are overworked, they do not have enough time to devote to recordkeeping, filing, correspondence, quality assurance, and other activities, which can also affect the quality and efficiency of the IRB. There is also inadequate support to educate and train IRB members and administrative staff. Inadequate education and training can have a negative impact on the quality and efficiency of IRB review, since IRB members and staff may not be familiar with the regulations, guidelines, and ethical issues related to protecting human subjects (Emanuel et al. 2004).

3. *Inadequate monitoring of research.* The approval of an IRB protocol is only the beginning of the process of research review. To ensure that the protocol is carried out appropriately and that regulations are complied with, it is important for IRBs and research institutions to monitor, audit, and continually review research. There is evidence, however, that many institutions and IRBs do not do this, and most do not do it well (Emanuel et al. 2004). Research institutions and sponsors need to ensure that there are sufficient resources to support continuing review and monitoring of research by the IRB.

4. *Inconsistent adverse event reporting.* An adverse event (AE) that occurs in research is an unexpected harm that happens to a human subject, such as death, severe injury, or any other unanticipated problem. Investigators are required to report AEs to sponsors, who have a duty to report them to regulatory agencies, such as the FDA or OHRP. Sponsors may also report AEs to IRBs or other investigators, who may also report AEs to IRBs. There have been some problems with the reporting of AEs, however. There is evidence that AEs are both underreported and overreported. There is evidence that investigators and sponsors often fail to report AEs in a timely fashion (Shamoo 2001). Conversely, there is also evidence that sponsors may be reporting too many AEs to IRBs. IRBs often receive hundreds of reports of AEs that they do not know how to evaluate. What might be more meaningful to the IRB would be a summary of AEs and what their significance is for the safety of research subjects. Additionally, FDA and DHHS regulations define AEs differently. Indeed, the DHHS regulations do not even include the term "adverse event" but instead refer to "unanticipated problems" (Shamoo 2001). Investigators, IRBs, and sponsors need clearer guidance on adverse event reporting. Better guidance will improve the efficiency of research and help to protect human subjects from harm.

5. *Low-risk research.* Some critics have argued that low-risk research, such as some types of social science research, oral history, student projects, journalism, and analyses of anonymous biological samples, should be relieved of the administrative burdens associated with full IRB review (Gunsalus 2004). These projects should have some other, less burdensome type of oversight, such as departmental review, according to these critics. Although there are procedures within the federal research regulations for allowing the IRB chair to review minimal risk research on an expedited basis, and for exempting some types of research from IRB review, such as research involving anonymous samples or data, following these procedures can still be complex

and uncertain. As a consequence, institutions may not be taking full advantage of these alternatives to full IRB review. Critics also argue that the federal research regulations were designed to deal with biomedical research, not social science research. Members of IRBs may prevent worthwhile social science research from going forward, due to their lack of understanding of its methods or design (National Bioethics Advisory Commission 2001).

6. *Loopholes in the regulations.* Unlike some countries, the United States has gaps in the system of human research protections. As mentioned earlier, the Common Rule applies to research conducted or sponsored by seventeen federal agencies, and the FDA regulations apply to research that will be used to support applications for new drugs, biologics, or medical devices. While these regulations cover most of the human subjects research conducted in the United States, they do not cover all of it (Shamoo and Schwartz 2007). For example, if a company sponsors a human research study, and it is not planning to use the data from the investigation to support an application to the FDA, then there are no federal laws that apply to the research, and there are probably no state laws as well. The research would be unregulated, under the current system. In the 1990s, pesticide companies conducted human experiments that were not governed by any federal regulations because the EPA had not adopted rules for human studies sponsored by private industry (National Research Council 2004). Other types of private research than can fall through the cracks include research on consumer psychology conducted by businesses, pharmaceutical research where the data will be used for marketing purposes, and educational research conducted by private institutions. It is not known how many human beings participate in studies that are not covered by the federal regulations, but the fact that some do should be a cause for concern (Shamoo 1999b). Ethical guidelines should be supplemented by laws and regulations. Though some people will do the right thing because they want to be ethical, others need the threat of legal liability. In response to the problem of gaps in the federal regulations, many commentators have argued that the United States should adopt a uniform system of human research regulations that applies to research subjects, regardless of the source of funding or the institutional affiliations of the investigators (Annas 1999, Emanuel et al. 2004, Shamoo and Schwartz 2007). In 2002, legislators introduced bills in the House of Representatives and the Senate to close the gaps in human research protections in the United States. The bills would have also required IRBs to be accredited and would have mandated that at least 20% of the IRB members come from outside the institution. So far no legislation has passed either house of Congress (Office of Legislative Policy and Analysis 2006).

It is worth noting that there could be some problems with extending federal regulations to cover all human research. Businesses conduct a considerable amount of marketing research and public opinion organizations conduct a considerable amount of research on public opinions, which are currently not covered by the regulations. If these categories of research are included under the federal regulations, this could greatly increase the amount of research that is regulated, which would increase IRB workloads and administrative burdens. To deal with this problem, the regulations would need to be developed in such a way that some types of low-risk research, such as anonymous opinion surveys, would be exempted from the regulations or would not require full IRB review, while other types of research, which entail greater risks, would be fully covered.

7. *Inconsistencies in the regulations.* Although there are many similarities between the DHHS regulations and the FDA regulations, there are also some significant differences (Emanuel et al. 2004). For example, the FDA regulations have special rules for emergency research, but the DHHS regulations do not. The FDA regulations require that consent always be documented, but the DHHS regulations have exceptions to documentation requirements. The FDA and DHHS regulations have different definitions of "research" and "human subject." Additionally, since the EPA has adopted its own special regulations concerning research with human subjects, there are differences between the EPA regulations and the DHHS and FDA regulations (Resnik 2007b). For example, the new EPA regulations do not allow the EPA to fund any studies that intentionally expose children to environmental agents, whereas the DHHS regulations allow intentional environmental exposure studies that pose only minimal risk to subjects (Resnik 2007a). Also, as noted earlier, the FDA and DHHS regulations have different definitions of AEs. Inconsistencies in regulations can undermine the quality and efficiency of IRB review by making it more difficult for researchers and IRB members to understand and apply legal

requirements. Harmonizing the regulations could improve the quality and efficiency of review and provide added protections for human subjects.

8. *Inadequate community input.* As noted earlier, IRBs are required to have at least one member from the community. The rationale for having community members is to provide an outside perspective on the IRB deliberations. A community member is less likely than an institutional member to have an interest in the research that the IRB evaluates. Though institutional members with direct involvement in research are required to abstain from IRB deliberations due to their conflict of interest, institutional members without a conflict of interest may have some biases due to their personal or professional relationships with investigators who submit protocols and their financial relationships with the institution (Shamoo 1999a, Shamoo and Resnik 2008).[3] Institutional IRB members may want to help their colleagues and their university, college, or medical center to succeed in research, and they may want to avoid being perceived as obstructing research. Community members can help IRBs to overcome these potential biases by voicing opinions different from those expressed by the institutional members. A community member may ask questions that an institutional member might overlook, or a community member may raise issues that an institutional member might not want to consider.

Even though there are good reasons for having outside members on IRBs, there is evidence that community participation in the review of research is often not very effective (Office of Inspector General 1998, Shamoo 1999a). One reason why community members are often not effective is that they are usually underrepresented on IRBs. Many IRBs comply with the federal regulations by having only one community member. Since the typical IRB has ten to fifteen members, on

3. An IRB member has a conflict of interest if he or she has direct involvement in the research that he or she is reviewing. For example, an IRB member who is an associate investigator on a research protocol being reviewed by the IRB would have a conflict of interest. An IRB member should not vote on a protocol if he or she has a conflict of interest, nor should he or she take part in any debate about the protocol. The IRB member may, however, provide the committee with information about the protocol (Amdur 2003, Shamoo and Resnik 2008).

some IRBs 10% or fewer members are from outside the institution (Office of Inspector General 1998). It is difficult for community members to make their opinions known when they are outnumbered on the IRB. Another reason why community members are sometimes not effective is they are usually not scientists or clinicians, and they may feel intimidated by the IRB members, who are scientists or clinicians and who may have considerable education, power, and social status. Community members may feel that their opinion isn't important, because they have less knowledge or expertise than other members. They may feel that institutional members don't respect them or even resent their presence on the board (Sengupta and Lo 2003).

Various commentators have made some suggestions for improving community input into IRB deliberations. First, the federal regulations could be changed to require that at least 20% of the IRB members are from the community. As noted earlier, the two research ethics bills included this requirement. Increasing the proportion of people from outside the institution will give community members more representation, visibility, and confidence. Second, IRBs should take steps to ensure that community members receive sufficient education and training in protecting human subjects in research (Sengupta and Lo 2003). While it is important for all IRB members to have adequate education and training, it is even more important for community members to have education and training because they may not have the background, experience, or knowledge that institutional members possess. Institutional members usually have expertise in science, medicine, law, or ethics, whereas community members are frequently laypeople with no particular expertise in any of these fields. Third, those who recruit community members should give careful consideration to their qualifications. A community member should have enough expertise or experience that he or she would feel comfortable debating with scientists, physicians, attorneys, or ethicists. Although many IRBs recruit laypeople to serve as community members, it would be desirable to also have some community members with professional standing, so that they will be able to converse with the institutional members on the board.

One option for improving community input that has been developed in recent years is for investigators to consult with community members when planning and implementing research (Goering,

Holland, and Fryer-Edwards 2008, Weijer and Emanuel 2000). Community advisory boards can help to protect the interests of the community, enhance community relations, assist with research design and subject recruitment, and help draft informed consent documents. Community consultation is especially important when a study is likely to have a significant impact on a particular, well-defined community. For example, genetic research pertaining to a specific racial, ethnic, or other group can have a significant impact on that group. The discovery that a genetic disease is more common in a particular ethnic group than in other ethnic groups may lead to stigma, discrimination, or bias against that group (Sharp and Foster 2000).

Although involving communities in the review of research can yield important benefits for science and society, some difficulties can also occur. First, following the counsel and advice of community members could compromise the objectivity of the research in some cases. For example, members of the community may not want researchers to study something that they fear may embarrass or stigmatize members of the community. For example, community members might not want researchers to study incest, alcoholism, or domestic violence. Community members may not want researchers to publish findings for similar reasons. If community members strongly object to the publication of some research findings, investigators will have to choose between respecting the community's preferences and contributing to the advancement of science. Second, it may be difficult to determine who (or what) represents the interests of the community, especially when the community does not have elected leaders and is scattered around the globe. Consulting with an organization that claims to represent the interests of a community (or population) may do more harm than good if the organization does not represent the interests of the community. Despite these and other problems, community consultation has become increasingly important in biomedical research (Weijer and Emanuel 2000).

9. *Lack of broad review of research.* While the federal regulations have established some ethical standards for research with human subjects and provided a mechanism for public oversight of research, they do not cover all of the ethical issues or concerns that might arise. The regulations focus on a fairly small range of ethical issues: risks to subjects, benefits to subjects and society, informed consent, privacy and confidentiality, protection of vulnerable subjects, and equitable subject selection. But there are many other important social and ethical issues that the regulations do not address, such as: risks to communities, society, and future generations; exploitation of individuals and populations; the sharing of benefits; human cloning; and embryonic stem cell research. Indeed, the federal regulations specifically prohibit the IRB from considering the risks to society of research: "In evaluating risks and benefits, the IRB should...not consider possible long-range effects of applying knowledge gained in the research (for example, the possible effects of the research on public policy) as among those research risks that fall within the purview of its responsibility" (Department of Health and Human Services 2005, 45 *C.F.R.* 46.111[a][2])." By excluding some issues from the IRB's domain, the federal regulations limit the government's ability to oversee research with human subjects. Some issues are not on the table, as far as the IRB is concerned.

There are some good reasons for limiting the range of the issues that the IRB may consider in its deliberations. First, IRBs lack the time to consider these larger issues. As noted earlier, many IRBs are already overworked. Increasing the workload could have a detrimental impact on the protection of human subjects, since IRBs might ignore their original mandate in order to consider these new issues. It is better for an IRB to do a good job of considering a few issues than to do a poor job of considering many issues. Second, IRBs may make inconsistent decisions if they tackle these other issues, since many of these other issues involve political concerns, not just ethical ones. For example, liberal and conservative IRBs would probably render very different opinions of a protocol involving research with human embryonic stem cells. Third, since these broader issues may have national implications, they should be debated at the national level, not the local level. Individual IRBs have neither the wisdom nor the authority to make national policy.

Even though there are good reasons for limiting the range of issues that IRBs may consider when evaluating research, there needs to be a forum for debating these issues to ensure that the public has adequate input into the regulation of research with human subjects. While the public has the ability to make its voice known by communicating with Congress or the president, these politicians may take a long time to respond to concerns about the ethics of research with human subjects, if they respond at all. The federal agencies charged with overseeing research with human subjects, such as the FDA and the OHRP, provide timely and competent responses to public concerns about ethical issues that are within the scope of IRB review. The FDA (2006) and the OHRP (2007b) provide investigators, IRB members, and research sponsors with useful guidance on interpreting and applying the federal regulations. Before developing new guidance documents, these agencies usually hold public hearings and have a public comment period. However, the guidance provided by these agencies usually sticks closely to the federal regulations and does not cover larger issues, such cloning, stem cell research, or genetic engineering.

The Recombinant DNA Advisory Committee (RAC) is a good example of an organization that provides the public with a forum for addressing concerns about research with human subjects that are not addressed in the federal regulations (National Institutes of Health 2006). The RAC, which was established by the NIH in 1974 in response to concerns about the dangers of genetic engineering, provides the NIH with advice about the safety and ethics of using recombinant DNA techniques to manipulate genetic material. The RAC holds public hearings that are attended by scientists, physicians, policy analysts, and laypeople. The RAC has addressed many topics not specifically covered in the federal regulations, such as somatic gene therapy clinical trials, human germline manipulation, and human cloning. The EPA recently established a Human Studies Review Board to provide the agency with advice on controversial human research studies and to serve as a public forum (Environmental Protection Agency 2007). Some writers have suggested that the federal government should establish an organization to provide advice on human embryonic stem cell research (Baylis and Robert 2006). Presidential commissions, such as the President's Council on Bioethics (or, as earlier, PCB), can also serve as a public forum for discussing human subjects research. However, as noted earlier, the politicalization of the PCB may affect its ability to serve as a fair and open public forum. A committee that preceded the PCB, the National Bioethics Advisory Commission (National Bioethics Advisory Commission 2001), which was established by President Clinton, held many hearings on research with human subjects and published several reports dealing with issues such as human embryonic stem cell research, cloning, international research involving human subjects, and research with mentally disabled subjects.

10. *Lack of IRB accreditation.* In the United States, IRBs are not required by law to be accredited. As a result, most are not. Accreditation can be a powerful mechanism for promoting integrity, quality control, quality improvement, and public engagement. In the accreditation process, an accrediting body develops standards for a particular area, and organizations conforming to those standards can receive accreditation. Accreditation must be renewed periodically. Members of the accrediting body usually include professionals and laypeople with expertise or interest in the accredited field. For example, under federal law, healthcare organizations, such as hospitals or nursing homes, must be accredited in order to receive Medicare or Medicaid funding. The Joint Commission on the Accreditation of Healthcare Organization (JCAHO) accredits most of the healthcare organizations in the United States. The JCAHO develops different standards for medical services, facilities, laboratory tests, patient safety, patients' rights, and so on. During an on-site visit of a healthcare organization, representatives from the JCAHO interview the staff and administrators, tour the facilities, and observe how the organization operates (Joint Commission on the Accreditation of Healthcare Organization 2006). Only of few of the JCAHO's standards address medical research. The Association for the Accreditation and Assessment of Laboratory Animal Care International (AAALAC) accredits animal research programs at research institutions. The AAALAC accreditation is not legally required, but over seven hundred institutions in twenty-eight countries have sought accreditation to affirm their commitment to the protection of animal welfare in research (Association for the Assessment and Accreditation of Laboratory Animal Care 2006).

In 2001, biomedical researchers concerned about the protection of human subjects formed the Association of Accreditation of Human Research Protection Programs (AAHRPP) to provide accreditation for organizations that conduct or review human research (Association of Accreditation of Human Research Protection Programs 2006). So far, a few dozen research institutions have voluntarily applied for and received AAHRPP accreditation, and the number seeking accreditation is growing. If the trend toward voluntary accreditation continues, it may not be necessary to make accreditation of human research protection programs legally required, since there will be sufficient social, political, and economic pressure to encourage most organizations that review or conduct human research to seek accreditation. As noted earlier, the AAALAC has accredited hundreds of organizations, even though accreditation of animal research programs is not legally required. Hopefully, AAHRPP will become as successful as AAALAC, and it will not be necessary to mandate accreditation for human research protection programs. If not, then legal action may be necessary (Emanuel et al. 2004).

11. *Lack of compensation plans for research-related injuries.* Compensating research subjects for research-related injuries is an important ethical requirement, because it helps to minimize harms that occur to research subjects and ensures that they receive fair treatment (Resnik 2006a). Although most commentators recognize the ethical importance of compensating research subjects for injuries, the federal research regulations do not require it. The regulations only require that subjects be informed if there are plans to compensate subject for injury when research poses more than minimal risks. The regulations also require that subjects not be asked to waive any of their legal rights to compensation. Many sponsors and institutions do not have compensation-for-injury plans, while some have provisions for providing specific types of compensation, such as short-term medical treatment. There is considerable variation in the language that researchers use to inform subjects about their compensation-for-injury policies (Paasche-Orlow and Brancati 2005, Resnik 2006a). To protect the rights and welfare of research subjects, the federal research regulations should require that sponsors and institutions provide at least a minimal form of compensation, such as the provision of short-term medical treatment. If a sponsor or institution does not have a compensation-for-injury plan, then subjects must file a lawsuit to receive compensation. Lawsuits can be costly and damaging to the research environment.

12. *Outdated regulations.* The human research regulations have not changed much since 1981, but the research environment has changed a great deal (Bankert and Amdur 2005). In 1981 most of the biomedical research was conducted by academic researchers at universities or medical centers. Today, a large proportion of research is conducted in physicians' offices, with the assistance of contract research organizations (CROs), which are involved in 64% of clinical trials (Snyder and

Mueller 2008). The CROs help to connect pharmaceutical or bio-technology companies with clinical investigators and research subjects. They collect and record data, monitor research, and conduct quality assurance studies. In 1981, there were no private, for-profit IRBs. Today, there are over a dozen in the United States. In 1981, there were not many multicenter clinical trials, but today most clinical trials include a dozen or more research sites. In 1981, most of the research for U.S. products was conducted in the United States. Today, companies outsource some of their clinical research to India and other countries (Gilbert 2008). One could argue that the regulations need to be revised in response to the changes in the research environment.

13. *The definition of research.* The federal regulations define research as "a systematic investigation, including research development, testing and evaluation, designed to develop or contribute to generalizable knowledge" (Department of Health and Human Services 2005, 45 C.F.R. 45.102d). There are many different data collection activities that may or may not fall under this definition, including innovative medical practices, healthcare quality improvement programs, public health interventions, and student projects, depending on how one interprets this definition. If IRBs, investigators, and institutes are not careful, then they may interpret the definition of research to include many activities that should not be categorized as research (Bankert and Amdur 2005). These IRBs, investigators, and institutes need additional guidance so the definition will be properly focused. The *Belmont Report* also includes a discussion of research:

> It is important to distinguish between biomedical and behavioral research, on the one hand, and the practice of accepted therapy on the other, in order to know what activities ought to undergo review for the protection of human subjects of research. The distinction between research and practice is blurred partly because both often occur together (as in research designed to evaluate a therapy) and partly because notable departures from standard practice are often called "experimental" when the terms "experimental" and "research" are not carefully defined. For the most part, the term "practice" refers to interventions that are designed solely to enhance the well-being of an individual patient or client

and that have a reasonable expectation of success. The purpose of medical or behavioral practice is to provide diagnosis, preventive treatment or therapy to particular individuals. By contrast, the term "research" designates an activity designed to test a hypothesis, permit conclusions to be drawn, and thereby to develop or contribute to generalizable knowledge (expressed, for example, in theories, principles, and statements of relationships). Research is usually described in a formal protocol that sets forth an objective and a set of procedures designed to reach that objective. (National Commission for the Protection of Human Subjects of Biomedical and Behavioral Research 1979, 6)

This discussion focuses on the purpose (or intent) of data collection activities: the purpose of practice is to benefit individuals, while the purpose of research is to contribute to generalizable knowledge. While this discussion clarifies matters somewhat, it still leaves some important questions unanswered, such as the meaning of "purpose." Federal agencies, such as the OHRP, have issued some guidance pertaining to this topic, but many investigators, administrators, IRB members, and practitioners are still confused about the definition of research and how to apply it to particular cases (Bankert and Amdur 2005). If the definition is not appropriately limited in scope, this could create additional administrative burdens for IRBs, healthcare professionals, healthcare institutions, and public health organizations, which could interfere with promoting public health, medical care, patient safety, and other important goals (Casarett, Karlawish, and Sugarman 2000, Lynn 2004, MacQueen and Buehler 2004).

Conclusion

The problems with the current U.S. system for protecting human research subjects, discussed above, demonstrate that in some ways the regulations provide too much oversight, and in some ways they provide too little oversight. Excessive paperwork, the review of low-risk research, and an overly broad definition of research show that there can be too much oversight in some areas. But inconsistencies and loopholes in the regulations, lack of compensation for injuries, inconsistent adverse event reporting, and a lack of broad research review demonstrate how there can be too little oversight in other areas. The federal research regulations and guidelines should be revised so that there is more emphasis on the protecting of human subjects and less emphasis on bureaucratic, administrative, and legal issues. Although the current system has some problems, it has operated very well for more than three decades. In many ways, the IRB system represents a judicious compromise between government oversight of human research and scientific autonomy. While there is no need to overhaul the system, changes should be made to improve the quality, scope, effectiveness, and fairness of research review and oversight.

8

Science Education

The purpose of education is to replace an empty mind with an open one.

—Malcolm S. Forbes

Education is one of society's most important functions. Each generation must provide the next with the knowledge, skills, and values necessary to make a living, raise a family, contribute to society, and seek happiness and fulfillment. The standard kindergarten through 12th grade (K–12) school curriculum includes classes in mathematics, language arts, social studies, fine arts, foreign languages, physical education, and, of course, natural science. Many educators and school administrators give high priority to education in science and mathematics, so that students can be prepared to live in the modern world, which is constantly transformed by science and technology. Politicians and educational leaders stress the importance of science education to enhance technological innovation, economic prosperity, and national security. Science education is also important for the scientific profession. Scientists (and science teachers) must educate, train, and mentor the next generation of scientists to ensure that old knowledge will not vanish, that new discoveries will be made, and that new methods and concepts will be developed. Education in science must begin in elementary school and continue through high school, college, and graduate school (American Association for the Advancement of Science 2007, National Academy of Sciences 1997).

Since scientists and members of the public have a great deal at stake in science education, it should come as no surprise that there have been disputes about how science should be taught. These battles have taken place on school boards, in courtrooms, and in the halls of Congress. For the most part, controversies concerning science education have focused not on pedagogy but on curriculum content. Many passionate debates have taken place in the United States concerning the teaching of evolution and human sexuality in the public schools. In other countries, there have been controversies concerning the teaching of Marxist ideology and Islamic religion. The reason that the content of the science education curriculum has generated so much debate is that scientific theories, hypotheses, and concepts sometimes conflict with religious teachings, political ideologies, or cultural traditions. This chapter will focus on the teaching of evolution in public schools, but the lessons learned from this debate also apply to other disputes concerning the content of the science curriculum.

Evolution: Some History

Most readers of this book are undoubtedly familiar with the theory of evolution by natural selection, which Charles Darwin (1809–82) proposed in *The Origin of Species* in 1859, but a quick review will be useful to illustrate the development of controversies concerning the teaching of evolution in the science curriculum. Darwin formed the idea of evolution by natural selection while he was a ship's naturalist on the H.M.S. *Beagle* from 1832 to 1837. During this voyage, Darwin was able to observe and catalogue many species of animals and plants that were adapted to different environments. He proposed a mechanism—natural selection—to explain adaptation, variation, and the origin of new species (Darwin 1859). Natural selection occurs when heritable, random variations in traits lead to differences in reproduction and survival. Those organisms that are best able to reproduce and survive in a given environment—the fittest—are most likely to survive. Over time, this process leads to changes in the population of organisms, and new species emerge. Darwin believed that natural selection is usually a gradual process, taking thousands or even millions of years to occur. He found support for gradualism in the work of Charles Lyell (1797–1875), who argued that geological changes take place over vast expanses of time as the result of uniform processes, such as weathering, rather than catastrophic processes, such as great floods (Eldredge 2005, Mayr 1982).

One of Darwin's key pieces of evidence for evolution was the diversity of finches he found on different islands in the Galapagos.

Darwin observed that the beaks of finches were different on each island: finches living on one island had short, strong beaks, while finches living on another island had long, thin beaks, and other finches had different beaks. He also observed that the beaks were useful for eating different types of seeds: finches with the short, strong beaks were able to eat large seeds, while finches with the long, weak beaks were able to eat small seeds, and so on. Darwin hypothesized that natural selection could explain the differences in the finches' beaks. At one time, a single population of finches migrated from the South American mainland to the Galapagos Islands. Over time, the populations living on different islands began to diverge, as natural selection favored finches that were better adapted to the environmental conditions on the different islands, such as the available food. Eventually, the populations became so different that they could no longer interbreed, and they became distinct species (Mayr 1982). Thus, natural selection could explain how the populations changed over time and how new species emerged.

Darwin was not the first scientist to defend the idea that life evolves. In the 18th century Jean-Baptiste Lamarck (1744–1829) had proposed that living things evolve by the inheritance of acquired characteristics. According to the theory, organisms can transmit traits that they acquire during their lifetime to their offspring. Evolution occurs because organisms adapt to their environments. For example, if a giraffe lengthens its neck by continually trying to reach a high branch on a tree, then its progeny will have longer necks too, because acquired traits are heritable. Darwin's grandfather, Erasmus Darwin (1731–1802), endorsed Lamarck's theory. Darwin rejected Lamarckian evolution and proposed that acquired traits are not heritable. Evolution occurs as a result of differential reproduction and the survival of organisms. Adaptation is a consequence of evolution, not a cause of evolution (Mayr 1982).

Darwin waited over twenty years before publishing his ideas. The main reason why he took so long is that he wanted to put together the best case for his theory. He gathered evidence from around the globe; studied and interpreted the fossil record; reflected on artificial evolutionary processes, such as selective breeding; and pondered the theological implications of his theory (Ruse 1979). He shared his ideas only with a few trusted scientists, such as Joseph Hooker (1817–1911). When

Darwin learned that Alfred Russel Wallace (1823–1913) had also come up with the idea of natural selection, he decided to publish the *Origin* earlier than he had wished to publish it, to avoid being scooped.

Darwin was concerned about how scientists and ordinary people would receive his theory, because it conflicted with prevailing religious views. Even though scientists had discussed evolution before Darwin's time, many still accepted the Judeo-Christian account of the origin of species and the human race found in the Bible's Book of Genesis. Many scientists and almost all laypeople believed that life does not evolve; that God created all species on the planet after He formed the earth, approximately 6,000 years ago; and that man has a special place in the creation (Mayr 1982). Darwin's theory asserted that life does evolve, that new species result from natural selection, that the earth is much older than 6,000 years old, and that man is descended from the apes. Darwin confessed in one his letters that he felt as if he would be committing a murder by publishing his theory (Ruse 1979).

Darwin knew a great deal about Christian theology. He had studied this subject in college and had planned to enter the clergy before he became interested in zoology, botany, and natural history. Darwin was familiar with William Paley's (1743–1805) version of the design argument for the existence of God, which asserts that one can infer the existence of an intelligent creator from the evidence of design and order found in the world. According to Paley, evidence for the existence of God can be found in the design of the universe, the stars and planets, and living things. Darwin's theory attacked one of the main pillars of Paley's theology by showing how one does not need to appeal to divine causes to explain the order and apparent design in the living world. The design that we observe in living things results from the blind mechanism of natural selection, not from an intelligent creator (Ruse 1979).

As Darwin had predicted, his theory of evolution generated enormous controversy and turmoil. Though many scientists embraced his ideas, religious leaders and members of the public rejected them. Caricatures of Darwin, satires of his book, and scathing editorials appeared in newspapers and periodicals. Though Darwin did not spend much time defending his theory in public, many scientists did, including Thomas Huxley, Hooker, Lyell, and Asa Gray. The theory was soon accepted by most scientists, even though members of the public and religious leaders continued to oppose it (Ruse 1979).

In the late 1800s, people began to apply Darwin's ideas to social problems. Some scientists, political theorists, and politicians, known as Social Darwinists, argued that the government should not provide assistance to poor, hungry, sick, or disabled people in society, since this would interfere with natural selection. They used Darwinism to justify laissez faire social and economic policies. Darwin's ideas also gave rise to the eugenics movement of the late 19th to early 20th centuries. According to this doctrine, the weakest members of society should not be allowed to reproduce, and the fittest members of society should be encouraged to reproduce, so the human race can become stronger and fitter. The eugenicists believed that it was possible to improve the human species through selective breeding (Ruse 1979).

Darwin's theory became a cornerstone of modern biology and influenced many other scientific fields, including psychology, anthropology, medicine, sociology, and economics. The theory stimulated a revolution in thought, and was recognized as one of the most important advances in the history of science. Darwinism also had significant impacts on philosophy, literature, and popular culture. Many great thinkers, including Friedrich Nietzsche (1844–1900), John Dewey (1859–1952), and Sigmund Freud (1856–1939) were influenced by Darwin (Ruse 1979).

One of the missing pieces in Darwin's account of evolution was the mechanism of inheritance. Biologists did not have a good understanding of inheritance until the early 1900s, when Carl Correns and Hugo DeVries rediscovered principles and concepts developed by Gregor Mendel (1822–84), an Austrian monk. Mendelian genetics explains how organisms transmit their traits to the next generation and how genetic variation arises in populations. By the mid-1900s, R. A. Fischer, G. H. Hardy, Wilhelm Weinberg, Ernest Mayr, Theodozius Dobzansky, M. Kimura, Richard Lewontin, Niles Eldridge, John Maynard Smith, George Williams, Stephen Jay Gould, and many other biologists had refined Darwin's ideas and related them with the emerging fields of population genetics, developmental biology, molecular genetics, and biostatistics to form what is known as evolutionary synthesis (Eldredge 2005, Mayr 1982).

Dobzansky (1973) once said that "nothing in biology makes sense except in the light of evolution" (125). What he meant by this provocative comment is that one needs evolutionary theory to explain the adaptation and variation present in the living world. Evolution provides ultimate explanations for the phenomena studied by other fields in biology, such as anatomy, physiology, development, cytology, molecular biology, zoology, botany, microbiology, and medicine. For example, one needs to have a basic understanding of natural selection to understand microbial resistance, since the application of antibiotics to a population of bacteria leads to increases in resistant bacteria in the population. Microbial resistance makes no sense at all unless one assumes that populations of bacteria can change over time in response to environmental conditions. Trying to understand the living world without evolutionary theory would be like trying to understand the solar system without Newton's laws of motion and gravity, or chemical reactions without the conservation of mass and energy (Sober 1993).

Although evolution is often referred to as a "theory," this does not mean that is speculative or without substantial evidence. The theory of evolution is no different from any other well-proven scientific theories, such as quantum mechanics, plate tectonics, relativity, or thermodynamics. Evolution is at least as well confirmed as any of these other theories with evidential support from the fossil record, phylogeny, comparative physiology and comparative anatomy, selective breeding, island biogeography, and molecular genetics. There are disputes among biologists about different aspects of evolutionary processes, such as the rate of evolutionary change, the units of evolution, and the prevalence of evolution by natural selection versus evolution by other mechanisms, such as random drift. However, these controversies do not undermine the overwhelming evidence for evolution or its widespread acceptance by biologists (Sober 1993).

Evolution versus Creationism

As noted earlier, religious opposition to evolutionary theory was very strong at first, especially among conservative Christian sects in the United Kingdom, the United States, and Europe. However, many liberal Christian sects eventually came to accept and accommodate Darwin's ideas. Today many Methodists, Lutherans, Episcopalians, Presbyterians, Unitarians, Congregationalists, Baptists, Catholics, and members of United Church of Christ accept Darwinian evolution and see no conflict between science and religion concerning the explanation of the adaptation, variation, and design found in the living world (Anderson 2006, Collins 2006, Ruse 2004). Even though many Christians and people from other religious traditions now accept evolution, many reject Darwin's ideas and accept a creationist account of the living world. According to one survey, only 40% of adults in the United States accept evolution, while 39% reject it and 21% are unsure. Among countries in the survey, only Turkey had a lower percentage of adults who accepted evolution. One reason why both Turkey and the United States had such a low acceptance rate of evolution is that there are many religious fundamentalists in these countries. In Turkey, Islamic fundamentalists oppose evolution. In several European countries and Japan, the percentage of adults who accept evolution is close to 80% (Miller et al. 2006).

In the United States, many battles have been fought over teaching evolution in public schools, but perhaps the most famous was the Scopes trial in 1925 (*Scopes v. State* 1925). In that case, John Scopes was charged with violating a Tennessee statute, the Tennessee Anti-Evolution Act, which prohibited the teaching of evolution in universities or public schools supported by state funds. The case drew tremendous publicity as two well-known lawyers faced off in the trial: Clarence Darrow, who represented Scopes, and William Jennings Bryan, who represented the State of Tennessee. The American Civil Liberties Union paid Scopes's legal fees. The attorneys debated such lofty topics as the compatibility of evolution and religion, the rationality of interpreting the Bible literally, and the morality of teaching evolution. The jury convicted Scopes of violating the law, and Scopes appealed the case to the Tennessee Supreme Court. The Tennessee Supreme Court interpreted the Tennessee Anti-Evolution Act as forbidding public school teachers from teaching that humans are descended from a lower order of animals. The Tennessee Supreme Court held that the main issue was whether the law violated Scopes's constitutional right to due process. The Court held that the law did not violate Scopes's right to due process because he was still free to teach evolution for a school not sponsored by the state. As a state employee, he had to abide by the contract he had with the state, which forbade him from teaching evolution. Though the Court upheld Tennessee's antievolution law, it urged the prosecution to drop the case because Scopes was no longer an employee of the state. The prosecution obliged and the matter ended (*Scopes v. State* 1925).

Because the Scopes case was not heard by the U.S. Supreme Court, the constitutional issues raised by the case were not decided by the highest tribunal in the land. Thus, other states were able to pass laws concerning the teaching of evolution in schools. These laws went unchallenged until 1968, when the U.S. Supreme Court invalidated an Arkansas statute that prohibited the teaching of evolution in public schools on the grounds that it violated the First Amendment to the U.S. Constitution (*Epperson v. Arkansas* 1968). Arkansas had passed a statute banning the teaching of evolution in public schools in 1928. In 1964, Susan Epperson, an Arkansas high-school biology teacher, decided to sue the state for its law prohibiting the teaching of evolution. If Epperson had been prosecuted under the law, she would have faced criminal sanctions as well as dismissal. A lower court upheld Epperson's claims against the state on the grounds that the statute violated her freedom of speech. However, the Arkansas Supreme Court ruled in favor of the state. The Arkansas Supreme Court held that the law did not violate Epperson's free speech rights because the state had the authority to establish the school curriculum. The case was appealed to the U.S. Supreme Court. The Court held that the Arkansas statute was unconstitutional because it violated the First Amendment's declaration that "Congress shall make no law respecting an establishment of religion, or prohibiting the free exercise thereof" (U.S. Constitution 1789). The First and Fourteenth Amendments, according to the Court, prevent the government from favoring a particular religion or interfering with religious freedom. The Arkansas statute favored the biblical version of creation in Genesis over other religious creation stories. Thus, it violated these amendments to the Constitution. The First Amendment makes it illegal for the federal government to establish a religion or restrict religious freedom. Under the Fourteenth Amendment, constitutional rights protected by the federal government also apply to state governments (Barron and Dienes 1999). Thus, state governments are also forbidden from establishing a religion or interfering with religious freedom.

The U.S. Supreme Court's decision in *Epperson* overturned the Scopes ruling and nullified laws passed by several states forbidding the teaching of evolution (Appleman 1979). After the ruling in this case, creationists continued to push their agenda, with little success. From 1972 to 2006, creationists suffered sixteen legal defeats. Some of these cases involved laws that states passed pertaining to the teaching of evolution, while others addressed the actions of school boards. Several attempts to require a balanced treatment of evolution and creationism in public schools were found to be unconstitutional, including laws passed by Arkansas, Louisiana, and Tennessee.[1] Creationists also lost cases in which they sued for the right to teach creationism in public schools (*Daniel v. Waters* 1975, *Edwards v. Arkansas* 1987).

In one of the most recent cases, a federal district court ruled that the actions by a Dover, Pennsylvania school board violated the establishment clause (*Kitzmiller v. Dover Area School District* 2005). The board had passed a resolution requiring students to be told about gaps in evolutionary theory and alternative theories, including intelligent design (ID). After hearing expert testimony from scientists, science historians, and philosophers of science, the court ruled that ID is not a scientific theory and that it is just a newfangled version of creationism (Mervis 2006b). Requiring schools to teach ID violates the First Amendment because ID is religion, not science. Though ID does not make any references to the Bible or God, the theory asserts that the existence of an intelligent cause is needed to explain some features of the universe and the living world and that some aspects of the universe and life cannot be explained by undirected processes, such as natural selection (Intelligent Design Network 2006).[2]

Actions taken by the Kansas Board of Education have survived legal challenges, however. In 1999, the board decided to drop the teaching of evolution and scientific cosmology from its required science

1. I define "creationism" as the view that a supernatural cause is needed to explain the origin of the whole universe or certain aspects of it, such as living things or intelligent beings. Judeo-Christian creationists believe that God created the whole universe, living things, and intelligent beings (man). Creationism is not necessarily associated with a belief in a Judeo-Christian God or a Muslim or Hindu God for that matter. I would regard a person who simply believes in some kind of intelligent, supernatural power that created the universe, or certain aspects of it, as a creationist.

2. Intelligent design theory would be a type of creationism, in my view. See note 1.

curriculum. This attack on evolutionary theory survived legal challenges because it did not prohibit schools from teaching evolution or
require schools to teach creationism. In 2005, the board put forth a
new definition of science that removed "natural explanations" from the
definition. Many commentators interpreted this move as leaving the
door open for supernatural explanations, such as divine creation or
intervention, in science classes (Overbye 2005).[3]

None of these legal battles affect the teaching of evolution or creationism in private schools. Since private schools are not agents of the
state, they do not have to respect the First Amendment's prohibition
against favoring a particular religion. Some private Christian schools
teach creationism; other private schools teach evolution; and some
teach both.

Assessing the Debate

In the United States, the Supreme Court's interpretation of the Constitution currently restricts the state's ability to forbid public school
teachers from teaching evolution or to require them to teach creationism. However, the current legal environment does not settle the general
policy questions concerning the teaching of evolution (or creationism), since the composition of the Supreme Court could change or
Congress could amend the Constitution. Also, the legal situation could
be different in countries that do not have constitutional limits on the
state's involvement with religion. Thus, the general questions still have
some currency: Should the government require public schools to teach
creationism, evolution, both, or neither? More generally, what is the
proper role of the government in science education?

These questions have important implications for the autonomy of
science, since scientists have a legitimate claim to have some control
over the education, training, and mentoring of the next generation of

3. Questions concerning the compatibility of science and religion are beyond
the scope of this book. Some prominent scientists, such as Francis Collins, director
of the Human Genome Project, believe that an intelligent being created the universe but that natural causes, such as natural selection and gravity, can explain what
happens in that universe. See Collins (2006), Ruse (2004).

scientists. Although most scientists do not teach K–12 students, they have a vested interest in how students are educated before they reach college or graduate school, because students who do not have an adequate education in scientific concepts, facts, ideas, theories, and methods will not be prepared to pursue careers in science. Deciding how to teach science to K–12 students is a scientific choice no less important than deciding how to design an experiment or analyze data. Members of the public also have a legitimate claim to have some control over science education, since science education plays a vital role in economic development, civic life, policy-making, public health, and many other areas of public concern. Also, scientific theories, concepts, hypotheses, and facts often have significant implications for human values. For example, biology has implications for religion and ethics, medicine has implications for sexual morality, and psychology has implications for criminal justice.

Most people, even most scientists, probably agree that the public should have some control over science education. But how much control should the public have? If we apply the analytical tools developed in chapter 3 to questions about the science curriculum, government control over science education raises two major concerns: (a) content restrictions, and (b) micromanagement. Government control of the science curriculum is a type of content restriction on science, because it attempts to dictate what science education should be about (that is, the topics that will be taught and so forth). Content restrictions on science are justified only if they serve an important social purpose. Public education is one of the key functions of government, and science education is an essential part of this endeavor. So, controlling the content of science education serves an important social purpose. However, since politicians and laypeople are not experts on science, the government needs advice from scientists to decide on the content of the science curriculum. In the United States, scientists and science educators play a major role in science education by developing textbooks and offering advice to school boards and other government committees at the state and federal levels.

Since content restrictions on the science curriculum are legitimate, the major issues concerning science education boil down to questions about micromanagement. What is the proper balance of political versus scientific control over the science curriculum? Should the government allow scientists to teach any topic that they decide is appropriate for science education, or should the government ban some topics or require others? As we have already seen in earlier chapters, micromanagement of scientific decisions by the public can undermine scientific research. The same point also applies to science education: granting the public too much control over science education could have disastrous effects on science education. The discussion in chapter 3 of the effects of Lysenkoism on Soviet science provides a vivid illustration of how politics and ideology can undermine science education. When the government micromanages science education, educators may feel constant pressure to meet various political demands and expectations. Teachers may worry that their actions will be subject to outside scrutiny and control. Writers and editors of science textbooks may avoid controversial subjects and censor their own textbooks to avoid potential confrontations with school boards, interest groups, or politicians. In short, excessive public input into science education can inhibit innovation, creativity, coherence, and quality in education.

To avoid these harmful effects, government control over science education must be kept in its proper place. The government should have general oversight over science education, but it should avoid micromanaging the science curriculum. The government can make decisions on the amount of science that should be taught in K–12 schools, when science is taught, how much money is spent on science education, and science requirements for graduation. The government should refrain from dictating specific details of science education, however, such as teaching methods, testing strategies, or specific topics (for example, evolution versus creationism). These decisions should be left to science educators and scientists, not politicians or school board members. If politicians have no business telling chemistry teachers whether they should teach students about a fundamental principle of chemistry, such as the conservation of energy, then they also have no business telling biology teachers whether they should teach a fundamental tenet of biology, that is, evolution by natural selection.

Limiting the government's control over science education need not imply that the public must relinquish control over the teaching of values in K–12 schools. The government has every right to insist that schoolchildren learn the values necessary to be productive members of society, such as honesty, integrity, civility, justice, tolerance, kindness, and courage. The government also has a right to demand that school-children learn about the philosophical, moral, political, and religious theories and traditions that influence human conduct and policy debates. However, these subjects should be taught in classes that are geared toward teaching children values, such as language arts, social studies, history, and civics. Thus, a public school system can teach children about doctrines held by different religious traditions, such as creationism, in a comparative religion class or a U.S. history class, but it should not teach these doctrines in a science class. Biology teachers may teach their students about creationism if they want to allow students to understand the historical and social context of Darwinism, but they should not teach it as a scientifically legitimate alternative to evolution. They can mention that creationism was a theory that many scientists accepted until Darwin published the *Origin of Species*, but they should not be compelled to teach it as a viable alternative to evolution. Science teachers may also inform their students about controversies in evolution theory, such as problems with the fossil record, random drift, explanations of the origins of life, and the rate of evolutionary change. But they should stress that there is considerable evidence for evolution, and that even well-established scientific theories have problems and shortcomings (Sober 1993).

Some of the points concerning the teaching of evolution also apply to the teaching of other topics, such as sex education. Sex education has been controversial in the United States and other nations (National Public Radio 2008). Some parents have opposed the teaching of human sexuality in public schools on the grounds that it undermines the moral or religious values they want to inculcate in their children, while health science educators have favored the teaching of human sexuality to promote sexual health and disease prevention. In thinking about this debate, it is useful to distinguish between the science of human sexuality and sexual morality. The science of human sexuality, including human anatomy, fertility, pregnancy, genetics, embryology, development, birth, endocrinology, and sexually transmitted diseases, should be taught in biology or public health classes. Scientists should be allowed to teach students about the science of human sexuality without political interference. Sexual morality, including topics of abstinence and safe sex, should be taught in a different type of class, such as courses in ethics or social studies. Controversies in sexual morality should be separated from the science of human sexuality, so that the politics of sex education need not affect education in the science of human sexuality.

Conclusion

In this chapter I have examined political versus scientific control over science education. I have argued that the government should have oversight over science education but that it should not micromanage the science curriculum. One implication of this view is that laypeople and politicians should not decide whether science teachers should teach evolution in K–12 public schools; this decision should be left to scientists and science educators. Though the government can teach values in public schools, these values should be taught in classes that are oriented toward humanistic education, such as language arts, social studies, history, and the fine arts. The next chapter will summarize some of the key points of the book and make some policy recommendations.

9

Conclusion

Balancing Scientific Autonomy and Government Control

> *The politicalization of science presents a severe challenge to modern democratic governments, which depend on a creative tension between elected representatives on the one hand, and unelected technocracies on the other. While we cannot allow scientific experts to rule us directly, we nevertheless need them desperately. Our leaders simply cannot do their jobs competently without considerable reliance on expertise that they themselves do not possess. But the politicalization of science—in essence, a corruption of the communication channels between credible experts and policymakers—weakens and ultimately destroys this necessary relationship.*
>
> —Chris Mooney

The quote from science journalist Chris Mooney's *The Republican War on Science* that serves as the epigraph to this chapter sketches some of the themes that I have explored in this book, in which I have addressed philosophical, ethical, and political questions pertaining to science and politics. Like Mooney, I oppose the politicalization of science. Like other science scholars, however, I realize the difficulties with trying to separate science and politics and the need for government oversight of scientific research. In this book, I have developed a framework that permits control of science by scientists and control of science by laypeople and politicians, and that gives distinct roles to scientists, laypeople, and politicians. Scientists should be free to make decisions pertaining to their work within the boundaries of government oversight and review. Excessive government control of science can inhibit scientific progress and undermine the reliability and objectivity of research. However, insufficient government oversight of science can threaten important social values, such as the rights and welfare of research subjects, public health and safety, and national security. There needs to be a proper balance between control of scientific research by scientists and control by the public that respects the unique contributions of each party.

In chapter 3, I developed a conceptual scheme for thinking about this balance. I made three distinctions relevant to government control of science:

1. Restrictions on the autonomy of scientists versus restrictions on the autonomy of scientific organizations or institutions
2. Restrictions on the content of science versus restrictions on the process of science
3. Micromanagement versus general oversight

I have argued that since individual scientists have rights to autonomy, restrictions on those rights are justified only if they serve a compelling social purpose and they are the least burdensome means necessary to achieve that purpose. Restrictions on scientific organizations or institutions, which do not significantly affect the autonomy of individuals, can be justified if the benefits of those restrictions outweigh the harms, including harms to the progress, reliability, and objectivity of science. Since content restrictions can have dire consequences for scientific progress, reliability, and objectivity, content restrictions are also justified only if they serve a compelling social purpose and they are the least burdensome means necessary to achieve that purpose. Process restrictions can be justified if the benefits of those restrictions outweigh the harms. Finally, since micromanagement of scientific decisions can have a negative impact on science, the government should avoid micromanagement of science, although micromanagement can be justified in some situations.

I have applied this framework to a variety of controversies concerning government control of science, including government science advice, science funding decisions, research with national security implications, protection of human research subjects, and science education. I have argued for the following points pertaining to these topics.

Government science advice. In an ideal world, the selection of experts to serve on government science committees would be depoliticized. Experts would be selected based on their knowledge and credentials, not based on their politics or ideology. Since we do not live in an ideal world, political considerations often enter into the selection of experts. One way to deal with the problem of politicalization of experts is to do our best to try to prevent political considerations from affecting the selection of experts. When this strategy falls short of the mark, a very different strategy may prove useful: allow political biases to counteract each other. If a committee has equal numbers of conservative and liberal scientists, then these political biases may cancel each other out. In Congress, bipartisan committees hold a great deal of respect because they are perceived to be more neutral than partisan committees. As noted earlier in this book, the president has a great deal of political power concerning appointments on federal advisory committees. When so much power rests in the hands of the president, or his or her administration, it may be difficult to prevent abuses of power. To buffer the effects of politics on appointments to federal scientific advisory committees, Congress should take steps to dilute the power of the executive branch. First, Congress should monitor the quality and integrity of government science advice, and hold the administration accountable for problems with government science advice. Second, Congress should pass legislation allowing a congressional subcommittee to approve appointments on some government science committees. Since there are hundreds of government science committees, congressional approval should be limited to the thirty most important committees.[1] Third, Congress should also have the power to investigate and criticize committee appointments, committee reports, and proceedings.

When an expert committee renders an opinion, the government should follow that advice, unless there is a compelling argument for not following it. The burden of proof should rest on those who plan to

---

1. The number thirty is somewhat arbitrary. One could argue that Congress should approve appointments on more than thirty or less than thirty committees. The best way to obtain a more objective estimate of the number of committees Congress should oversee is to experiment with different numbers and see what works best. If thirty is too many, it can be reduced; if thirty is too few, it can be increased.

ignore the advice of experts. If an advisory committee is evenly split, with a slight majority favoring a particular position, government officials may choose to adopt the minority position. But officials should not ignore a position adopted by a clear majority (66% or more). Governments should not distort, manipulate, falsify, or censor reports prepared by scientific advisory committees or scientific agencies. Committee reports and proceedings should be open to the public. If the administration disagrees with a committee report, it can publish a contrary opinion. The government should provide adequate funding to agencies, such as the FDA and EPA, which review data submitted by industry for regulatory purposes. Providing adequate funding for these agencies is necessary to assess and counterbalance research submitted by private industry. The government should also support agencies that provide independent science advice, such as the NAS. Congress should consider reviving the OTA or some other office to provide additional, independent science advice (see below).

Government funding of science. The government should use expert peer review committees to make science funding decisions. The government should set funding priorities and oversee the funding process, but it should avoid micromanaging the funding of science. The government should not second-guess the decisions of peer review committees, except in unusual circumstances where the peer review system breaks down and external control is necessary to protect human rights, prevent violations of the law, or ensure scientific integrity. Some micromanagement of science may also be necessary for the purposes of accounting for the use of government funds via contracts or grants. Since earmarked funding bypasses the normal peer review process, the government should avoid the earmarking of science funding. When projects are too large, innovative, or complex to fund through normal peer review channels, special expert panels should be used to evaluate these projects. Specific funding restrictions, such as restrictions on embryonic stem cell research, should be avoided unless they have widespread popular support and a sunset clause. Scientists who are government employees (that is, intramural researchers) should be free to publish articles or communicate with the public without government interference or intimidation. Intramural scientists' freedom of expression may be restricted only to ensure the quality or integrity of government-funded research, or to enable the administration to develop clear and consistent communications with the public. Government agencies may require that articles written by intramural researchers undergo internal peer review prior to submission to a journal. Also, government agencies may request that intramural scientists inform public relations officials about media interviews. In publications and other communications, intramural researchers should indicate that they are expressing their own opinions, not the official views of the federal government or one of its agencies. An independent organization, such as the American Association for the Advancement of Science (AAAS), should monitor and review the government's treatment of intramural scientists.

Science with national security implications. Protecting national security implications is a legitimate reason for restricting the autonomy of scientists, scientific organizations, and scientific institutions. To avoid misusing the national security justification for controlling scientific research, it must be clearly defined and limited in scope. The government should classify research only when a clearly defined national security interest is at stake. Research should not be classified for political expediency. Research should be declassified when classification is no longer necessary. Although the government may control access to classified research, it should not, as a general rule, censor unclassified research, even if that research may threaten national security. Censorship is justified only when a publication would definitely pose a grave and irreparable harm to national security, such as publishing information about troop movements or weapons systems. For most research with national security implications, the government should refrain from restricting publication and scientists should decide whether (or how) the research should be published. In making publication decisions, scientist should carefully consider the benefits and risks of publication to science and society, and they should consider the different options for publication. Scientists should take reasonable precautions to prevent plausible threats to national security. The government should sponsor agencies that help scientists to evaluate research with national security implications. The agencies can also help to develop ethics guidelines and can provide scientists with information and resources for decision-making. The government may control access to dangerous biological, chemical, and radiological agents, but should take care to avoid hampering scientific research. To avoid the manipulation of intelligence with national security implications, intelligence analysts, committees, and agencies must be allowed to make judgments and decisions free from political pressure, manipulation, or control. Intelligence assessment should be structured to allow for ample room for dissension and debate. Though military intelligence is not a science, it should aspire to be objective and reliable and should use some of the methods of science.

Protection of human subjects in research. Regulations and guidelines pertaining to research with human subjects should protect the rights and welfare of human beings without placing undue burdens on scientific research. While under-regulation can threaten the rights and welfare of human subjects, over-regulation can hinder the progress of science. In some ways, the U.S. regulations provide both too much control of science and too little. Excessive paperwork and bureaucracy, the review of low risk research, and excessively broad applications of the definition of research are examples of too much regulation, while loopholes in the regulations, no requirements for compensation for injuries, and lack of broad research review are examples of too little regulation. The U.S. federal research regulations and guidelines should be revised so that there is more emphasis on the protecting of human subjects and less emphasis on bureaucratic, administrative, technical, and legal issues.

Science education. The government should have oversight over science education but it should not micromanage the science curriculum. Laypeople and politicians should not decide whether science teachers should teach evolution in K–12 public schools; this decision should be left to scientists and science educators. Though the government can teach values in public schools, these values should be taught in classes that are oriented toward humanistic education, such as language arts, social studies, history, and the fine arts.

To help implement the recommendations made in the previous paragraphs and further protect science from politicalization, I also recommend the following:

Forming a new government agency to provide much needed independent scientific advice. Currently, the NAS provides scientific advice to the government on various topics, but that organization does not fulfill all of the government's needs. The NAS does not cover all of the topics that need to be addressed, and it usually does not provide immediate advice (because NAS reports can take several years to prepare.) The OTA at one time played an important role in providing science advice to Congress, but that office has been closed for many years. One of the problems with the OTA is that its funding was always in peril, and this caused administrators at the office to avoid taking controversial positions out of fear that the office would lose funding (Bimber 1996). Congress should create an agency similar to the OTA and ensure that it has a secure source of long-term funding and political independence. The agency should be named the Office of Science and Technology Advice (OSTA) to reflect its main mission, which would be to provide science and technology advice to the government and private citizens. To ensure that the agency has political independence, it should be designed like the Federal Reserve System, which oversees financial institutions in the United States, controls the nation's money supply, and helps to stabilize the U.S. economy. The Federal Reserve does not report to the president and its members are not appointed by the president. The Federal Reserve System is governed by an independent board of governors, who have the authority to appoint board members and name a chairman of the board. Congress has oversight authority over the Federal Reserve, however (Federal Reserve System 2005). Like the Federal Reserve, the OSTA should be governed by an independent board, which appoints its own members, but is overseen by Congress. Staff and committee appointments within the OSTA should be handled internally, with no outside political influence. Appointments should be based on experience, expertise, and other nonpolitical considerations. The OSTA should compliment the NAS by covering topics not covered by the NAS and by providing timely advice to the government and citizens. Like the EPA, CDC, FDA, and NIH, the OSTA would also provide information directly to the public via reports, articles, books, video programs, or Web sites. The OSTA should have standing committees on perennial issues, such as energy, the environment, and education, as well as ad hoc committees on emerging or temporary problems. The OSTA could also help to reduce some of the politicalization on federal scientific advisory committees by recommending potential candidates for advisory committee appointments. Some federal advisory committees could even be eliminated and/or consolidated within the OSTA. There would be no need for a president's council on bioethics, for example, if there is a council on bioethics within the OSTA. The OSTA should also include members of the public on its advisory committees and hold meetings, focus groups, and other forums for soliciting public opinion on various issues. All committee meeting documents should be open to the public.

Depoliticizing appointments to leadership positions at science agencies. In the United States, many of the appointments to leadership positions at science agencies are political appointments decided by the executive branch. For example, the president appoints the director of the NIH as well as the directors of the NIH's twenty-seven institutes and centers. Other political appointments include the directors of the EPA, FDA, NASA, NSF, and CDC. To reduce the political pressure on government science agencies, political appointments should be kept to a minimum. Ideally, only agency heads who are members of the cabinet should be political appointees. All other leadership positions should be nonpolitical. For example, the secretary of the DHHS is a cabinet position and should be a political appointment. But leadership positions at agencies within DHHS, such as the NIH, FDA, and CDC, should not be political appointments. These appointments should be decided by scientists and administrators within these agencies who understand the expertise, knowledge, and temperament necessary for effective leadership.

Developing policies to provide scientists with guidance concerning research with national security implications. The policies and codes should address issues concerning publication and publication dissemination of information, risk assessment, and publication options. Universities, professional societies, and journals should develop guidelines and rules that encourage researchers to take their responsibilities seriously and to be mindful of the risks of publication.

Teaching students and trainees about the political aspects of science. Education in the politics of science is important to prepare students for the issues and challenges they are likely to face when they enter the scientific profession, such as serving on advisory committees, dealing with science funding agencies, communicating with the media and politicians, and encountering political pressures. Universities and research institutes can meet these educational objectives by developing a separate course on the politics of science, incorporating discussions of political issues into standard courses in research ethics, methods or practice, or mentoring students in the politics of science (National Academy of Sciences 1997, 2002).

Scientists becoming more knowledgeable about the politics of science and more involved in political issues relating to science. Scientists are the ones who must deal with censorship, funding restrictions, distortion of science advice, and other types of politicalization (Pielke 2007). They should be prepared to defend the scientific profession against the threat posed by politicalization. In 2006, a group of scientists and engineers who were concerned about the politicalization of science under the Bush administration formed a nonprofit organization, Scientists and Engineers for America (SEA), to promote respect for evidence-based decision-making in all levels of government. The organization plans to achieve its mission by educating the public and members of the scientific community about science policy issues and participation in political processes and by holding politicians accountable for distributing accurate information on the positions they take on sciences issues (Scientists and Engineers for America 2008). According to Henry Kelly, chairman of the board of the SEA, "The principal role of the science and technology community is to advance human understanding. But there are times when this is not enough. Scientists and engineers have a right, indeed an obligation, to enter the political debate when the nation's leaders systematically ignore scientific evidence and analysis, put ideological interests ahead of scientific truths, suppress valid scientific evidence, and harass and threaten scientists for speaking honestly about their research" (Scientists and Engineers for America 2008). To promote its mission and objectives, the SEA has adopted the following Bill of Rights for Scientists and Engineers:

1. Public policy shall be made using the best available scientific, technical, and engineering knowledge.

2. No government organization shall knowingly distribute false or misleading information.

3. Government funding for science, technology, engineering, and mathematics (STEM) education shall only be used for evidence-based curricula.

4. No one should fear reprisals or intimidation because of the results of his or her research.

5. Scientists, technologists, and engineers conducting research or analysis with public funding shall be free of unreasonable

restrictions in discussing and publishing their work, and the results of governmentally-funded research and analysis shall be made open to the public without unreasonable delay.

6. A clear, public, and transparent process shall be used to make decisions about restricting public access to information for reasons of national security. There shall be a process for challenging decisions, and remedial measures to correct mistakes and abuses of the classification system.

7. Employees exposing what they believe to be manipulation of research and analysis for political or ideological reasons shall be protected from intimidation, retribution, or adverse personnel action resulting from the decision to speak out.

8. Appointments to publicly funded advisory committees shall be based on professional and academic qualifications, not political affiliation or ideology. (Scientists and Engineers for America 2006)

As one can see, the statements contained in the SEA's Bill of Rights are very similar to many of the recommendations I have made in this book.

★★★

This concludes my discussion of the relationship between science and politics. I don't expect that everyone who has read this book will agree with everything I have said here, and I expect that some people will disagree with almost everything I have said. Be that as it may, I am hopeful most people will find something useful and illuminating in the book. There is much more that can be said about the topic of science and politics, of course, but I will leave that task for another day or another writer. I will close the book with two quotes. The first is from American biologist Thomas Huxley (1825–95), who said that "science is nothing but trained and organized common sense" (Huxley 2006). The second is from Prussian politician Otto Von Bismarck (1815–98), who said that "politics is the art of the possible" (Von Bismarck 2006). I hope that in some way my book can help politicians acquire some common sense when dealing with science and can help scientists to understand the possibilities (both good and bad) of politics.

References

ABC News. 2004. Stem cell backing holds at six in ten. Available at: http://abcnews.go.com/sections/politics/DailyNews/po11010803.html (accessed March 31, 2008).

Advisory Committee on Human Radiation Experiments (ACHRE). 1995. *The human radiation experiments*. Washington, DC: DOE.

Alberts, B. 2005. Modeling attacks on the food supply. *Proceedings of the National Academy of Sciences* 102: 9737–38.

Amdur, R. 2003. *Institutional review board guidebook*. Boston: Jones and Bartlett.

American Association for the Advancement of Science (AAAS). 2006. AAAS funding update, August 9, 2006. Available at: http://www.aaas.org/spp/rd/upd806.htm (accessed March 31, 2008).

American Association for the Advancement of Science (AAAS). 2007. *Project 2061: A long-term AAAS initiative to advance literacy in science, mathematics, and technology*. Available at: http://www.project2061.org/ (accessed March 25, 2008).

American Association of University Professors (AAUP). 2003. Academic freedom and national security in a time of crisis. *Academe* 89, 6: 34–59.

American Heritage Dictionary of the English Language. 2008. 4th ed. Available at: http://dictionary.reference.com (accessed April 7, 2008).

Amnesty International. 2006. *Report 2006: The state of the world's human rights*. New York: Amnesty International.

Anderson, L. 2006. Churches to mark Darwin's birthday. *Chicago Tribune*, February 11: A1.

Angell, M. 2004. *The truth about drug companies*. New York: Random House.

Annas, G. 1999. Why we need a national human experimentation agency. *Accountability in Research* 7: 293–302.

Appleman, P. 1979. Darwin among the moralists. In P. Appleman (ed.), *Darwin*, 2nd ed., 551–71. New York: W. W. Norton.

Aristotle. [350 B.C.] 2000. *Posterior analytics*. Available at: http://classics.mit.edu/Aristotle/posterior.html (accessed March 5, 2008).

Association of Accreditation of Human Research Protection Programs (AAHRPP). 2006. About AAHRPP. Available at: http://www.aahrpp.org/www.aspx?PageID=5 (accessed March 31, 2008).

Association for the Assessment and Accreditation of Laboratory Animal Care International (AAALAC). 2006. What is AAALAC? Available at: http://www.aaalac.org/about/index.cfm (accessed March 31, 2008).

Atkinson, R. 1994. *Crusade: The untold story of the Persian Gulf War.* New York: Mariner.

Babington, C. 2006. Stem cell bill gets Bush's first veto. *Washington Post*, July 19: A4.

Bacon, F. [1620] 2005. *The new organon.* Available at: http://etext.library.adelaide.edu.au/b/bacon/francis/organon/ (accessed March 5, 2008).

Bankert, E., and Amdur, R. (eds.). 2005. *Institutional review board: Management and function*, 2nd ed. Boston: Jones and Bartlett.

Baram, M. 2007. An inconvenient verdict for Gore. ABC News, October 12, 2007. Available at: http://abcnews.go.com/US/story?id=3719791&page=1 (accessed February 18, 2008).

Barnes, B. 1977. *Interests and the growth of knowledge.* London: Routledge.

Barron, J., and Dienes, C. 1999. *Constitutional law*, 5th ed. Minneapolis: West.

Bayles, M. 1988. *Professional ethics*, 2nd ed. Belmont, CA: Wadsworth.

Baylis, F., and Robert, J. 2006. Human embryonic stem cell research: An argument for national research review. *Accountability in Research* 13: 207–24.

Beecher, H. 1966. Ethics and clinical research. *New England Journal of Medicine* 274: 1354–60.

Beitz, C. 1999. *Political theory and international relations.* Princeton, NJ: Princeton University Press.

Benham, B. 2008. The ubiquity of deception and the ethics of deceptive research. *Bioethics* 22: 147–56.

Berlin, I. 2002. *Liberty*, H. Hardy (ed.). New York: Oxford University Press.

Bhattacharjee, Y. 2006. Should academics self-censor their findings on terrorism? *Science* 312: 993–94.

Bimber, B. 1996. *The politics of expertise in Congress: The rise and fall of the Office of Technology Assessment.* Albany: State University of New York Press.

Biotechnology Industry Organization (BIO). 2006. History of BIO. Available at: http://www.bio.org/aboutbio/history.asp (accessed March 5, 2008).

Blackburn, E. 2004. Bioethics and the political distortion of biomedical science. *New England Journal of Medicine* 350: 1379–80.

Blackburn, E., and Rowley, J. 2004. Reason as our guide. *PLoS Biology* 2, 4: e116.

Boorstin, D. 1983. *The discoverers.* New York: Vintage.

Boureston, J. 2002. Center for Contemporary Conflict, assessing Al Qaeda's WMD capabilities. Available at: http://www.ccc.nps.navy.mil/rsepResources/si/sep02/wmd.asp (accessed March 31, 2008).

Boyd, R. 1983. On the current status of the issue of scientific realism. *Erkenntnis* 19: 45–90.

Broad, W. 2007. From a rapt audience, a call to cool the hype. *New York Times*, March 13: A1.

Brumfiel, G. 2006. The scientific balance of power. *Nature* 439: 646–47.

Bullock, A. 1962. *Hitler: A study in tyranny*. New York: Penguin.

Burke, J. 1995. *The day the universe changed*. Boston: Little and Brown.

Bush, G. 2001. Executive Order 13237. Available at: http://www.bioethics. gov/about/executive.html (accessed March 7, 2008).

Bush, V. 1945. *Science: The endless frontier*. Washington, DC: U.S. Government Printing Office. Available at: http://www.nsf.gov/about/history/vbush1945. htm#summary (accessed March 5, 2008).

Butterfield, H. 1997. *The origins of modern science*. New York: Free Press.

Byrnes, W. 2005. Why human "altered nuclear transfer" is unethical: A holistic systems view. *National Catholic Bioethics Quarterly* 5: 271–9.

Cartwright, N. 1983. *How the laws of physics lie*. New York: Oxford University Press.

Casarett, D., Karlawish, J., and Sugarman, J. 2000. Determining when quality improvement initiatives should be considered research: Proposed criteria and potential implications. *Journal of the American Medical Association* 283: 2275–80.

Cello, J., Paul, A., and Wimmer, E. 2002. Chemical synthesis of poliovirus cDNA: Generation of infectious virus in the absence of natural template. *Science* 297: 1016–18.

Chambers, H. 2004. *My way or the highway: The micromanagement survival guide*. San Francisco: Berrett-Koehler.

Cho, M., and Bero, L. 1996. The quality of drug studies published in symposium proceedings. *Annals of Internal Medicine* 124: 485–89.

Chubin, D., and Hackett, E. 1990. *Peerless review: Peer review and U.S. science policy*. Albany: State University of New York Press.

Citizens against Government Waste. 2006. 2006 pig book summary. Available at: http://www.cagw.org/site/PageServer?pagename=reports_pigbook2006 #criteria (accessed March 5, 2008).

Cohen, J. 2005. House "peer review" kills two NIH grants. *Science* 309: 29–30.

Coleman, C., Menikoff, J., Goldner, J., and Dubler, N. (eds.). 2005. *The ethics and regulation of research with human subjects*. Newark, NJ: Lexis Nexis.

Collins, F. 2006. *The language of God*. New York: Free Press.

Copi. I. 1986. *Introduction to logic*, 7th ed. New York: Macmillan.

Couzin, J. 2005. Plan B: A collision of science and politics. *Science* 310: 38–39.

Couzin, J. 2006. Texas earmark allots millions to disputed theory of Gulf War illness. *Science* 312: 668.

Daley, G. 2004. Missed opportunities in embryonic stem-cell research. *New England Journal of Medicine* 351: 627–28.

Daniel v. Waters. 515 F.2d 485 (6th Cir. 1975).

Darwin, C. 1859. *On the origin of species by means of natural selection, or the preservation of favored races in the struggle for life.* London: John Murray.

Daubert v. Dow Merrell Pharmaceuticals, Inc. 509 U.S. 579 (1993).

Deichmann, U. 1999. *Biologists under Hitler.* Cambridge, MA: Harvard University Press.

Dennis v. United States. 341 U.S. 494 (1951).

Department of Health and Human Services (DHHS). 1998. *Office of Inspector General: Institutional review boards: A time for reform.* Available at: http://oig. hhs.gov/oei/reports/oei-01-97-00193.pdf (accessed March 20, 2008).

Dessler, A., and Parson, E. 2006. *The science and politics of global climate change.* Cambridge: Cambridge University Press.

Dobzansky, T. 1973. Nothing in biology makes sense except in the light of evolution. *American Biology Teacher* 35: 125–29.

Dresser, R. 2001. *When science offers salvation: Patient advocacy and research ethics.* New York: Oxford University Press.

Dupre, J. 1993. *The disorder of things: Metaphysical foundations for the disunity of science.* Cambridge, MA: Harvard University Press.

Dworkin, G. 1988. *The theory and practice of autonomy.* Cambridge: Cambridge University Press.

Earman, J. 1992. *Bayes or bust.* Cambridge, MA: MIT Press.

Edwards v. Arkansas. 482 U.S. 578 (1987).

Eilperin, J. 2006. Censorship is alleged at NOAA. *Washington Post*, February 6: A7.

Eldredge, N. 2005. *Darwin: Discovering the tree of life.* New York: W. W. Norton.

Emanuel, E., Crouch, R., Arras, J., and Moreno, J. (eds.). 2004. *Ethical and regulatory aspects of clinical research.* Baltimore, MD: Johns Hopkins University Press.

Emanuel, E., and Emanuel, L. 1992. Four models of the physician-patient relationship. *Journal of the American Medical Association* 267: 2221–26.

Emanuel, E., Wendler, D., and Grady, C. 2000. What makes clinical research ethical? *Journal of the American Medical Association* 283: 2701–11.

Emanuel, E., Wood, A., Fleischman, A., Bowen, A., Getz, K., Grady, C., Levine, C., Hammerschmidt, D., Faden, R., Eckenwiler, L., et al. 2004. Oversight of human participants research: Identifying problems to evaluate reform proposals. *Annals of Internal Medicine* 141: 282–91.

Environmental Protection Agency (EPA). 2006. What we do. Available at: http://www.epa.gov/epahome/aboutepa.htm (accessed March 31, 2008).

Environmental Protection Agency (EPA). 2007. EPA Human Studies Review Board. Available at: http://www.epa.gov/OSA/hsrb/ (accessed March 31, 2008).

Epperson v. Arkansas. 393 U.S. 97 (1968).

Federal Advisory Committee Act. 1972. Available at: http://www.gsa.gov/gsa/cm_attachments/GSA_BASIC/without_annotations_R2G-b4T_0Z5RDZ-i34K-pR.pdf (accessed March 7, 2008).

Federal Reserve System. 2005. Purpose and function. Available at: http://www.federalreserve.gov/pf/pdf/pf_1.pdf (accessed April 10, 2008).

Feinberg, J. 1987. *Harm to others.* New York: Oxford University Press.

Food and Drug Administration (FDA). 2006. Guidance for institutional review boards, clinical investigators, and sponsors. Available at: http://www.fda.gov/oc/ohrt/irbs/ (accessed March 31, 2008).

42 C.F.R. 93: Public Health Service policies on research misconduct. 2005. *Code of Federal Regulations* Title 42, Pt. 93 (Public Health Service, Department of Health and Human Services).

45 C.F.R. 46: Protection of health and human subjects. 2005. *Code of Federal Regulations* Title 45, Pt. 46 (Department of Health and Human Services). Available at: http://www.hhs.gov/ohrp/humansubjects/guidance/45cfr46.htm#46.107 (accessed April 7, 2008).

Fost, N., and Levine, R. 2007. The dysregulation of human subjects research. *Journal of the American Medical Association* 298: 2196–98.

Freedom of Information Act (FOIA). 1996. 5 U.S.C. 532. Available at: http://www.usdoj.gov/oip/foia_updates/Vol_XVII_4/page2.htm (accessed March 12, 2008).

Friedberg, M., Saffran, B., Stinson, T.. Nelson, W., and Bennett, C. 1999. Evaluation of conflict of interest in new drugs used in oncology. *Journal of the American Medical Association* 282: 1453–57.

Gallin, J. 2002. *Principles and practice of clinical research.* New York: Academic Press.

Gert, B. 2007. *Common morality.* New York: Oxford University Press.

Gibbs, W., and Lyall, S. 2007. Gore shares peace prize for climate change work. *New York Times,* October 13: A1.

Giere, R. 1988. *Explaining science.* Chicago: University of Chicago Press.

Gilbert, M. 2004. *The Second World War.* New York: Holt.

Gilbert, S. 2008. Trials and tribulations. *Hastings Center Report* 38, 2: 14–18.

Goering, S., Holland, S., and Fryer-Edwards, K. 2008. Transforming genetic research practices with marginalized communities: A case for responsive justice. *Hastings Center Report* 38, 2: 43–53.

Godlee, F., and Jefferson, T. (eds.). 2003. *Peer review in health sciences.* New York: Blackwell.

Goklany, I. 2001. *The precautionary principle: A critical appraisal of environmental risk assessment.* Washington, DC: Cato Institute.

Goldman, A. 1986. *Epistemology and cognition.* Cambridge, MA: Harvard University Press.

Gould, S. 1981. *The mismeasure of man.* New York: W. W. Norton.

Government Accounting Office (GAO). 2004. Federal advisory committees: Additional guidance could help agencies better ensure independence and balance. Available at: http://www.gao.gov/new.items/d04328.pdf (accessed March 7, 2008).

Green, R. 2001. *The human embryo research debates.* New York: Oxford University Press.

Green, R. 2007. Can we develop ethically universal embryonic stem-cell lines? *Nature Reviews Genetics* 8: 480–85.

Greenberg, D. 2001. *Science, money, and politics.* Chicago: University of Chicago Press.

Gunsalus, C. 2004. The nanny state meets the inner lawyer: Overregulating while underprotecting human participants in research. *Ethics and Behavior* 14: 369–82.

Guston, D. 2000. *Between politics and science.* Cambridge: Cambridge University Press.

Gutmann, A., and Thompson, D. 1996. *Democracy and disagreement.* Cambridge, MA: Harvard University Press.

Haack, S. 2003. *Defending science within reason.* New York: Prometheus.

Hacking, I. 1983. *Representing and intervening.* Cambridge: Cambridge University Press.

Hamilton, A. 1788. *Federalist* number 76. Available at: http://www.foundingfathers.info/federalistpapers/fedindex.htm (accessed March 30, 2008).

Hamilton, A., and Madison, J. 1788. *Federalist* number 51. Available at: http://www.foundingfathers.info/federalistpapers/fedindex.htm (accessed March 30, 2008).

Harris, G. 2006. Morning after pill is cleared for wider sales. *New York Times*, August 24: A1.

Harris, G. 2007. Surgeon general sees 4-year term as compromised. *New York Times*, July 11: A1.

Harris Interactive. 2004. The Harris poll #58, August 18, 2004. Available at: http://www.harrisinteractive.com/harris_poll/index.asp?PID=488 (accessed March 5, 2008).

Harris, R., and Paxman, J. 2002. *A higher form of killing: The secret history of chemical and biological warfare.* New York: Random House.

Hawthorne, F. 2005. *Inside the FDA: The business and politics behind the drugs we take and the food we eat.* New York: John Wiley.

Hempel, C. 1965. *Aspects of scientific explanation*. New York: Free Press.

Hoffman, B. 2006. *Inside terrorism*, 2nd ed. New York: Columbia University Press.

Holden, C. 2005. Pellegrino to replace Kass on U.S. panel. *Science* 309: 1800.

Holden, C. 2006. States, foundations lead the way after Bush vetoes stem cell bill. *Science* 313: 420–21.

Hooker, B. 2003. *Ideal code, real world: A rule-consequentialist theory of morality*. New York: Oxford University Press.

Hossfeld, U., and Olsson, L. 2002. From the modern synthesis to Lysenkoism, and back? *Science* 297: 55–56.

Howson, C., and Urbach, P. 2005. *Scientific reasoning: The Bayesian approach*, 3rd ed. New York: Open Court.

Hurlbut, W., George, R., and Grompe, M. 2006. Seeking consensus: A clarification and defense of altered nuclear transfer. *Hastings Center Report* 36, 5: 42–49.

Human Genome Project. 2005. What is the Human Genome Project? Available at: http://www.ornl.gov/sci/techresources/Human_Genome/project/about.shtml (accessed April 5, 2008).

Huxley, T. 2006. The quotations page. Available at: http://www.quotationspage.com/quote/26215.html (accessed March 31, 2008).

Intelligent Design Network. 2006. Intelligent design. Available at: http://www.intelligentdesignnetwork.org/ (accessed March 31, 2008).

Institute of Medicine. 2002. *Responsible research: A systems approach to protecting research participants*. Washington, DC: National Academy Press.

Jackson, R., Ramsay, A., Christensen, C., Beaton, S., Hall, D., and Ramshaw, I. 2001. Expression of mouse interleukin-4 by a recombinant ectromelia virus suppresses cytolytic lymphocyte responses and overcomes genetic resistance to mousepox. *Journal of Virology* 75: 1205–10.

Janofsky, M. 2005. Nominee is grilled over program on pesticides. *New York Times*, April 7: A1.

Jasanoff, S. 1990. *The fifth branch: Science advisors as policymakers*. Cambridge, MA: Harvard University Press.

Jasanoff, S. 1997. *Science at the bar: Science and technology in American law*. Cambridge, MA: Harvard University Press.

Joint Commission for Accreditation of Healthcare Organizations (JCAHO). 2006. About the commission. Available at: http://www.jointcommission.org/AboutUs/ (accessed December 5, 2006).

Jones, J. 1993. *Bad blood: The Tuskegee syphilis experiment*, 2nd ed. New York: Free Press.

Joravsky, D. 1986. *The Lysenko affair*. Chicago: University of Chicago Press.

Jordan, A., Taylor, W. Jr., and Mazarr, M. 1998. *American national security*, 5th ed. Baltimore, MD: Johns Hopkins University Press.

Journal Editors and Authors Group. 2003. Uncensored exchange of scientific results. *Proceedings of the National Academy of Sciences* 100: 1464.

Kaiser, J. 2004. Sex studies "properly" approved. *Science* 303: 741.

Kaiser, J. 2005. Forty-four researchers broke NIH consulting rules. *Science* 309: 546.

Kant, I. [1785] 1981. *Groundwork of the metaphysic of morals*, J. Ellington (trans.). Indianapolis, IN: Hackett.

Kant, I. [1781] 2003. *Critique of pure reason*, N. K. Smith (trans.). New York: Macmillan.

Kantorovich, A. 1993. *Scientific discovery: Logic and tinkering*. Albany: State University of New York Press.

Kass, L. 2004. *Life, liberty, and the defense of dignity*. Washington, DC: American Enterprise Institute.

Kempner, J., Perlis, C., and Merz, J. 2005. Forbidden knowledge. *Science* 307: 854.

King, C. 2007. Scientific productivity and citation of scientific papers: Where do we stand? *Current Science* 93, 6: 750–51.

Kintisch, E. 2007. CDC director's message on risk runs afoul of White House edits. *Science* 318: 726–27.

Kintisch, E., and Mervis, J. 2006. A budget with big winners and losers. *Science* 311: 762–64.

Kitcher, P. 1983. *The case against creationism*. Cambridge, MA: MIT Press.

Kitcher, P. 1993. *The advancement of science*. New York: Oxford University Press.

Kitcher, P. 2001. *Science, truth, and democracy*. New York: Oxford University Press.

Kitzmiller v. Dover Area School District. Case No. 04cv2688 (December 20, 2005).

Klee, R. 1997. *Introduction to the philosophy of science*. New York: Oxford University Press.

Klimanskaya, I., Chung, Y., Becker, S., Lu, S., and Lanza, R. 2006. Human embryonic stem cell lines derived from single blastomeres. *Nature* 442: 1–5.

Knorr-Cetina, K. 1981. *The manufacture of knowledge*. Oxford, UK: Pergamon Press.

Krimsky, S. 2003. *Science in the private interest*. Lanham, MD: Rowman and Littlefield.

Kuhn, T. 1970. *The structure of scientific revolutions*, 2nd ed. Chicago: University of Chicago Press.

Kuhn, T. 1977. *The essential tension*. Chicago: University of Chicago Press.

Kumho Tire Co. v. Carmichael. 526 U.S. 137 (1999).

Lakatos, I. 1970. Falsificationism and the methodology of scientific research programmes. In: I. Lakatos and A. Musgrave (eds.), *Criticism and the growth of knowledge*, 91–195. Cambridge: Cambridge University Press.

Latour, B., and Woolgar, S. 1986. *Laboratory life: The social construction of scientific facts*. Princeton, NJ: Princeton University Press.

Laudan, L. 1977. *Progress and its problems*. Berkeley: University of California Press.

Lee, C., and Kaufman, M. 2007. Bush aide blocked report. *Washington Post*, July 29: A1.

Lenard, J. 2006. Two facets of peer review and the proper role of study sections. *Accountability in Research* 13: 277–83.

Lemmens, T., and Thompson, A. 2001. Noninstitutional commercial review boards in North America: A critical appraisal and comparison with IRBs. *IRB: Ethics and Human Research* 23, 2: 1–12.

Levine, R. 1986. *Ethics and the regulation of clinical research*. New Haven, CT: Yale University Press.

Lewis, S. 2001. History of biowarfare. *Nova Online*. Available at: http://www.pbs.org/wgbh/nova/bioterror/history.html (accessed March 31, 2008).

Licinio, J., and Wong, M. 2002. *Pharmacogenomics*. New York: Wiley.

Locke, J. [1689] 2004. *Two treatises of government*. Whitefish, MT: Kessinger.

Longino, H. 1990. *Science as social knowledge*. Princeton, NJ: Princeton University Press.

Lynn, J. 2004. When does quality improvement count as research? Human subject protection and theories of knowledge. *Quality and Safety in Health Care* 13: 67–70.

MacQueen, K., and Buehler, J. 2004. Ethics, practice, and research in public health. *American Journal of Public Health* 96: 928–31.

Malakoff, D. 2001. White House asks community to oppose earmark projects. *Science* 293: 2364.

Mayer, T. 2006. The biological weapon: A poor man's weapon of mass destruction. *Air and Space Power Journal*. Available at: http://www.airpower.maxwell.af.mil/airchronicles/battle/chp8.html (accessed March 31, 2008).

Mayr, E. 1982. *The growth of biological thought*. Cambridge, MA: Harvard University Press.

Melton, D., Daley, G., and Jennings, C. 2004. Altered nuclear transfer in stem-cell research—a flawed proposal. *New England Journal of Medicine* 351: 2791–92.

Mervis, J. 2006a. Academic earmarks: The money schools love to hate. *Science* 313: 1374.

Mervis, J. 2006b. Judge Jones defines science—and why intelligent design isn't. *Science* 311: 34.

Mervis, J. 2006c. Senate panel chair asks why NSF funds social sciences. *Science* 312: 829.

Merton, R. 1973. *The sociology of science.* Chicago: University of Chicago Press.

Mill, J. [1859] 1956. *On liberty.* New York: Liberal Arts Press.

Miller, J., Scott, E., and Okamoto, S. 2006. Public acceptance of evolution. *Science* 313: 765–66.

Miller, S., and Selgelid, M. 2007. Ethical and philosophical consideration of the dual-use dilemma in the biological sciences. *Science and Engineering Ethics* 13: 523–80.

Mooney, C. 2005. *The Republican war on science.* New York: Basic Books.

Moynihan, D. 1999. *Secrecy: The American experience.* New Haven, CT: Yale University Press.

Nagel, E. 1961. *The structure of science.* New York: Harcourt and Brace.

National Academy of Sciences (NAS). 1997. *Advisor, teacher, role model, friend: On being a mentor to students in science and engineering.* Washington, DC: National Academy Press.

National Academy of Sciences (NAS). 2002. *Integrity in science.* Washington, DC: National Academy Press.

National Academy of Sciences (NAS). 2006. *Understanding and responding to climate change.* Available at: http://dels.nas.edu/basc/Climate-HIGH.pdf (accessed March 30, 2008).

National Bioethics Advisory Commission (NBAC). 2001. *Ethical and policy issues in research involving human participants.* Available at: http://bioethics. georgetown.edu/nbac/human/overvo11.html (accessed March 20, 2008).

National Cancer Institute. 1999. *Health effects of exposure to environmental tobacco smoke.* Available at: http://cancercontrol.cancer.gov/tcrb/monographs/10/ m10_complete.pdf (accessed July 11, 2008).

National Commission for the Protection of Human Subjects of Biomedical and Behavioral Research. *The Belmont report: Ethical principles and guidelines for the protection of human subjects of research.* Available at: http://www.hhs. gov/ohrp/humansubjects/guidance/belmont.htm (accessed April 7, 2008).

National Institutes of Health (NIH). 2006a. About NIH. Available at: http://www.nih.gov/about/ (accessed March 31, 2008).

National Institutes of Health (NIH). 2006b. Office of extramural research. Available at: http://grants1.nih.gov/grants/oer.htm (accessed March 31, 2008).

National Institutes of Health (NIH). 2006c. Recombinant DNA advisory committee. Available at: http://www4.od.nih.gov/oba/rac/aboutrdagt.htm (accessed March 31, 2008).

National Institutes of Health (NIH). 2006d. A short history of the NIH. Available at: http://history.nih.gov/exhibits/history/docs/page_04.html (accessed March 31, 2008).

National Institutes of Health (NIH). 2008. HIPAA privacy rule: Information for researchers. Available at: http://privacyruleandresearch.nih.gov/faq.asp (accessed March 20, 2008).

National Nanotechnology Initiative (NNI). 2006. About the NNI. Available at: http://www.nano.gov/ (accessed March 31, 2008).

National Public Radio. 2008. Sex education in America. Available at: http://www.npr.org/templates/story/story.php?storyId=1622610 (accessed March 25, 2008).

National Research Council (NRC). 2003. *Biotechnology research in an age of terrorism: Confronting the dual use dilemma.* Washington, DC: National Academy of Sciences.

National Research Council (NRC). 2004. *Intentional human dosing studies for EPA regulatory purposes: Scientific and ethical issues.* Washington, DC: National Academy Press, 2004.

National Science Advisory Board for Biosecurity (NSABB). 2005. Welcome. Available at: http://www.biosecurityboard.gov/index.asp (accessed March 31, 2008).

National Science Advisory Board for Biosecurity (NSABB). 2006. Draft guidance documents. Available at: http://www.biosecurityboard.gov/pdf/NSABB%20Draft%20Guidance%20Documents.pdf (accessed March 31, 2008).

National Science Foundation (NSF). 2006. Science indicators 2006. Available at: http://www.nsf.gov/statistics/seind06/toc.htm (accessed March 31, 2008).

New York Times Co. v. United States. 403 U.S. 713 (1971).

Niiniluoto, I. 1987. *Truthlikeness.* Dordrecht, Netherlands: Reidel.

Nobel Prize Foundation. 2008. Nobel Prize winners. Available at: http://nobelprize.org/ (accessed February 26, 2008).

Novak, M. 1997. *The fire of invention: Civil society and the future of the corporation.* Lanham, MD: Rowman and Littlefield.

Nuremberg Code. 1949. Available at: http://ohsr.od.nih.gov/guidelines/nuremberg.html (accessed March 31, 2008).

Office of Human Research Protections (OHRP). 2007a. International compilation of human subject research protections. Available at: http://www.hhs.gov/ohrp/international/HSPCompilation.pdf (accessed March 31, 2008).

Office of Human Research Protections (OHRP). 2007b. Policy and guidance. Available at: http://www.hhs.gov/ohrp/policy/index.html (accessed March 31, 2008).

Office of Inspector General, Department of Health and Human Services. 1998. *IRBs: A system in jeopardy.* Bethesda, MD: Department of Health and Human Services.

Office of Legislative Policy and Analysis. 2006. Human subjects legislation. Available at: http://olpa.od.nih.gov/legislation/107/pendinglegislation/humansubjects.asp (accessed March 31, 2008).

Online Ethics Center. 2005. Roger Boisjoly and the shuttle Challenger disaster. Available at: http://www.mae.ncsu.edu/courses/mae415/eischen/docs/OnlineEthics.pdf (accessed March 31, 2008).

Overbye, D. 2005. Philosophers notwithstanding, Kansas school board redefines science. *New York Times*, November 15: A1.

Paasche-Orlow, M., and Brancati, F. 2005. Assessment of medical school institutional review board policies regarding compensation of subjects for research-related injury. *American Journal of Medicine* 118: 175–80.

Pellegrino, E., and Thomasma, D. 1981. *A philosophical basis of medical practice.* New York: Oxford University Press.

Pharmaceutical Research and Manufacturers of America (PHrMA). 2006. Who we are. Available at: http://www.phrma.org/about_phrma/ (accessed March 31, 2008).

Pielke, R. 2007. *The honest broker: Making sense of science in policy and politics.* Cambridge: Cambridge University Press.

Pitt, R., and Ritter, S. 2002. *War on Iraq.* New York: Context Books.

Pojman, L. 2005. *Ethics*, 5th ed. Belmont, CA: Wadsworth.

Popper, K. 1959. *The logic of scientific discovery.* London: Routledge.

Powaski, R. 1997. *The Cold War.* New York: Oxford University Press.

Powell, C. 2003. Transcript of Colin Powell's presentation to the U.N. on February 3, 2003. Available at: http://www.cnn.com/2003/US/02/05/sprj.irq.powell.transcript.10/index.html (accessed March 14, 2008).

President's Council on Bioethics. 2002. *Human cloning and human dignity: An ethical inquiry.* Available at: http://www.bioethics.gov/reports/cloningreport/index.html (accessed March 31, 2008).

Proctor, R. 2003. *Racial hygiene: Medicine under the Nazis.* Cambridge, MA: Harvard University Press.

Pucéat, M., and Ballis, A. 2007. Embryonic stem cells: From bench to bedside. *Clinical Pharmacology and Therapeutics* 82: 337–39.

Quine, W., and Ullian, J. 1978. *The web of belief.* New York: Random House.

Rampton, S.. and Stauber, J. 2003. *Weapons of mass deception.* New York: Tarcher Penguin.

Rawls, J. 1971. *A theory of justice.* Cambridge, MA: Harvard University Press.

Rawls, J. 2001. *The law of peoples.* Cambridge, MA: Harvard University Press.

Rawls, J. 2005. *Political liberalism*, 2nd ed. New York: Columbia University Press.

Resnik, D. 1998. *The ethics of science: An introduction.* New York: Routledge.

Resnik, D. 2000. A pragmatic approach to the demarcation problem. *Studies in the History and Philosophy of Science* 31: 249–67.

Resnik, D. 2001. Setting biomedical research priorities: Justice, science, and public participation. *Kennedy Institute for Ethics Journal* 11: 181–205.

Resnik, D. 2003a. From Baltimore to Bell Labs: Reflections on two decades of debate about scientific misconduct. *Accountability in Research* 10: 123–35.

Resnik, D. 2003b. Is the precautionary principle unscientific? *Studies in the History and Philosophy of Biology and the Biomedical Sciences* 34: 329–44.

Resnik, D. 2005. The patient's duty to adhere to prescribed treatment: An ethical analysis. *Journal of Medicine and Philosophy* 30: 167–88.

Resnik, D. 2006a. Compensation of research-related injuries: Ethical and legal issues. *Journal of Legal Medicine* 27: 263–87.

Resnik, D. 2006b. Openness versus secrecy in scientific research. *Episteme* 2: 135–47.

Resnik, D. 2007a. Are the new EPA regulations concerning intentional exposure studies with children overprotective? *IRB: Ethics and Human Research* 29, 5: 5–7.

Resnik, D. 2007b. The new EPA regulations for protecting human subjects: Haste makes waste. *Hastings Center Report* 37, 1: 17–21.

Resnik, D. 2007c. *The price of truth: How money affects the norms of science.* New York: Oxford University Press.

Resnik, D. 2008. Freedom of speech in government science. *Issues in Science and Technology* 24, 2: 31–34.

Resnik, D., and Shamoo, A. 2005. Bioterrorism and the responsible conduct of research. *Drug Development Research* 63: 121–33.

Resnik, D., Shamoo, A., and Krimsky, S. 2006. Fraudulent human embryonic stem cell research in South Korea: Lessons learned. *Accountability in Research* 13: 101–9.

Resnik, D., and Wing, S. 2007. Lessons learned from the Children's Environmental Exposure Research Study. *American Journal of Public Health* 97: 414–18.

Revkin, A. 2006. Climate expert says NASA tried to silence him. *New York Times*, January 29: A1.

Revkin, A. 2007. Climate change testimony was edited by White House. *New York Times*, October 25: A1.

Ridker, P., and Torres, J. 2006. Reported outcomes in major cardiovascular clinical trials funded by for-profit and not-for-profit organizations: 2000–2005. *Journal of the American Medical Association* 295: 2270–74.

Robertson, J. 1977. The scientist's right to research: A constitutional analysis. *Southern California Law Review* 51: 1203–78.

Ronan, C. 1982. *Science: Its history and development among the world's cultures.* New York: Facts on File.

Rosenberg, A. 1985. *The structure of biological science*. Cambridge: Cambridge University Press.

Rosenberg, A. 1994. *Instrumental biology or the disunity of science*. Chicago: University of Chicago Press.

Rosenberg, A. 1995. *Philosophy of the social sciences*, 2nd ed. Boulder, CO: Westview.

Rosengard, A., Liu, Y., Nie, Z., and Jimenez, R. 2002. Variola virus immune evasion design: Expression of a highly efficient inhibitor of human complement. *Proceedings of the National Academy of Sciences* 99: 8808–13.

Ross, W. [1930] 1988. *The right and the good*. Indianapolis, IN: Hackett.

Ruse, M. 1979. *The Darwinian revolution*. Chicago: University of Chicago Press.

Ruse, M. 2004. *Can a Darwinian be a Christian?* Cambridge: Cambridge University Press.

Scientists and Engineers for America. 2006. Bill of rights for scientists and engineers. Available at: http://sharp.sefora.org/bill-of-rights/ (accessed March 30, 2008).

Scientists and Engineers for America. 2008. Mission and vision. Available at: http://sharp.sefora.org/mission/ (accessed March 30, 2008).

Scopes v. State. 152 Tenn. 424, 278 S.W. 57 (Tenn. 1925).

Sen, A., and Williams, B. (eds.). 1982. *Utilitarianism and beyond*. Cambridge: Cambridge University Press.

Sengupta, S., and Lo, B. 2003. The roles and experiences of nonaffiliated and non-scientist members of institutional review boards. *Academic Medicine* 78: 212–18.

Shamoo, A. 1999a. Institutional review boards (IRBs) and conflict of interest. *Accountability in Research* 7: 201–12.

Shamoo, A. 1999b. Unregulated research with human subjects. *Accountability in Research* 6: 205–14.

Shamoo, A. 2001. Adverse event reporting: The tip of an iceberg. *Accountability in Research* 8: 197–218.

Shamoo, A., and Resnik, D. 2008. *Responsible conduct of research*, 2nd ed. New York: Oxford University Press.

Shamoo, A., and Schwartz, J. 2007. Universal and uniform protections of human subjects in research. *American Journal of Bioethics* 7: 7–9.

Sharp, R., and Foster, M. 2000. Involving study populations in the review of genetic research. *Journal of Law, Medicine, and Ethics* 28: 41–51.

Sheehan, H. 1993. *Marxism and the philosophy of science*. Amherst, NY: Humanity.

Shirer, W. 1990. *The rise and fall of the Third Reich*. New York: Simon and Schuster.

Shrader-Frechette, K. 1994. *Ethics of scientific research*. Lanham, MD: Rowman and Littlefield.

Shulman, S. 2007. *Undermining science: Suppression and distortion in the Bush administration*. Berkeley: University of California Press.

Shulsky, A., and Schmitt, G. 2002. *Silent warfare: Understanding the world of intelligence*, 3rd ed. Dulles, VA: Potomac Books.

Simpson, S. 2006. *Francis Bacon: The Internet encyclopedia of philosophy*. Available at: http://www.iep.utm.edu/b/bacon.htm#H3 (accessed March 31, 2008).

Singer, P. 1999. *Practical ethics*, 2nd ed. Cambridge: Cambridge University Press.

Snyder, L., and Mueller, P. 2008. Research in the physician's office: Navigating the minefield. *Hastings Center Report* 38, 2: 23–25.

Sober, E. 1993. *The philosophy of biology*. Boulder, CO: Westview.

Solomon, M. 2007. *Social empiricism*, 2nd ed. Cambridge, MA: MIT Press.

Spitz, V. 2005. *Doctors from hell: The horrific account of the Nazi experiments on humans*. Boulder, CO: Sentient.

State of California. 2007. Protection of Human Subjects in Medical Experimentation Act. Available at: http://www.rgs.uci.edu/ora/rp/hrpp/medicalexperimentation.htm (accessed March 31, 2008).

Steneck, N. 2004. *ORI introduction to responsible conduct of research*. Washington, DC: ORI.

Stokstad, E. 2004. House cuts EPA R & D, restores STAR grants. *Science* 305: 591.

Stokstad, E. 2008. EPA adjusts a smog standard to White House preference. *Science* 319: 1602–3.

Stout, D. 2006. In first veto, Bush blocks stem cell bill. *New York Times*, July 19: A1.

Supreme Court Historical Society. 2006. FDR and the court-packing controversy. Available at: http://www.supremecourthistory.org/02_history/02.html (accessed March 31, 2008).

Thagard, P. 1978. Why astrology is a pseudoscience. In: P. Asquith and I. Hacking (eds.), *PSA 1978*, vol. 1, 223–33. East Lansing, MI: Philosophy of Science Association.

Union of Concerned Scientists. 2004. *Scientific integrity in policymaking*. Washington, DC: Union of Concerned Scientists. Available at: http://www.ucsusa.org/scientific_integrity/interference/reports-scientific-integrity-in-policy-making.html (accessed March 31, 2008).

United Nations. 1948. Universal declaration of human rights. Available at: http://www.un.org/Overview/rights.html (accessed February 18, 2008).

United Nations. 2002. Nuclear non-proliferation treaty. Available at: http://www.un.org/Depts/dda/WMD/treaty/ (accessed March 31, 2008).

U.S. Constitution. 1787. Available at: http://www.law.cornell.edu/constitution/constitution.overview.html (accessed February 18, 2008).

U.S. Patent and Trademark Office (USPTO). 2006. Calendar year 2006 patent counts by patent types and by state and country of origin. Available at: http://0-www.uspto.gov.mi111.sjlibrary.org/web/offices/ac/ido/oeip/taf/st_co_06.htm (accessed February 26, 2008).

Vedantam, S. 2005. Kyoto treaty takes effect today. *Washington Post*, June 16: A04.

Vestag, B. 2008. EPA feels heat over flame retardant. *Nature* 452: 513.

Von Bismark, O. 2006. The quotations page. Available at: http://www.quotationspage.com/quote/24903.html (accessed March 31, 2008).

Wald, M. 2008. Environmental agency tightens smog standards. *New York Times*, March 13: A1.

Weijer, C., and Emanuel, E. 2000. Protecting communities in biomedical research. *Science* 289: 1142–44.

Wein, L., and Liu, Y. 2005. Analyzing a bioterror attack on the food supply: The case of botulinum toxin in milk. *Proceedings of the National Academy of Sciences* 102: 9984–89.

Weiss, R. 2006. NIH official takes the fifth on tissue sharing. *Washington Post*, June 15: A10.

Weissman, P. 2006. Politic stem cells. *Nature* 439: 145–47.

White House press release. 2002. President names members of bioethics council, January 16, 2002. Available at: http://www.bioethics.gov/about/whpress.html (accessed March 31, 2008).

Wittgenstein, L. [1922] 2001. *Tractatus logico philosophicus*. New York: Routledge.

Woodward, R. 2004. *Plan of attack*. New York: Simon and Schuster.

World Bank. 2006. GNI per capita 2006. Available at: http://siteresources.worldbank.org/DATASTATISTICS/Resources/GNIPC.pdf (accessed March 31, 2008).

World Medical Association. 2004. Declaration at Helsinki: Ethical principles for medical research involving human subjects. Available at: http://www.wma.net/e/policy/b3.htm. (accessed March 5, 2008).

Ziman, J. 2000. *Real science*. Cambridge: Cambridge University Press.

Index